P9-BZH-450

Aha!

The Moments of Insight that Shape Our World

William B. Irvine

OXFORD

UNIVERSITY PRESS

OXFORD
UNIVERSITY PRESS

Oxford University Press is a department of the University of Oxford.
It furthers the University's objective of excellence in research, scholarship,
and education by publishing worldwide.

Oxford   New York

Auckland   Cape Town   Dar es Salaam   Hong Kong   Karachi
Kuala Lumpur   Madrid   Melbourne   Mexico City   Nairobi
New Delhi   Shanghai   Taipei   Toronto

With offices in

Argentina   Austria   Brazil   Chile   Czech Republic   France   Greece
Guatemala   Hungary   Italy   Japan   Poland   Portugal   Singapore
South Korea   Switzerland   Thailand   Turkey   Ukraine   Vietnam

Oxford is a registered trademark of Oxford University Press
in the UK and certain other countries.

Published in the United States of America by
Oxford University Press
198 Madison Avenue, New York, NY 10016

© William B. Irvine 2015

All rights reserved. No part of this publication may be reproduced, stored in
a retrieval system, or transmitted, in any form or by any means, without
the prior permission in writing of Oxford University Press, or as expressly
permitted by law, by license, or under terms agreed with the appropriate
reproduction rights organization. Inquiries concerning reproduction
outside the scope of the above should be sent to the Rights Department,
Oxford University Press, at the address above.

You must not circulate this work in any other form
and you must impose this same condition on any acquirer.

Library of Congress Cataloging-in-Publication Data
Irvine, William Braxton, 1952–
Aha!: the moments of insight that shape our world/William B. Irvine.
pages cm
ISBN 978–0–19–933887–0 (hardback)
1. Insight. 2. Epiphanies. I. Title.
BF449.5.I78 2015
153.4—dc23
2014013504

1 3 5 7 9 8 6 4 2
Printed in the United States of America
on acid-free paper

To Jamie,
For being the source of so many aha moments

CONTENTS

Aha!

ACKNOWLEDGMENTS

This book would not have been possible without the various forms of assistance I have received. Thanks, to begin with, to Wright State University for granting me the leave during which most of this book was written. Thanks to Lois W. Madden, a high-school math teacher in Yerington, Nevada, who nearly half a century ago introduced me to the aha moment experienced by mathematician Henri Poincaré and thereby inadvertently set into motion the long chain of investigations that resulted in this book. And thanks to Byrd Leavell for finding a home for this book and to Lucy Randall at Oxford University Press for helping it grow.

I also want to offer a special thanks to my muse. Although this is a work of nonfiction rather than a novel, writing it required an ongoing stream of aha moments, with which you generously supplied me. At least on most days you did. On some days, you were nowhere to be seen. It would have been nice if I had been told of those occasions in advance, since it would have spared me the drudgery of sitting for hours at my computer with nothing to show for it. But mind you, I'm not complaining. I'm grateful for all you've done for me.

Part of my problem is that I don't understand how the muse business works. I'm guessing that you are like a social worker who has been assigned a caseload. This means that on some days, you are able to help me but that on other days, you have to help other clients. Or maybe you think of your authors not as clients but as patients? And while we are on the muse business, how do you get paid? Will I be billed?

But whoever you are and whatever your terms of employment may be, I am indebted to you: without your assistance, this book would not have been possible.

Aha!

Introduction

IN THE LATE EIGHTEENTH CENTURY, Thomas Clarkson, the son of a minister, was a student at Cambridge University. He entered an essay-writing competition on the topic of slavery's moral status. At that time, slavery had been abolished in Britain, but many Brits were nevertheless profiting from the slave trade. In preparing to write his essay, Clarkson discovered how little he knew about slavery and thereby came to realize what an abomination it was. Much to his surprise, he found himself undergoing a moral awakening. He wrote, "I had expected pleasure from the invention of the arguments, from the arrangement of them, from the putting of them together, and from the thought in the interim that I was engaged in an innocent contest for literary honour. But all my pleasure was damped by the facts which were now continually before me. It was but one gloomy subject from morning to night."[1] He nevertheless finished writing the essay. It won the contest.

A short time later, while Clarkson was riding horseback between Cambridge and London, his moral awakening transformed into a full-blown moral crisis.

> I became at times very seriously affected....I stopped my horse
> occasionally, and dismounted and walked. I frequently tried to per-
> suade myself in these intervals that the contents of my Essay could
> not be true. The more however I reflected upon them...the more
> I gave them credit. Coming in sight of Wades Mill in Hertfordshire,
> I sat down disconsolate on the turf by the roadside and held my
> horse. Here a thought came into my mind, that if the contents of the
> Essay were true, it was time some person should see these calami-
> ties to their end.[2]

Not long thereafter, Clarkson realized that *he* was that person. He threw himself into the British abolitionist movement
and soon became one of its leading figures.

AT AGE SIXTEEN, Albert Einstein had a puzzling thought: what
would a light beam look like if you could travel alongside it?
Over the next decade, as he gained a much deeper understanding of physics, the question continued to bother him. It
was a question, he came to realize, that revealed an inconsistency in the views held by his fellow physicists. They were
convinced—quite sensibly, most people would say—that time
is absolute, that it passes at the same rate for everyone, regardless of where they are or how they happen to be moving.

While working as a clerk at the patent office in Berne,
Switzerland, Einstein threw himself into the task of resolving
this inconsistency. After a year of intense but fruitless effort,
he was ready to give up. As a last-gasp measure, he decided
to describe the problem and his efforts to solve it to his friend
Michele Besso. They met on a beautiful spring morning in
1905. During their conversation, Einstein later wrote, "a

storm broke loose in my mind." It dawned on him that he could resolve the inconsistency by giving up the assumption that time is absolute. He went home to ponder this insight and the next day paid Besso another visit. Without even saying hello, Einstein blurted out, "Thank you. I've completely solved the problem."[3] Five weeks later, Einstein sent off the paper containing his solution and thereby laid the foundation for the theory of relativity.

IN THE SUMMER OF 1905, Gustav Mahler was struggling to finish his *Seventh Symphony*. After two weeks of fruitless effort, he decided that a change of place would do him good. He traveled to the Dolomites but remained musically blocked. On the journey home, his creative prayers were answered, but in an unexpected manner. His route required that he be rowed across a lake, and as he later wrote to his wife, "At the first stroke of the oars the theme...of the introduction to the first movement came into my head—and in four weeks the first, third and fifth movements were done."[4]

Not long before this, French mathematician Henri Poincaré experienced a curiously similar moment of insight. He had been working hard to solve a problem concerning so-called Fuchsian functions. He decided to take a break from his research to go on a geological excursion.

> The meanderings of the trip made me forget my mathematical work. When I arrived at Coutances we embarked on a bus for some trip or other. At the moment that I put my foot on the step, the idea came to me, without anything of my previous thoughts appearing

to have prepared me, that the transformations that I had used to define fuchsian functions were the same as those of non-euclidean geometry.[5]

On returning to his home in Caen, he wrote down the resulting proof. Poincaré thereby made a key contribution to the development of the geometric theory of functions.[6]

HIERO, RULER OF SYRACUSE, gave a goldsmith a certain amount of gold with which to make a crown. The goldsmith returned an exquisite and intricately crafted crown that weighed exactly as much as the gold Hiero had given him. Yet rumors circulated, claiming that the goldsmith had cheated Hiero, that the crown contained gold mixed with silver, and that the goldsmith had kept some of the gold for himself. The obvious way to find out whether the rumors were true was by melting part of the crown to see if it contained any silver, but this would ruin the crown. Was there, Hiero wondered, a nondestructive way to determine whether or not the crown contained pure gold? He turned to Archimedes for an answer to this question.

After pondering the question Hiero had posed, Archimedes went off to take a bath. As he slid into the tub, he saw something he had seen hundreds of times before: the level of the water in the tub rose. This was when Archimedes had his aha moment. Because gold is denser than silver, gold would displace less water than an equal weight of silver. Therefore, by measuring how much water the crown displaced when it was submerged, he could determine the gold content of the crown without damaging it. According to the account of this event offered two centuries later by architect and engineer Vitruvius, Archimedes responded to this insight in rather dramatic fashion: "Transported with joy, he jumped out of the tub and rushed home naked." As he ran, he repeatedly cried out "Eureka," meaning "I have found it."[7] Archimedes subsequently demonstrated that the goldsmith had indeed cheated Hiero.

IN THE EARLY SPRING OF 1820, fourteen-year-old Joseph Smith went into the woods to pray for guidance regarding which religion he should practice. The divine response to his prayers was rather more complete and compelling than he had expected. Before he could finish praying, he discovered that he had lost the ability to speak. Darkness, he later wrote, gathered around him, and he felt doomed to a sudden destruction. Just when things seemed hopeless, he had a vision:

> I saw a pillar of light exactly over my head, above the brightness of the sun, which descended gradually until it fell upon me. It no sooner appeared than I found myself delivered from the enemy which held me bound. When the light rested upon me I saw two Personages, whose brightness and glory defy all description, standing above me in the air. One of them spake unto me, calling me by name and said, pointing to the other—This is My Beloved Son. Hear Him![8]

And what advice did the Son offer? He informed Smith that all currently existing religions were corrupt, meaning that he should join none of them. The obvious solution, reinforced by subsequent revelations, was for Smith to start a new religion, which he did. The Church of Jesus Christ of the Latter-day Saints—more commonly known as the Mormon Church—is not unusual in its ability to trace its history back to a religious revelation.

IN EACH OF THE CASES DESCRIBED ABOVE, a person experienced what I shall call an "aha moment." What, exactly, transpires during such moments is a bit of a mystery. Consider again the aha moments experienced by Einstein, Mahler, Archimedes, and Poincaré. We have an expression to describe such incidents: we say that an idea "came to them." But when an idea "comes to us," where does it come from? Or consider Clarkson's aha moment. We might say that he had a moral epiphany, but this expression seems syntactically backwards: *he* didn't have the epiphany; *it* had him. The same is true of Smith's revelation. He was the passive recipient of a message from a mysterious outside force.

We have all experienced the aha phenomenon. While doing a crossword puzzle, for example, you might find yourself stumped: what's a three-letter word meaning *eggs*? You turn your attention to another part of the puzzle, only to have the answer come to you: *ova*! This is, to be sure, a trivial aha moment. In other cases, though, our moments of insight have a profound personal impact on us. Suppose, for example, you discover that you are in love with someone. It is a discovery that might overturn the plan you had for your life. Or suppose that after staring idly at a nearby cow while eating a hamburger at a picnic, it dawns on you that if you continue your carnivorous ways, you might someday eat a portion of *that very cow*. This realization might be sufficiently disturbing to transform you into a vegetarian.

Besides these personal epiphanies, there are aha moments that change the world. This is certainly true of the moments experienced by Clarkson, Einstein, Mahler, Poincaré, and Smith.

Imagine a world in which such moments didn't take place. That world would be radically different from ours. It would be an amoral, irreligious world, devoid of science and art. It would also be devoid of the inventions we take for granted. There would be no antibiotics, no light bulbs—indeed, not even any candles—and no drive-through windows at fast-food restaurants. For that matter, there wouldn't even be restaurants, fast-food or otherwise.

Although we can argue about the historical significance of any particular aha moment, the role these moments collectively play in human progress is indisputable. Indeed, the fact that humans are capable of having these moments and sharing them with other people is one of the most significant characteristics of our species. Consequently, if we wish to understand the human experience, we would do well to examine the aha phenomenon. In the pages that follow, I will do just that.

This book is an outgrowth of my research for *On Desire: Why We Want What We Want*. In that book, I explore human desire. I argue that in many cases, people don't consciously choose their desires; instead, desires form in their unconscious minds and then emerge, unbidden, in their conscious minds. People tend to take ownership of the desires they thereby discover within themselves, and they set to work trying to fulfill them. It's a recipe for an unhappy existence.

In this book, I explore the way our unconscious minds give rise not to desires but to ideas. Like our desires, our ideas have lives of their own. They can come to us out of the blue when we aren't seeking them; and when we *are* seeking them, they can play coy and refuse to appear. Aha moments can't be summoned like waiters at a restaurant. As a result, many novelists spend their days staring at a blank computer screen, and many mathematicians spend their days filling wastebaskets with the crumpled remains of stillborn proofs. Why is this the case? Why do intelligent and dedicated individuals have to endure such frustration in order to elicit an aha moment? This is one of the questions I attempt to answer in the pages that follow.

TO KEEP MY TASK MANAGEABLE, I will focus my attention on the aha phenomenon as it occurs in five different *domains*: religion, morality, science, mathematics, and art. In the course of my investigation, I will attempt to answer the following questions:

What is it like to have an aha moment? As we shall see, people experience the aha moment in different ways within different domains. When a mathematician finally succeeds, after an extended period of intense effort, in proving a theorem, he experiences a profound delight; indeed, some mathematicians would have us believe that the pleasures afforded by mathematics surpass those of sex and drugs. It is in part for this reason that one mathematician, on being told by his doctor that he had only a few months to live, chose to spend those months not in hedonistic revelry but sitting in a quiet room, doggedly proving theorems.

In the moral domain, by way of contrast, having an aha moment can be quite disconcerting: someone who has an important moral epiphany will in most cases have to change her lifestyle and in some cases have to radically alter the plan she had made for her life. In religion, experiencing an aha moment can be downright terrifying: the prophet Ezekiel responded to his encounter with God by falling to the ground in fear.

What process or activity precedes a significant aha moment? The answer to this question again varies by domain. Mathematicians, for example, spend years studying math, followed by more years mastering some particular field within math, followed by still more years studying some problem within that field, before they experience an aha moment worthy of sharing with the world—if, that is, they are lucky enough ever to experience such a moment. For every mathematician who makes a breakthrough discovery, there might be hundreds of other mathematicians who invested similar effort trying to make that discovery but never experienced the requisite moment of enlightenment. What is it, one wonders, that separates the mathematicians who succeed from those who don't?

And here is another curious thing about the process that precedes an aha moment: the breakthrough idea often comes not when mathematicians are consciously trying to solve a problem but during intervals of rest between problem-solving sessions. It would appear that a mathematician's unconscious mind works on math problems when his conscious mind is otherwise occupied, and that his unconscious mind is a better mathematician than his conscious mind is! Would-be mathematicians, if they are to be successful in their field, must learn how to make use of this process of "mental incubation."

In the moral domain, unlike in math, a person doesn't need to spend years taking classes in order to experience an epiphany; he need only have moral beliefs and then become cognizant of an apparent inconsistency in those beliefs. Similarly, people experience religious revelations not because of anything they do but because God has chosen them. I should add that God's criteria for selecting individuals to be his representatives on earth can be difficult to fathom. In particular, if it came as a surprise to Joseph Smith that God would choose him, it was an even bigger surprise to many of his neighbors.

What brain processes give rise to aha moments? In the pages that follow, I explore the neuroscience of idea formation. I examine, for example, the manner in which mental illness can unleash creative impulses in artists. I examine hallucinations and show how easily they can be mistaken for religious revelations. And I explore how our hominid ancestors could have developed the ability to innovate or do math. I should caution readers, though, that much of my exploration of the science behind ideas can best be characterized as speculative. Although neuroscientists have ideas about how ideas happen, there is much that they don't know.

Besides exploring the neuroscience that lies behind aha moments, I explore their psychological dimensions. Consider, for example, the use both mathematicians and artists make of trial and error. In most cases, this is not just the best way but the only way for them to accomplish their creative endeavors. A mathematician might try very many ways to solve a problem before finding one that works, and a painter might need to paint over a portrait many times before it looks right. One recurring theme in the pages that follow is that if you are to succeed in your creative efforts, you must develop a tolerance for failure.

How does a person respond to his experience of an aha moment? What does he do with it? We might think that someone, on experiencing an aha moment, would rush to share it with the world. By doing this, he can do a public service, especially if his aha moment enables him to invent, say, a life-saving drug. He can also do himself a service: by being the first to make a discovery, he can gain fame and fortune. And indeed, the individuals whose names are linked with historically significant aha moments almost always did share the discoveries they made as a result of those moments; otherwise, it is unlikely that we would have heard of them or their work.

In many cases, though, someone who experiences an aha moment is reluctant to publicize it. He might worry that the moment is not all that it seems to be. A scientist, for example, might worry that because of a mistake in his calculations, he has not, in fact, discovered what he thinks he has discovered.

And a person who experiences a religious aha moment might be reluctant to share it with the world; those who have done so in the past have in many cases paid with their lives.

How does the world respond to the revelation of an aha moment? Often quite badly. Suppose a scientist experiences an intellectual breakthrough that leads him to formulate a radical new theory. He might think that his fellow scientists, being thoughtful, rational individuals, will welcome his theory. What he will often find, though, is that his colleagues react with skepticism, and the more radical his theory is, the more skeptical they will be. By way of illustration, many of Albert Einstein's fellow physicists were quite skeptical of his theory of relativity. In fact, Einstein's 1921 Nobel Prize in physics was not for what we now regard as his greatest scientific accomplishment—namely, his work on relativity—but for his work on the photoelectric effect.

In some cases, a scientist has more to worry about than his colleagues' response to a theory. Although the public is indifferent—indeed, is oblivious to—much of science, it cares intensely about certain areas of research. It is quite interested, for example, in research regarding the origin of our species. Charles Darwin's fear of public reaction to his theory of evolution was doubtless one of the reasons he waited two decades to share that theory with the world. Significantly, this fear was subsequently overcome only by another, more compelling fear—that if he didn't publish, Alfred Russel Wallace, who had independently had the same insight, would publish ahead of him and would thereby go down in history as the father of evolution.

Like scientists, artists have to worry about the response to their work from both inside and outside their profession. Of course, there is one important respect in which new ideas in art differ from new ideas in science: it is possible for an artist to advance rather than hinder his career prospects by becoming the target of either public or critical condemnation. Andres Serrano, the artist who achieved notoriety for photographing a crucifix immersed in what looked like urine, probably would have been horrified to receive fan mail from the local Catholic bishop.

Someone who experiences a religious aha moment is likely to find that other people don't want to hear about it. Joseph Smith's revelations, for example, implied that his neighbors' religious views were seriously mistaken and therefore that their souls were in jeopardy. Similarly, sharing a moral epiphany is unlikely to make you popular. Other people might worry that you are going to pass judgment on their moral values or, even worse, force them to live in accordance with yours. Consider, for example, the investors who, though not directly involved in the British slave trade, made a good living from it. These individuals were rather annoyed by Clarkson's ongoing disclosure of the horrors of slavery. Life would have been so much simpler for them if he had just minded his own business and kept his mouth shut.

Finally, how does the person who had and reveals an aha moment deal with the world's response to that moment? Suppose someone reveals a major breakthrough to his colleagues or to the world at large, and suppose their response to this revelation is negative or even hostile. At first he is likely to be puzzled that others are resisting the insight that he finds so compelling. Once he recovers from his puzzlement, though, he has an important decision to make: how should he respond to their negativity?

One option is to succumb to it. A scientist might renounce the theory he proposed, a painter might return to more conventional styles of painting, and someone who had a moral epiphany or religious revelation might stop trying to convert the masses.

Alternatively, someone who has experienced an aha moment might decide that she will do whatever it takes to bring her colleagues or the world at large around to her way of thinking. A scientist, rather than backing away from the radical theory she proposed, might publish papers and give talks in support of it; indeed, she might spend the remainder of her career defending her theory. Biologist Lynn Margulis was in her late twenties when, after having it rejected fifteen times, she published the landmark paper in which she proposed her endosymbiotic theory. This theory explains how we came to have in our cells those little powerhouses known as mitochondria. Margulis spent the next four decades of her career defending this theory, the way a mama grizzly would defend its cub. Likewise, someone who has had an unpopular moral epiphany might start a campaign of moral reform, and someone who has had a religious revelation might start a new religion, even though doing so exposes him to the hostility of those who feel threatened by it.

For an aha moment to transform the world, it isn't enough for someone to experience it; the person who experienced it must subsequently do something with that moment. She must publicize it and then, quite possibly, fight for its acceptance. When we examine the individuals who experienced the aha moments that made our world what it is, we find in most cases that although they may be remarkable for their intelligence or creativity, what really sets them apart from other people is their courage and persistence. In other words, character counts.

Although we won't all experience a significant aha moment in the course of our lifetimes, every one of us has a role to play as a consumer of other people's insights. New ideas abound, and when we encounter one, we have an important choice to make: should we embrace the idea or reject it?

Most of us like to think that had we lived in the past, we would have been early and staunch supporters of the individuals we now revere for the aha moments they experienced. If we are artists, we like to think that had we been on the jury of the 1863 Salon de Paris, we would have fought bravely for acceptance of Manet's *Déjeuner sur l'Herbe*. If we are scientists, we like to think that had we been around in the early twentieth century, we would have instantly appreciated Einstein's theory of relativity. If we are Christians, we like to think that had we lived in Jerusalem around the year 30, we would have become one of Jesus's followers. Likewise, unless we are racists, we like to think that had we lived in Britain in the early nineteenth century, we would have supported Thomas Clarkson in his fight against the slave trade.

The sad truth, though, is that in many cases, if we had been around in the past, we would have found ourselves on the wrong side of the greatest aha moments in history. We would have attacked the very individuals we now admire. This is the only conclusion one can draw after witnessing the way we respond to the aha moments that take place around us during our lifetime. Indeed, it is altogether likely that in the same way as we are astonished and dismayed by the hostility our ancestors expressed in response to the aha moments of their time, our descendants will look back on us in wonder: "How could my grandparents have been so blind as not to recognize the brilliance of [fill in the name of the innovative thinker you most recently ridiculed]?"

Although intolerance for aha moments can slow human progress, lack of skepticism toward such moments can also be hazardous. Imagine a world in which people uncritically accepted whatever new ideas were expressed. Every crackpot suggestion, every delusional rambling would be given full consideration: "Have you heard? Cousin Bob has decided that the earth is hollow!" Such a world would quickly be swamped by false insights, and there would cease to be a generally accepted body of knowledge. Human progress would grind to a halt.

In a perfect world, people will take aha moments seriously while simultaneously harboring skepticism toward them. The trick is finding the proper balance between acceptance and rejection, which, I think, is one of the great challenges confronting any society. It is for this reason that I examine not just the psychology of aha moments but their political ramifications as well. If society benefits from aha moments, and if people are inclined to suppress the expression of these moments, it can be argued that governments should take steps to protect people from the social consequences of expressing them.

IN THIS BOOK, as I've said, I will consider aha moments as they take place in five different domains—religion, morality, science, mathematics, and art. The order in which I examine these domains is somewhat arbitrary, but not entirely. A case can be made, in particular, for putting religion and morality in one group and for putting science, math, and art in another. Here's why.

The aha moments that take place in connection with religion and morality are *unbidden*. In most cases, those who experience them do nothing to bring them on. Furthermore, these moments are unlikely to trigger delight in those who experience them; to the contrary, it is usually frightening to have a religious revelation and annoying to have a moral epiphany.

On the other hand, the aha moments that take place in science, math, and art are *bidden*, in the sense that it almost always takes years of training followed by years of intensely directed effort before a person has a chance of experiencing one. If a scientist or mathematician is rewarded with one, the resulting aha moment is likely to take the form of a "thunderbolt": she experiences a single, profound flash of insight that enables her to solve the problem she is working on. Experiencing such an aha moment is likely to be the source of considerable delight.

In art, aha moments are also likely to be bidden, but they differ in certain respects from those that take place in science and math. Most significantly, it is quite unusual for them to arrive in the form of a thunderbolt. Instead, artistic creativity tends to proceed by means of a long series of lesser aha moments. Thus, an artist might, in the process of painting a portrait, repaint sections of it a dozen times. At no point in this process is he likely to say, "Eureka, that's it!" Instead, he will feel that something he has done is an improvement. He might stop working on a portrait not because he thinks he has achieved artistic perfection but because he can't think of any way to improve it.

Each of the five sections of this book comprises three chapters. The first chapter focuses on the aha moment as it takes place in the domain covered in that section. What process or activity brings it on? What does it feel like to have it? The second chapter examines the psychology and neuroscience behind those aha moments. In the third chapter of each section, we explore the world's resistance to new ideas. Why do we resist them? And what must the person who experiences an aha moment do to overcome this resistance?

Let us, then, embark on our investigation of aha moments, beginning with an examination of religious revelations. People who have experienced a full-blown revelation in which they saw and talked to God are in an enviable position: they know exactly what he wants them to do—or at least they think they know. Most of us, though, have not experienced such a revelation. This means that if we want to do what God wants us to do, we must rely on other people's revelations regarding God's wishes. We are, in particular, faced with the task of choosing among the religions God instructed them to start. But as we shall see in the pages that follow, making this choice is no easy task.

PART ONE

The Aha Moment in Religion

CHAPTER 1

Seeing the Light

AUTHOR C. S. LEWIS was an atheist for the first three decades of his life. Then, after much soul searching, he concluded that God exists. This wasn't, however, the end of his religious transformation. On September 28, 1931, at age 33, he got into the sidecar of his brother's motorcycle to travel to Whipsnade Zoo near London. "When we set out," he says, "I did not believe that Jesus Christ is the son of God, and when we reached the zoo I did. Yet I had not exactly spent the journey in thought. Nor in great emotion.... It was more like when a man, after a long sleep, still lying motionless in bed, becomes aware that he is now awake."[1] As a result of this experience, Lewis became a committed Anglican.

This is only one of many forms a religious aha moment can take. Consider, for example, that of David Brainerd, an eighteenth-century missionary to the American Indians. He had been experiencing what we today would call a meaning-of-life crisis. In an attempt to resolve it, he resorted to prayer, even though he thought the activity was pointless. But then, he writes,

> As I was walking in a thick grove, unspeakable glory seemed to open to the apprehension of my soul. I do not mean any external

brightness, nor any imagination of a body of light, but it was a new inward apprehension or view that I had of God, such as I never had before, nor anything which had the least resemblance to it. I had no particular apprehension of any one person in the Trinity, either the Father, the Son, or the Holy Ghost; but it appeared to be Divine glory. My soul rejoiced with joy unspeakable, to see such a God, such a glorious Divine Being.... I continued in this state of inward joy, peace, and astonishing, till near dark without any sensible abatement.... I felt myself in a new world, and everything about me appeared with a different aspect from what it was wont to do.[2]

In this case, although Brainerd at one point remarks on how joyous it was to "see such a God," the rest of his account indicates that he did not see or hear anything during his revelation; he instead *felt* something within his soul. As a result, he regained his conviction that there was a God and thereby found meaning for his life. It was a transformative event.

Psychologist Chana Ullman has investigated religious conversions. One young man she interviewed had attended a prayer meeting at which Christian friends laid hands over his head and prayed that he would receive the Holy Spirit. This ceremony, he said, caused him to feel "flooded with joy," with "a blissful feeling of being drunk, of being fed." Later that night, lying in bed, he had an even more profound experience: "All this intensity started hitting me from above, like intense warmth, like a blanket of love. It was almost like it made noise, like it hit me on top of my head, surged all the way down my body and just filled it. I would have been knocked down by the power if I had not been lying down already."[3]

In other, more dramatic revelations, a person hears or sees something rather than feeling something in his body or soul. Consider, for example, Moses's first encounter with God:

> The angel of the Lord appeared to him in the flame of a burning bush. Moses noticed that, although the bush was on fire, it was not being burnt up; so he said to himself, "I must go across to see this wonderful sight. Why does not the bush burn away?" When the Lord saw that Moses had turned aside to look, he called to him out of the bush, "Moses, Moses." And Moses answered, "Yes, I am here." God said, "Come no nearer; take off your sandals; the place where you are standing is holy ground." Then he said, "I am the God of your forefathers, the God of Abraham, the God of Isaac, the God of Jacob." Moses covered his face, for he was afraid to gaze on God.[4]

Or consider the aha moment experienced by Saint Augustine of Hippo. In the middle of a personal crisis, Augustine sat crying and praying for divine guidance under a fig tree, when he heard a child chanting, "Pick it up and read, pick it up and read." It was a very strange thing, he thought, for a child to say. He therefore interpreted it to be "a divine command to me to open the [Bible] and read the first chapter I might find." On doing this, Augustine encountered the following passage: "Not in riots and drunken parties, not in eroticism and indecencies, not in strife and rivalry, but put on the Lord Jesus Christ and make no provision for the flesh in its lusts." The effect of reading this was instant and profound: "With the last words of this sentence, it was as if a light of relief from all anxiety flooded into my heart."[5]

Augustine's aha moment, it should be noted, was triggered by two mundane events: hearing the sound of a child playing and opening the Bible to a randomly chosen page and reading what was on it. He took the concurrence of these events as a sign from God.

In many cases, those who claim to have seen or heard something supernatural are disappointingly inarticulate when they describe what they saw or heard. Consider, by way of illustration, American revivalist C. G. Finney's description of his encounter with God. It was early in the morning. He had gone to the meeting house to pray, when "All at once the glory of God shone upon and round about me in a manner almost marvelous.... A light perfectly ineffable shone in my soul, that almost prostrated me on the ground.... This light seemed like the brightness of the sun in every direction. It was too intense for the eyes.... It was surely a light such as I could not have endured long."[6]

The light he saw, Finney is certain, wasn't natural; someone hadn't simply turned on a lamp. He fails to make it clear, though, whether the light in question would have been visible to other people, had they been present. He says that the light he perceived "shone in my soul," which suggests that it was internal and therefore invisible to others, but he also says that "it was too intense for the eyes," which suggests that it existed in the external world, where it would have been visible to others. So maybe the light was both external and internal: it could have entered his soul through his eyes. In the end, the event is as mysterious to us as it must have been for Finney.

Finney's is only one of many reported revelations in which light played an important role. When people have revelations in which they see a divine figure, that figure is often illuminated by a powerful beam of light, or is itself glowing and therefore a source of light. In other revelations, a person sees only a bright light. The most famous of these is probably the revelation experienced by Saul of Tarsus on the road to Damascus: "A light from heaven flashed around him; and he fell to the ground and heard a voice saying to him, 'Saul, Saul, why are you persecuting Me?' And he said, 'Who are You, Lord?' And He said, 'I am Jesus whom you are persecuting, but get up and enter the city, and it will be told you what you must do.'"[7] Saul then went blind until a Christian named Ananias came to heal him. Saul not only converted to Christianity as a result of this experience but became the apostle Paul. This conversion was particularly notable because of Saul's previous reputation for thoroughness in persecuting Christians.[8]

BEFORE WE INVESTIGATE religious aha moments further, it will be useful to distinguish between moments that involve *epiphanies* and those that involve *revelations*. Consider again the moment C. S. Lewis experienced. It wasn't something Lewis saw or heard during his sidecar ride that changed his mind; instead, his mind simply changed itself, to Lewis's surprise. What happened to Lewis that day can best be described as an *epiphany*: he had been harboring doubts with respect to his faith and suddenly discovered, *without any seemingly supernatural event taking place*, that those doubts had been replaced by a feeling of conviction. The epiphany Lewis experienced was religious in nature, but it is also possible to have a moral or scientific epiphany. Indeed, the realization that one has fallen in love—or out of love, for that matter—would count as an emotional epiphany.

In the other religious aha moments I have described, something seemingly supernatural transpires: a divine being reveals itself, thereby revealing an important religious truth to a person. It is therefore fitting to reserve the term *revelation* for such events.

Although the revelations I have described above took place when people were awake, they can also take place when a person is asleep. Joseph, the husband of Mary, Jesus's mother, saw and heard an angel in his dreams. This angel explained to him how it was that Mary, although a virgin, could be pregnant: she was carrying the child of the Holy Spirit.[9] Joseph took this dream seriously. He was convinced that it was God's vehicle for communicating with him.

Mohammed, founder of Islam, also experienced a dream revelation. Every year, Mohammed would go up Mount Hira to pray in seclusion during the month of Ramadan. During one of these retreats, when he was about forty years old, the angel Gabriel came to him while he lay sleeping. Gabriel carried a coverlet of brocade on which words were written. He commanded Mohammed to read it, and after experiencing both confusion and distress, Mohammed succeeded in doing so. The words in question later became a verse in the Quran.

If this dream had been the only revelation Mohammed experienced, it is unlikely that he would have succeeded in founding a new religion. Others would have likely dismissed this story as nothing more than a strange dream. But this dream revelation turned out to be only the prelude to a grander revelation. Mohammed woke from his sleep and, thinking he was somehow possessed, started climbing Hira with the object of throwing himself from the mountain. During his ascent, however, he had a vision. Turning his eyes toward the heavens, he saw a man apparently floating in mid-air. No matter which way Mohammed directed his vision, the man stayed before him. The man announced that he was Gabriel and that Mohammed had been chosen as the apostle of God.[10] Waking revelations like this one carry far more weight, both among those who experience them and those who are told of them, than dream revelations.

Among waking revelations, we can distinguish between those that are sensory and those that are mental. In a mental revelation, we involuntarily see or hear something in our mind. Thus, if I pause in my writing to call up a mental image of Jesus, I can't be said to have had a religious revelation: I was clearly the cause of what I saw. But if, without willing it, I see a mental image of Jesus and if I am powerless to make that image go away, I might conclude that I have experienced a religious revelation that was mental rather than sensory.

Mohammed's second encounter with Gabriel—during which he saw Gabriel floating in front of him—was a sensory revelation. This does not seem to have been the case with the revelations he subsequently had in which Allah dictated the Quran to him. The voice Mohammed heard in those revelations appears to have been in his mind. In saying this, I am not denying the possibility that the voice had a divine origin; I am simply pointing out that other people who were present when he heard the voice heard nothing.[11]

IN A RELIGIOUS REVELATION, a divine being reveals himself to a human being. I had assumed that such events were rare. Then I found out about evangelical Christians who believe that God routinely reveals himself to them. The revelations in question are mental rather than sensory, and they consist not in mentally seeing or hearing God but in simply having a thought. Allow me to explain.

People pray for any number of reasons. Some pray in an attempt to affect events: they might pray for world peace, pray that an ill friend recovers, or pray that they win the lottery. Some pray to offer thanks. Some pray for help in dealing with a difficult situation; they might pray, for example, for strength to resist temptation. There are also prayers in which people ask for divine guidance in making a decision.

The decision in question might be whether to marry someone, whether to have children, or whether to join a certain religion. The decision might also be something mundane, such as whether to paint a table or wear a certain outfit.[12] God can, of course, give us guidance by causing us to hear his voice, either with our ears or in our mind. According to some evangelicals, though, God can also guide us simply by causing us to have a thought. As a result of having it, we will know what we should do. And thanks to our belief that God is responsible for this thought, we will have a high degree of confidence that we have made the right decision. Indeed, if someone questions the wisdom of our decision—"Do you really think it is a good idea to marry George?"—we will have a ready response: "It's what God wants me to do."

According to this line of thinking, God reveals himself to us by causing us to have thoughts that we wouldn't otherwise have had. This belief, however, raises obvious questions. We humans are prone to spontaneous thoughts; indeed, ideas "come to us" throughout the day. The source of these thoughts is our unconscious mind. How can we be sure, then, that the thoughts we have after praying for guidance aren't also the product of our unconscious mind, in which case they might represent wishful thinking on our part rather than revelations of the will of God? And even if we are confident that thoughts were planted in us by a supernatural source, how can we be certain the source is God rather than, say, Satan?

To be sure, those in the evangelical community admit that it is possible for us to mistakenly attribute *our* thoughts to God. According to Tanya Luhrmann, an anthropologist who has studied members of the evangelical Vineyard Movement, newcomers "soon learn that God is understood to speak to congregants inside their own minds. They learn that someone who worships God at the Vineyard must develop the ability to recognize thoughts in their own mind that are not in fact their thoughts, but God's. They learn that this is a skill they should master." She adds that "at the beginning, they usually find both the skill and the very idea of the skill perplexing."[13]

It would be difficult for someone to establish a new religion solely on the basis of mental revelations. Although the person who experienced them might be supremely confident about his interpretation of these revelations, other people would likely be skeptical. They would assume that he, not God, was responsible for the images, voices, or thoughts he had. Likewise, it would be difficult to establish a new religion solely on the basis of a dream; people would be likely to dismiss it as "just a dream," the kind we have every night. Indeed, the world's great religions all seem to have been founded on the basis of sensory revelations in which someone saw or heard God, or some other divine being, and the seeing and hearing was done not within his mind but with his eyes and ears. Let us, therefore, take a closer look at sensory revelations.

WE HAVE EXAMINED sensory revelations in which people see or hear a divine being, but what about the other senses? We can certainly imagine them being involved. We can, for example, imagine someone telling us that she not only saw God standing before her but that when God held out his hand to be kissed, she also touched, smelled, and tasted him: "The skin of his hand was smoother than silk. It had an aroma more intoxicating than the finest perfume, and when I kissed that hand, it tasted sweeter than honey." But when we look at revelations people have reported, we rarely find mention of the senses of touch, smell, and taste; instead, sight and hearing dominate. It is not clear why this should be the case.

Although it is quite unusual for a person experiencing a revelation to feel a divine being *externally*—for example, by touching it with his fingertips—it is not at all unusual for a revelation to consist of feeling the presence of a divine being *internally*. This is what happened to David Brainerd: he felt joy.

This is also what happened to the young man whose friends laid hands over his head and prayed for him. His revelation consisted of a feeling of "intense warmth." I should add that the warmth people experience during a religious revelation is different from the warmth they experience when a sunbeam hits their cheek, when they have a fever, or when they down a shot of whiskey. The warmth of a religious revelation is felt not on their skin or in their body, but in their soul.

Most sensory revelations involve not *direct* but *indirect* encounters with a divine being. In these encounters, a person doesn't see or hear a divine being—or touch, smell, or taste one, either. Instead, he sees or hears something natural—the way Saint Augustine heard the children and saw the line in the Bible—and concludes that a divine being is causally responsible for what he sees or hears. He concludes, in other words, that a divine being has revealed itself to him by means of "a sign."

Sometimes when people experience a sign, they themselves bring the sign into existence. This is presumably what happens when people speak in tongues. What they hear is not the voice of God but something perfectly natural—their own voice. They believe, however, that it is God who is making them speak. What makes the event remarkable is the fact that they aren't choosing what words they speak and don't know the language those words are in. It is evidence, they argue, of the presence of the Holy Spirit within them, and it therefore constitutes a revelation.

It turns out that your tongue isn't the only thing that can give rise to a sign from God; your fingers can as well. Along these lines, consider the indirect revelations experienced by Ron Lafferty, a Mormon who, in the 1980s, thought his church needed radical reform. The Mormon Church not only rejected his reforms but excommunicated him.[14] Lafferty thereafter started receiving "high-tech revelations" from God: he would sit at a computer keyboard with eyes closed and wait for his fingertips to be moved by the spirit of the Lord. "It's like a blanket falls over you," he said, "and you can feel the Lord's thoughts, and you write them down."[15] It was in this manner that Lafferty, early in 1984, received a revelation in which God commanded him to kill various people. In response to it, he brutally murdered his brother's wife and her fifteen-month-old baby.[16]

As we have seen, sensory revelations can take many forms. The ones that are most persuasive and therefore most likely to give rise to a new religion are those in which you see God or some other divine being with your eyes. I will henceforth reserve the word *vision* for this kind of revelation. And among visions, the most persuasive are those in which you not only see a divine being with your eyes, but hear it speak as well. Allow me to explain why.

Suppose you try to start a new religion on the basis of a being appearing silently before you. Although you will likely be impressed by this event, potential converts will be skeptical: "Well, who was it, and what did it want?" they will ask. If the being was mute, the most you will be able to do in response to such questions is tell them who you *think* it was and what you *think* it wants. Even if you feel confident that these thoughts were planted in your mind by the speechless being, many people will understandably be skeptical. If, however, you can tell people that the being introduced itself (the way God introduced himself to Moses) and issued direct commands to you, people will probably pay attention and might even be inclined to join the new religion that this being told you to start.

Having said this, though, I hasten to add that even "audible visions," in which you both see and hear a divine being, raise many important questions about the identity and objectives of that being, questions we shall return to in Chapter 3.

SUPPOSE SOMEONE IS INSTRUCTED, in a vision, to start a new religion, but that this is the end of divine contact: the being never makes another appearance and never even sends an angel to deliver messages. It would be very difficult, under these circumstances, for the prophet to succeed. This is because the process of starting a new religion raises a number of questions. What should the leadership structure be, and who should fill the leadership roles? How should the church be financed? How should people pray? Where should the followers live? What should the rules of conduct be? How should internal disputes be settled?

Thus, when he was leading the Jews, Moses was faced with the question of where to store the tablets of stone on which the Ten Commandments were inscribed. Here is the answer he came up with:

> Make an ark of acacia wood—two and a half cubits long, a cubit and a half wide, and a cubit and a half high. Overlay it with pure gold, both inside and out, and make a gold molding around it. Cast

four gold rings for it and fasten them to its four feet, with two rings on one side and two rings on the other. Then make poles of acacia wood and overlay them with gold. Insert the poles into the rings on the sides of the ark to carry it. The poles are to remain in the rings of this ark; they are not to be removed. Then put in the ark the tablets of the covenant law, which I will give you.[17]

The instructions go on to specify how to make a cover for the ark, where to keep the ark, and so forth.

In 1841, Joseph Smith, the founding prophet of the Mormon religion, was faced with the question of how to build a boarding house in Nauvoo, Illinois. Here is part of his answer:

Behold, verily I say unto you, let my servant George Miller, and my servant Lyman Wight, and my servant John Snider, and my servant Peter Haws, organize themselves, and appoint one of them to be a president over their quorum for the purpose of building that house. And they shall form a constitution, whereby they may receive stock for the building of that house. And they shall not receive less than fifty dollars for a share of stock in that house, and they shall be permitted to receive fifteen thousand dollars from any one man for stock in that house.[18]

It is important to realize that in these cases, Moses and Smith weren't telling their followers what *they* wanted done, what *they* thought would be a good idea to do. Had they done so, their followers might have responded by coming up with ideas of their own, and there might have been a debate over how best to do things. Moses and Smith avoided such debates by informing followers that in giving these directives, they were speaking for God. Moses was simply quoting what God had told him on Mount Sinai, and Smith was simply passing on instructions he had been given in a revelation.[19]

By having these ongoing revelations, the prophet not only maintains control over the direction the church takes but provides followers with evidence that he remains God's chosen prophet. After a founding prophet dies, whoever takes his place sometimes inherits his prophetic ability. This is the case in the Mormon Church, for example: whoever gains the position of president thereby becomes the church's official prophet, seer, and revelator.[20]

Gordon B. Hinckley was the fifteenth person to hold the position of president. In a 1997 interview, he described the role revelations played in his own administrative efforts: "Let me say first that we have a great body of revelation, the vast majority of which came from the prophet Joseph Smith. We don't need much revelation. We need to pay more attention to the revelation we've already received." He went on to describe his own experience with revelations: "If a problem should arise on which we don't have an answer, we pray about it, we may fast about it, and it comes. Quietly. Usually no voice of any kind, but just a perception in the mind." He called it "a still, small voice," like the one heard by the Old Testament prophet Elijah.[21]

I will have more to say about these and other revelations in Chapter 3, but first let us take a look at what might be going on in our brain when we experience a religious revelation. As it turns out, our brains are a prolific source of what appear to be religious aha moments.

CHAPTER 2

Vision or Hallucination?

A THIRTY-ONE-YEAR-OLD WOMAN was at a party, enjoying the pool. She decided to see how far she could swim underwater. She was turning after completing her first lap when another partygoer jumped into the pool and landed on her. Rather than apologize, this person—apparently in a spirit of drunken playfulness—dragged her to the bottom of the pool. She soon blacked out, at least as far as the world around her was concerned.

At this point, she started seeing scenes from her childhood. Then she saw a distant light and started moving toward it, but to get to it she had to go through what seemed like a dark tunnel. As she got closer to the light, she felt overcome with feelings of awe, peace, and love. Then she noticed that standing within the light was an angel with blonde hair and blue eyes, wearing a white dress. This angel reached out to touch her but, just as they were about to make contact, told her "through her eyes" that it was not yet her time and that she had to go back.[1]

This woman had what is called a *near-death experience* (NDE). The number of people who have been near death and revived is quite small, but within this select group, a rather high percentage report having had NDEs. Thus, in one survey, only 18 out of 6,340 people had experienced a near-death recovery, but of these 18, 13 experienced NDEs.[2]

Significantly, what people experience during NDEs depends on their culture. The survey just mentioned was done in India, and the people in it were Hindu.[3] Some reported encountering yamadoots, the messengers of Yamaraj, the god of death,[4] and one reported encountering an irritable man with papers who resembled an Indian bureaucrat. But none reported encountering Jesus, God, or blonde-haired, blue-eyed angels. And yet, the Indian NDEs did have things in common with those reported by, say, Americans. In both cultures, for example, subjects reported seeing deceased relatives and "beings of light."[5]

ASK A SCIENTIST what happens during an NDE, and she might dismiss supernatural explanations involving God, angels, or yamadoots, and instead offer a natural explanation: these near-death "visions" are mere hallucinations. She might go on to explain that they are the result of a diminished supply of oxygen and glucose to the brain.

Such hallucinations are a consequence of the manner in which the human brain evolved. Our early ancestors had brains consisting of a brain stem and cerebellum. These "reptilian" brains were reflexive and intuitive but were incapable of engaging in higher thought processes. As these reptilian brains evolved into mammalian brains, the reptilian brain did not disappear; instead, a cerebrum, capable of higher thought processes, grew around it. The reptilian brain continued to play its original role.

Because of its simplicity, the reptilian brain doesn't consume much energy. It also has very wide "operating parameters." It can, for example, function in a wide range of temperatures, as well as for a time after its energy supply (the glucose and oxygen in the blood) have been cut off. The mammalian brain, by way of contrast, is quite sensitive to its environment and is an energy hog; indeed, to perform its sophisticated functions, the mammalian brain requires—under normal circumstances—20 percent of the body's glucose and oxygen. Cut off its energy supply, and it stops functioning within ten seconds.[6]

This explains why, when a human brain is deprived of oxygen and glucose, its mammalian portion quickly shuts down, but its reptilian portion will, for a time, continue to operate. Under normal circumstances, a human sees the world as it is interpreted to him by the mammalian portion of his brain. During an NDE, though, he sees the world as it is interpreted to him by the reptilian portion. As a result, the world he sees and hears may have little bearing on reality—if by "reality" we mean the world as interpreted by our higher brain functions.

If we want to see what it is like to shut down our mammalian brain, we can take a ride in a giant centrifuge. Test subjects who have done so ultimately black out because the high G-forces generated by the spinning deprive their brain of blood and thereby deprive it of oxygen and glucose. Subjects reported that as they were blacking out, they lost their peripheral vision, which caused them to experience tunnel vision. They also reported feeling euphoric and having what researchers described as "dreamlets" in which they might see relatives.[7]

If you don't have access to a centrifuge, you can climb a very high mountain. At high altitudes little oxygen is available. A climber might become disoriented, with potentially fatal consequences. And if there are no nearby mountains, you can shut down the mammalian portion of your brain by running a four-hundred-meter sprint as fast as you can. By the end of the sprint, you will almost certainly be experiencing "tunnel hearing": you either won't hear or won't be able to understand things people are yelling at you. In addition, you might experience tunnel vision and might slip into a dream-like state.

IT IS PRETTY REMARKABLE to encounter one angel in the course of a lifetime. Fifteen years after nearly drowning, however, the woman described above had a second such encounter. The circumstances were quite different, though.

The woman, who had completely recovered from her earlier brush with death, was in a hospital room cradling her seriously injured daughter, when she suddenly saw, standing nearby, the same "angel" as she had seen before. (She knew they were the same because they looked exactly alike, except for their hairdos.[8]) This time, the angel telepathically told her that the daughter would be all right. When the woman blinked her eyes in disbelief, the angel vanished.[9] The woman concluded that the angel had been sent by God to comfort her.[10] In other words, she experienced a revelation in which she not only saw a divine being with her own eyes but also had a thought planted in her mind by that being. This, at any rate, is the most obvious way to understand the "telepathic telling" she describes.

As I have said, a scientist might attribute this woman's earlier angel encounter to an oxygen-starved brain. In this second angel encounter, though, the woman's brain was fully oxygenated. But still, a scientific explanation is possible: perhaps what the woman was experiencing was a mental state known as *hypnagogia*.

I happen to be subject to hypnagogia: when I am drifting off to sleep, especially for a nap, I often go through a stage during which I see things. Because I am not yet fully asleep, I know that the things I am seeing are not really there. And yet I am seeing them not in my mind but with my eyes—that is, the eyes that I know to be closed.

Hypnagogic episodes are fascinating; indeed, I have become a collector of them. When I am trying to take a nap, I relax with my eyes closed. Before long, I realize that I am seeing something. It is as if someone has turned on a movie projector in my head, with the movie being projected onto the insides of my eyelids. I have no control at all over what "film" is going to be shown during a hypnagogic episode. In one of them, I saw five people ride past me on bicycles. They were wearing colorful cycling attire and helmets. They were moving quickly and were together in one group, so I assumed that they were racing.

This sort of imagery, of course, can happen during a dream, but in a dream, I am unaware that I am dreaming. Instead, I think that what I am seeing is really happening. In an episode of hypnagogia, though, I am fully aware that I am not in fact seeing what I seem to be seeing, even though the images look as real as they would if my eyes were open. I am routinely deceived by dreams; I am never deceived by hypnagogic states.

That hypnagogic states are possible tells us something about the creative power of the human brain. In the case just described, my unconscious mind apparently decided to make a ten-second "movie." In doing so, it decided that it would be about cyclists, how many cyclists there would be, what they would be doing, what they would be wearing, whether or not they would have helmets, and so on. It created the environment through which the cyclists would be riding, complete with asphalt, sidewalks, lawns, trees, and houses. And it decided that the film would be in high-definition 3D color. For a movie studio to come up with such a "film" might take a week of effort by a talented group of filmmakers who have access to a very powerful computer. My unconscious mind apparently came up with the idea for this hypnagogic film on the spur of the moment, and the resulting film was presumably made as it was being shown.

I am not, by the way, unusual in experiencing hypnagogia. Many people, on reading the above account, will recognize in themselves the phenomenon I have described.

It is conceivable that, while cradling her child, the angel-seeing woman closed her eyes and drifted into a hypnagogic state in which she "saw" an angel. I think it is significant that on "seeing" the angel, she blinked her eyes, and the angel vanished. Perhaps the woman didn't so much blink her eyes as open them, an action that would have shattered the hypnagogic state. If this is indeed what happened, the woman's vision of an "angel" has a natural explanation.

But this explanation sounds inconsistent: if the woman was experiencing a hypnagogic state, wouldn't she be aware that she wasn't really seeing the things she seemed to be seeing, the way I am aware? Perhaps not. If someone is unfamiliar with hypnagogic states or eager to give supernatural explanations for natural phenomena, it might not occur to her that what she sees is mere hypnagogia. She might therefore sincerely believe that something supernatural has just happened.

WE HAVE CONSIDERED the way hallucinations can be interpreted as religious revelations. The hallucinations in question might be triggered by depriving the brain of blood or oxygen, or by drifting off to sleep. But this is just the beginning. Certain substances, if ingested, smoked, snorted, injected, or otherwise internalized, can cause people to experience hallucinations. In some cultures, these hallucinations are thought to have religious significance.

The Mixtec people of Mexico, for example, have long used psilocybin mushrooms in religious ceremonies. In 1957, Robert G. Wasson, then a vice president of J. P. Morgan, participated in these ceremonies and published a description of them in *Life* magazine. It is unclear whether ingesting the mushrooms allowed the Mixtecans to "see God"; they did think, however, that the mushrooms had the power to "carry you there where God is."[11] The mushrooms could also turn a person into an oracle, through whom God could speak.

Wasson doesn't claim to have seen God or any other divine being, but what he saw was nevertheless spectacular:

> I saw river estuaries, pellucid water flowing through an endless expanse of reeds down to a measureless sea, all by the pastel light of a horizontal sun. This time a human figure appeared, a woman in primitive costume, standing and staring across the water, enigmatic, beautiful, like a sculpture except that she breathed and was wearing woven colored garments. It seemed as though I was viewing a world of which I was not a part and with which I could not hope to establish contact. There I was, poised in space, a disembodied eye, invisible, incorporeal, seeing but not seen.[12]

He adds, "For the first time the word *ecstasy* took on real meaning. For the first time, it did not mean someone else's state of mind."[13]

In 1962, before Good Friday services commenced in Boston University's Marsh Chapel, twenty Protestant divinity students participated in an experiment in which half were given psilocybin and the other half were given a placebo.[14] None of those who took the psilocybin reported seeing God, but they did report having a profoundly spiritual experience. And even after a quarter of a century, those who got the hallucinogen unanimously described the experience as "one of the high points of their spiritual life."[15] In another, similar experiment, published in 2006, 71 percent of the subjects rated their psilocybin trip as being either the most spiritually significant or one of the top five most spiritually significant experiences of their lifetime.[16] But again, they did not claim to have seen God or some other divine being.

These examples make it clear that use of a hallucinogen can trigger a profound religious experience. When we examine the world's religions, though, we don't find many that are based on hallucinogen-induced revelations. This is because these revelations tend to be *contentless*, in the sense that they don't provide us with a specific divine being to worship, and they don't reveal that being's expectations of us. These are things that most people seek in a religion.

SEIZURES ARE ANOTHER SOURCE of hallucinations that potentially have religious significance. Of particular interest are epileptic seizures. Early symptoms of such seizures might include hallucinatory smells, say of frying meat or perfume.[17] These might be accompanied by hallucinatory sounds, perhaps of hissing, ringing, or rustling.[18] In some cases, an auditory hallucination will involve hearing a voice calling your name. According to one epileptic, "This is not like hearing a voice in a dream. It is a *real* voice. Every time I hear it I fall for it. It is not a man's voice or a woman's voice. I don't recognize it. There is one thing that I do know and that is if I turn towards the voice I have a convulsion."[19]

Researchers have found that the religious revelations epileptics experience depend partly on their religious views. In the West, an epileptic might, during a seizure, have a vision of Jesus, God, or an angel. Likewise, the voice he hears might instruct him to convert to Christianity. In Japan, however, someone experiencing an epileptic seizure might hear a voice that instructs him to pray to Buddha.[20] And in one case, an epileptic who was a devout Buddhist experienced a revelation that was remarkable for its religious diversity. He says that he "saw different divine worlds structured around folk beliefs, a new sect of Christianity, and other kinds of contemporary religions." He "heard the voices of the objects of worship of every religion and saw how the heavens and the earth were created according to each religion."[21]

During seizures, people can become convinced that they have personally encountered God. Emboldened by this encounter, they might do something they normally wouldn't have done. Oliver Sacks describes one epileptic who, after encountering God during a seizure, not only ran for Congress but nearly won, since she could look voters in the eye and tell them that God had commanded her to run.[22] Sacks also mentions a woman who had converted not once but five times as the result of seizures, and a man who started believing in the existence of God as the result of one seizure and then stopped believing as the result of another.[23]

History gives us several notable examples of people who seem to have been suffering from epilepsy and also experienced religious revelations. Joan of Arc was one of these. She had her first vision as a teenager, when she heard a voice from without, accompanied by a bright light. She says that she "recognized that it was the Voice of an Angel."[24] The prophet Ezekiel, who was subject to visions, was also arguably an epileptic.[25]

Some—most famously, novelist Fyodor Dostoevsky—have suggested that Mohammed would fall into this same category.[26] After experiencing the revelations on Mount Hira, Mohammad started receiving the verses that became the

Quran: they were "sent down" to him by Allah.[27] The revelations in question, he explained, came in two ways: "Sometimes Gabriel visits me and tells it to me as though one man were speaking to another, but then what he speaks is lost to me. But sometimes it comes to me as with the noise of a bell, so that my heart is confused. But what is revealed to me in this way never leaves me."[28] He also explained how he knew a revelation was coming: "I hear loud noises, and then it seems as if I am struck by a blow. I never receive a revelation without the consciousness that my soul is being taken away from me."[29]

There will be those, I suspect, who think it impious for me to entertain the thought that the revelations that gave rise to Islam are nothing more than a byproduct of epileptic seizures. Realize, though, that I am making no such claim. I will explain why in a moment.

WHETHER OR NOT Mohammed suffered from epilepsy, it seems clear that Dostoevsky did. In fact, Dostoevsky experienced a form of epilepsy that triggers what are called "ecstatic seizures."[30] In his novel *The Idiot*, Dostoevsky describes—fictionally, but presumably based on his own experience[31]—a seizure had by the character Myshkin: "Amidst the sadness, the mental darkness, the pressure, his brain suddenly seemed to burst into flame at moments, and with an extraordinary jolt all his vital forces seemed tensed together. The sensation of life and of self-awareness increased almost tenfold at those moments, which had a duration like that of lightning." In these moments, "the mind, the heart were flooded with an extraordinary light; all his unrest, all his doubts, all his anxieties were as if pacified at once, were resolved into a kind of higher calm, full of a serene, harmonious joy and hope." This moment, according to Dostoevsky, represents "the highest degree of harmony and beauty" and "yields a hitherto unheard-of and undreamed-of sense of completeness, proportion, reconciliation and an ecstatic, prayerful fusion with the highest synthesis of life." The feeling is so intensely pleasurable that one is inclined to say, "Yes, for this moment one could give up one's whole life!"[32]

The medical literature offers many other examples of religiously significant seizures. In one case, a woman reported feeling a sudden rush of elation, accompanied by a feeling that she was "about to find out knowledge no one else shares—something to do with the line between life and death."[33] In another case, a woman experienced a seizure in which she had the sensation of being simultaneously in two different worlds. In one of these worlds, she encountered a wise woman who tried to present her with the ultimate mission of her life. Since this wise woman didn't use words, the message wasn't very clear. It had something to do with saving children.[34]

As we saw earlier, Saul of Tarsus experienced a religious revelation that caused him to go blind for a time and thereby compelled him to convert to Christianity. Fourteen years after this event, he had another revelation in which he felt "caught up to the third heaven" and heard "sacred secrets which no human lips can repeat."[35] After studying Saul's "symptoms," some have concluded that he was an epileptic who sometimes experienced ecstatic seizures. Epileptic seizures, it is worth noting, can cause temporary blindness, which would explain why Saul temporarily went blind after Jesus "spoke to him" on the road to Damascus.[36]

In addition to observing epileptics, scientists have experimented on them. In the 1930s, Wilder Penfield performed a number of experimental operations on epileptics.[37] His patients' scalps were pulled back and their skulls opened, so Penfield could move an electrode over the surface of their brain. Since the patients, who had been given only a local analgesic,[38] were fully conscious during the operation, they could tell Penfield what, if anything, the electrode made them think or feel. Penfield's goal in performing this operation was to find a spot on the brain, stimulation of which would trigger an epileptic seizure in the patient. That part of the brain could then be removed, hopefully putting an end to the patient's seizures.[39] (Thus, Penfield was not so much experimenting on his patients as attempting to cure them.)

While stimulating brains in this manner, Penfield made an astonishing discovery: stimulation sometimes triggered strange thoughts and sensations in patients. One woman, when a particular spot of her brain was stimulated, said she suddenly felt like she was in her kitchen and could hear the voice of her son playing outside.[40] Another woman experienced mystical feelings. She had "just a tiny flash of a feeling of familiarity and a feeling that I knew everything that was going to happen in the near future."[41] Penfield could also trigger in patients the feeling that they were in two places at the same time.[42]

Wilder Penfield had to open people's skulls to stimulate their brains, but modern technology allows researchers to stimulate brains without resorting to surgery. Transcranial magnetic stimulators, for example, can send pulsating magnetic fields through people's skulls and thereby stimulate regions of the brain. Depending on what region is stimulated and on the strength and pulse rate of the field, a subject might experience an involuntary contraction of his muscles or intense pleasure "like a thousand orgasms rolled into one."[43] And if a subject's temporal lobe is stimulated, he might even experience God, as Canadian psychologist Michael Persinger did. For the record, before his experience with transcranial magnetic stimulation, Persinger had not been particularly religious.[44]

AFTER CONSIDERING ALL THE WAYS in which a hallucination can resemble a revelation, we might be tempted to conclude that *all* religious revelations—even those that launched the world's great religions—were in fact hallucinations that can be explained in straightforward, scientific terms. But it would be a mistake to draw such a conclusion. We don't, after all, know the circumstances under which the great religious revelations of the past took place: Abraham, Moses, Mohammed, Joseph Smith, and all the other historically significant prophets weren't hooked up to EEG or MRI machines when they had their revelations. Nor were they being observed by blue-ribbon panels of neurologists. As a result, their mental state at the time of their revelations is a matter of speculation.

And even if we could prove that a prophet was having an epileptic seizure when he had the vision that lay the foundation for the religion he started, it would not follow that the revelation in question wasn't "genuine." Someone could argue, after all, that just as God gives us eyes so we can see the world around us, he gives some people the ability to experience seizures by means of which they can see or hear him.

In making such a claim, though, we have moved outside the realm of science. There is, after all, no way to test this claim to see if it is true. If a perception has a supernatural cause, then science, which concerns itself only with natural things and events, won't be able to detect that cause and therefore won't be able to determine whether it really is the cause. In much the same way, a person's claim that God caused his favorite soccer team to win is outside the realm of science: there is no observation we can make, no experiment we can do, that would confirm or refute this claim.

If we ourselves have a vision, it won't occur to us—unless we are unusually skeptical and analytical—to try to confirm or refute it; we are likely to not only accept it but also to feel quite confident that God appeared before us. But suppose we aren't the ones who had the vision; suppose someone else did. Suppose, too, that the person in question lived long ago and far away, suppose he is one among many people who have had visions, and suppose, finally, that the visions of these prophets appear to be incompatible. This leaves the rest of us with a conundrum: which vision—if any!—shall we accept as genuine? It is to this question that we will turn our attention in the next chapter.

CHAPTER 3

Other People's Visions

ADAM WAS LUCKY. He not only got to live in the Garden of Eden but knew exactly what God wanted of him. His job was to take care of the garden, and he was given permission to eat from any tree in the garden except for the tree of the knowledge of good and evil.[1] Adam would apparently encounter God when the latter came for a walk "in the cool of the day."[2] At that time, one imagines, Adam would get feedback on his performance, both as a gardener and as a human being.

We descendants of Adam don't live in the Garden of Eden—thanks to Adam's failure to follow God's directives—nor do we have direct contact with God, the way Adam did. It may be true that if we pray to him, our prayers will be answered with internal feelings of warmth or with spontaneous thoughts. But these phenomena can easily be misconstrued. We can never be sure, after all, that God is responsible for a feeling or thought; maybe the thought that suddenly appeared in our mind is wishful thinking on our part rather than a message from God, and maybe the warm feeling we experienced is, well, indigestion.

What would be wonderful is face time with God, one or more meetings in which he would tell us, in no uncertain terms, what he wants of us. It is clear that God *can* do this; after all, he did it for Adam, as well as for any number of prophets. In other cases, God didn't make a personal appearance but instead sent Jesus or an angel with a message. This raises an obvious question: if God can provide divine contact to *some* people, why not to *all* people? It would make it much easier for us to know what he wanted of us, and thereby make it much more likely that we would do his bidding.

Someone might respond to this suggestion by asserting that God is too busy to put in seven billion personal appearances. Realize, though, that because he is an infinite being, he can easily do this: he need only will that it be done. Indeed, it is arguably easier for God to put in multiple daily appearances before every person on earth than it is for me to mow my lawn. Unfortunately, I cannot cut my grass by willing that it be short; I must instead go out into the heat and push around a lawn mower for half an hour. And yet God is stinting with his personal appearances. Why?

THIS LAST QUESTION might sound impious, but in any discussion of religious aha moments, it is one that must be raised. If God gave us the kind of direct contact I have described, all of us would experience full-blown religious visions—religious revelations in which we see and converse with a divine being. As things are, though, most of us go through life without even one such encounter. If we seek to serve God, we must rely on the visions other people claim to have had. In this respect, we resemble a group of blind people in a desert who must rely on the eyesight of others to guide them to water.

Our task of sorting through other people's visions would be easy if only one person claimed to have been visited by God and instructed to found a religion. That religion would be our only option: if we wanted to be religious, that would be the one we would follow. Returning to the blind-people-in-the-desert analogy, suppose a group of one hundred people was lost in the desert. Suppose one of these people could see but the other ninety-nine were blind. The blind people would quickly conclude that their best option was to follow the directions of the sighted person.

Our task of choosing a religion would also be straight-forward if several people, at scattered locations around the world, claimed to have been visited by God and instructed to start a new religion, and if, when these prophets compared notes, they discovered that they had all been given the same instructions. A sensible person would conclude that the most likely way for this to have happened is if a single divine being had revealed itself to all of them. By employing this multiple-prophet communication strategy, the being would not only be conveying its desires to people all over the world but would simultaneously be providing us with compelling evidence of its existence. As a result, our decision to follow a religion and our choice of which religion to follow would be a no-brainer. Returning once again to our desert analogy, suppose that in the group of one hundred people, ten could see and all agreed on which way to head for water. This is the direction any sensible blind person would want to head.

When we explore the history of religion, though, we find that there have not only been lots—certainly thousands, and maybe millions—of people who claim to have been instructed by God to start a new religion, but the religions they founded or wanted to found are incompatible with each other. (I know there are people who claim that all religions are "at base the same." My response is to suggest that these individuals try practicing orthodox Judaism and Islam, or Islam and Mormonism, simultaneously.) From the perspective of someone trying to choose a religion, this is the worst possible state of affairs. To see why, consider, one last time, the desert analogy. Suppose each of the ten people who could see has a different idea about which way to head for water. The blind people would be in a quandary: which of these "seers," if any, should they follow?

Those of us who have never been blessed with a vision are in a similar predicament. Lots of people claim to have had face time with a divine being and have founded incompatible religions on the basis of their encounter. Which of them should we follow? Stated more bluntly, how can we determine which of the self-proclaimed prophets is in fact God's Chosen One?

AT THIS POINT, clarification is in order. The question just asked is misleading. It assumes that of all the people who have claimed to be God's Chosen One, exactly one person was in fact chosen. This assumption can be challenged.

It is possible, after all, that *none* of the people claiming to be God's prophet were in fact contacted by God. Then how can we explain their revelations? They might all be mentally ill.

Or maybe, despite being of sound mind, they experienced a hallucination. It is also possible that their claims to have had a vision are fraudulent—that they just made up their visions to get other people's attention or to gain power over them. And finally, it is possible that their visions do have a supernatural origin, but that it was Satan rather than God who caused them. I will have more to say about this possibility in a moment.

It is also possible that *many* or even *all* of the self-proclaimed prophets were chosen by God. But wait a minute! I just pointed out that different prophets offer different, often glaringly incompatible messages about what God wants us to do. Mohammed, for example, tells us one thing, and Joseph Smith tells us another. And now I am suggesting that both can be recipients of a "genuine" revelation. How could this be?

God works in mysterious ways. He lets innocent children die in fiery bus crashes that he could easily have prevented. (He is, after all, omniscient, meaning that he knows when a bus is about to crash, and omnipotent, meaning that he can easily intervene to prevent the crash.) He lets diseases sweep the globe, when he could easily prevent them from spreading. He lets hundreds of thousands of people drown in tsunamis that take place only because of how he chose to construct the earth. It is baffling that God would behave in this manner, but he does. Believers often try to explain this behavior by saying that all human suffering is part of a bigger plan that we mere mortals cannot hope to understand. They maintain, in other words, that some greater good arises out of all this suffering.

Someone could argue, along these lines, that God is behind many of the world's religions—including Judaism, Islam, and Mormonism—and that he made these religions incompatible as part of some larger plan. Perhaps he did it as a test, to see whether we humans can sort through the competing religions to find the "correct" one and thereby prove ourselves worthy of salvation. Thus, from the mere fact that different religions are incompatible, it does not follow that their founding prophets did not all have "genuine" visions: God could have visited them all and given them incompatible instructions, for reasons known only to him.

IN DOING THE RESEARCH for this book, I examined many visions. To me, the single most striking thing about visions is the ability of the people who have had them to identify the divine being who appeared to them. Thus, a person might describe a vision in which he saw God, Jesus, the angel Gabriel, or some other being. Such a description raises an obvious but often unasked question: how is it possible for a mere mortal to identify a divine being?

Consider claims of having encountered Jesus. If you knew what Jesus looked like, and if that is how the being you saw in your revelation looked, you could conclude that you saw Jesus. But we don't know what Jesus looked like! We have no photographs of him. Nor do we have contemporaneously made paintings of him. What we have are artists' conceptions, made hundreds of years after his crucifixion, of what he might have looked like. And if we turn to the Bible for a physical description of Jesus, we will be disappointed. We are told, for example, that Jesus "had no form or majesty that we should look at him, and no beauty that we should desire him."[3]

If it is hard to know what Jesus looks like, it is harder still to know what God looks like. After all, God is incorporeal, meaning that when he decides to reveal himself to someone, he must choose a body to use in the vision. This could be any human body you can imagine: a man's or a woman's body, an old or young body, a dark- or fair-skinned body. It could also be a nonhuman body: God could, if he chose, appear as a talking turtle. He could even appear—as he did to Moses—as a talking bush. So how can someone know that what he sees in a revelation is God?

As I have explained, it is easier to base a new religion on an "audible vision" than on a vision in which a person sees but does not hear the being he encounters: by hearing the being, a prophet can find out what the being wants done. But "audible visions" have another advantage: they allow the being to identify himself. Thus it was that God introduced himself to Abraham—"I am God Almighty"[4]—and to Moses—"I am the God of your father, the God of Abraham, the God of Isaac and the God of Jacob."[5] Joseph Smith was not as lucky as these Old Testament figures. When a divine being first appeared to him in a pillar of light, the being didn't introduce himself but instead introduced a second being as "my Beloved Son." Smith inferred that it was God and Jesus who hovered before him.

This raises a new question: can a prophet trust these divine self-introductions? How does he know some other supernatural being isn't impersonating a divine being? As the Apostle Paul reminds us, "even Satan disguises himself as an angel of light."[6] Furthermore, identifying himself as God or Jesus is just the kind of trick we would expect Satan to play. Someone might argue that if you see God in a revelation, he will cause you to feel confident that you are seeing him. But again, you could never be sure that it wasn't the devil trying to fool you.

FOR THE SAKE OF ARGUMENT, let us overlook this difficulty. Suppose you experience a full-blown vision: you see and talk to God—or rather, you are convinced that you have seen and talked to a divine being and that the being in question is God. You are now faced with the question of what to do with this aha moment. Should you tell other people what has happened? Doing this will doubtless have an impact on your relationships. Many people will conclude that you have gone crazy and will start avoiding you. So perhaps it is wisest to keep your encounter with God to yourself.

This, one suspects, is what most recipients of religious revelations do. If they share their revelations, they do so only with family members. They worry that if they share a revelation with outsiders, they will be met with hostility. This is what happened to Joseph Smith. As you'll remember, God and Jesus informed him that all existing religions were wrong; indeed, their creeds were an abomination and their professors were corrupt, and Smith should join none of them.[7] When Smith, who was then fourteen years old, told a Methodist preacher about his vision, the preacher's response surprised him: "He treated my communication not only lightly, but with great contempt, saying it was all of the devil, that there were no such things as visions or revelations in these days; that all such things had ceased with the apostles, and that there would never be any more of them."[8]

Faced with this sort of reception, it is perfectly understandable that the recipient of a vision would keep it to himself. Indeed, it may be that many or even most people who experience a vision take it to the grave with them. In some cases, though, people are given a compelling reason to spread word of their vision: they have a subsequent vision in which a divine being commands that they start a new religion. This is what happened to both Mohammed and Joseph Smith. According to the former, the Lord's instructions were accompanied by a threat: "Gabriel came to me and told me that if I did not do as I was ordered my Lord would punish me."[9]

A prophet who is instructed to start a new religion is faced with the challenge of convincing skeptical people. These skeptics will think that the prophet has simply made up the religion he is promoting and that they would be foolish to join it. If the prophet happens to be charismatic, he might be able to overcome this initial distrust and win followers. No matter how charismatic he is, though, he will likely find that to have a chance of convincing others of his legitimacy, he will have to tell them about his encounters with God.

People tend to let other people think on their behalf. If a claim is widely accepted, they assume—often mistakenly—that its believers researched the claim and found it credible.

They therefore feel comfortable in believing it themselves. Psychologists call this the *bandwagon effect*: belief begets additional belief. Conversely, if almost no one believes a claim, people will assume that there is a good reason why they don't, and they will reject it themselves.

It therefore requires considerable courage to abandon a widely held religious belief in favor of an unpopular one. When a new religion is being launched and the prophet's reputation is just beginning to spread, there will be few believers and many nonbelievers. A prophet will have to work very hard to gain his first "real" adherent, drawn from outside of his circle of family and friends.

This was Mohammed's experience. In response to God's command to start a new religion, he called together forty members of his tribe to ask that they abandon their religious views in favor of his. The meeting did not go well. He made but one convert, an individual described as "the youngest, most rheumy-eyed, fattest in body and thinnest in legs." The other men, we are told, responded to his appeal with laughter.[10]

As a prophet starts gaining followers, he may notice a new phenomenon. People who previously were indifferent to the religion he was promoting will become openly hostile to it. Mohammed and his followers made a point of praying in public, in part so that people would see them and take note. Rather than attract followers, though, this practice made the early Muslims susceptible to harassment.[11] Non-Muslims would interrupt their prayers with rude remarks. Even worse, they would throw things at the person who was praying: on one occasion, Mohammed was pelted with a sheep uterus.[12] And even when they were not openly practicing their religion, Muslims were threatened and harassed. Muslim businessmen became the targets of boycotts,[13] and Muslims of lower social standing were beaten[14] or even tortured.[15] Indeed, at one point, Mohammed himself was nearly killed by his tribesmen.[16]

Why such hostility? Because many people feel threatened by a new religion. They realize that if the new religion is correct, their current religion must be mistaken, and this is something that they not only don't want to admit but also don't even want to have to think about. At a deeper level, they might worry that they will be compelled to follow the new religion. It therefore seems best to fight the new religion while it is still small enough to extinguish.

A prophet will typically try to start his new religion wherever he happens to be living when he receives the divine command. The problem with this strategy is that the local people knew him before God chose him, and as Jesus noted— I paraphrase—it is hard to be a prophet in your home town.[17] Thus, when Mohammed abandoned Mecca for Yathrib, he found the people there much more receptive to his religious message. To the residents of Yathrib, after all, Mohammad was a man who had come from afar to enlighten them.[18] He possessed a mystique that no local could claim. Joseph Smith also found that the best strategy for growing a religion was to leave the people who knew him best. Even after he gained followers, they often had to move again because of local hostility to their religion.

THERE IS A DANGER that as a prophet gains power, his followers will want to seize it for themselves. They could start a new religion of their own, of course, but it is much easier to take over an existing religion or cause a schism and thereby gain control over a portion of its members. One way to do this is to challenge the prophet's authority. This is another reason that it is beneficial to a prophet to experience ongoing revelations. That he has such revelations is evidence that he remains God's Chosen One. It also provides him with a potent tool for dealing with those who challenge his authority with revelations of their own: he can have a revelation in which God declares their revelations to be null and void.

Joseph Smith's authority was challenged when two of his closest associates, Oliver Cowdery and Hiram Page, started having revelations.[19] Smith subsequently had a revelation in which God announced to him that "no one shall be appointed to receive commandments and revelations in this Church, excepting my servant Joseph Smith, Jun., for he receiveth them even as Moses."[20] Mohammed likewise had a revelation in which he was declared to be the "last of the prophets,"[21] meaning that anyone who has revelations that contradict his is not a true prophet. (There are, to be sure, other interpretations of this "Seal of the Prophets" passage.)

Although a religion's founding prophet will want to suppress many of his followers' revelations, he might want to encourage some of them. In 1843, Smith experienced a revelation in which God told him that "if any man espouse a virgin, and desire to espouse another, and the first give her consent, and if he espouse the second, and they are virgins, and have vowed to no other man, then is he justified."[22] (This revelation was later "rescinded" by the Mormon Church,[23] although there continue to be Mormons who practice polygamy.)

Smith subsequently started acquiring additional wives. He told one young woman that an angel had appeared to him three times, commanding him to take her as his wife, and that on the third visit, the angel had a drawn sword and threatened him with death if he didn't take her. In response, the woman asked—quite reasonably—why she had not likewise been visited. Thereafter, she *was* visited, by an angel that she said went through her like lightning, and she consented to become Smith's wife.[24] From Smith's point of view, it was a useful revelation for her to have had.

In another case, Smith needed people who could attest to the existence of the golden plates that were the source of the *Book of Mormon*. He settled on three close associates—Martin Harris, Oliver Cowdery, and David Whitmer—as witnesses. Rather than simply showing them the plates, Smith took them into the woods and had them pray. Nothing happened. They prayed again, but still nothing happened. Harris then left, blaming himself (and his doubts) for their failure to see the plates. The remaining three prayed yet again, and this time they were successful: they saw above them a light of exceeding brightness, and then an angel, who held the plates. Smith then turned his attention to Harris, whom he found praying in the distance. Smith joined him in prayer, and before long, Harris had the vision that Smith and the others had previously experienced. "Mine eyes have beheld," Harris exclaimed.[25]

These cases are examples of what I call *confirming revelations*. The founder of a religion, as we have seen, typically experiences a revelation in which he encounters God and then experiences subsequent revelations in which God tells him what he must do. When the prophet informs other people of these revelations he will often be met with skepticism. But then something remarkable can happen: other people start experiencing revelations of their own that confirm the revelations experienced by the prophet!

Confirming revelations will likely have a profound impact on the prophet. If he is sincere in his prophecy, he will take them as evidence that he isn't delusional, that God is in fact speaking through him. And if he is a false prophet—if he is simply making up revelations in order to gain power over other people—he will take their confirming revelations as evidence that his efforts are succeeding: he is fooling people so thoroughly that they are fooling themselves!

FOR A RELIGION TO TRULY SUCCEED, it must outlast its founding prophet. If, however, the founding prophet owes his position in the church to having been chosen by God, as demonstrated by his ongoing stream of revelations, questions will arise over whether the person who takes control of the church after the founder's death will be likewise blessed by God.

When Smith died, there was a battle for succession within the Mormon Church. Those who wanted to take his place claimed to have received authorizing revelations. The church could at this point simply have disappeared, the way countless religions with charismatic founders have, or broken into rival sects, the way Islam did after the death of Mohammed. Brigham Young, however, prevented this from happening to the Mormons: he reminded people that he was president of the apostles and as such had authority to lead the church. People listened and followed.[26]

A Mormon named James Jesse Strang subsequently managed to draw away seven hundred Mormons including, significantly, Joseph Smith's mother and his associate Martin Harris. Strang claimed that at the exact moment of Smith's death, an angel visited him and appointed him Smith's successor. Strang later claimed to have discovered brass plates that contained the ancient *Book of the Law of the Lord*—a document, he asserted, that had originally been part of the buried document Smith had found. The sorts of claims that had worked so well for Smith failed to work for Strang, though. His plans went awry when some of his disgruntled followers ambushed and shot him.[27]

IN THE PRECEDING CHAPTERS, we have considered religious aha moments of various kinds. Some of these moments transform a person. As the result of praying for guidance, someone might feel internal joy and become, say, a devout Catholic. In other cases, a religious aha moment, besides transforming a person, transforms the world in which he lives. On the basis of this aha moment—which typically involves seeing and hearing (with his eyes and ears, not with his mind) a divine being—he feels that he is serving as God's agent on earth and therefore must start a new religion. After having this foundational revelation, he will typically have others in which God tells him what he needs to do for his religion to flourish. This is how Judaism, Islam, Mormonism, and many other religions got their start.

It will be obvious to a religion's founding prophet that he is doing what God wants him to do. Those of us who haven't been blessed with a vision, though, are in a less fortunate situation. We must decide who, among the rival prophets, is God's Chosen One, and making this decision won't be easy. It is apparently a decision on which reasonable minds can differ; otherwise, the world's people wouldn't be divided into Mormons, Muslims, Jews, and so forth.

It is unlikely, I think, that my remarks in this and the preceding two chapters will cause anyone to abandon his or her religious beliefs. Such beliefs tend to be easy to acquire but difficult to abandon. At the same time, I hope that readers will come away from this text with a much deeper understanding of religious aha moments and the role they have played in human history.

Religious aha moments are different from the aha moments we will explore in subsequent chapters. Religious revelations have a sensory component—we see or hear something. They also feel like they are imposed on us from without. This is not the case, though, with the insights had by scientists, mathematicians, and artists. It is also not the case with the moral epiphanies to which we now turn our attention.

PART TWO

The Aha Moment in Morality

CHAPTER 4

The Two Kinds of Moral Epiphany

AS A YOUNG LAWYER, Mohandas Gandhi knew about racial discrimination but had never really experienced it. This all changed when he went to South Africa in 1893 to take on a legal case. He purchased a first-class train ticket, but when he entered the first-class car, a passenger objected to traveling with a "colored person." Gandhi was asked to leave the car, and when he refused to go, a constable pushed him out. In his autobiography, Gandhi describes the impact this incident had on him: "I began to think of my duty. Should I fight for my rights or go back to India, or should I go on to Pretoria without minding the insults, and return to India after finishing the case?" He concluded that he "should try, if possible, to root out the disease and suffer hardships in the process."[1]

On the next leg of his journey, Gandhi took a stagecoach and encountered more discrimination. He was told by the white "leader" of the coach that he couldn't sit inside, even though there were seats available. He instead had to sit outside with the coachman, a demand to which Gandhi acceded. This same leader subsequently decided that he wanted to have a smoke and get some fresh air, meaning that Gandhi would have to vacate the seat next to the coachman and sit on the floor of the footboard for a while. Gandhi replied that he wouldn't do this and offered to move to an inside seat instead, at which point the leader started cursing and beating him. Later in his trip, a hotel turned Gandhi away, with the excuse that they were full.

When Gandhi told the South African Indians he met what had happened to him, they were not surprised. Indeed, they had little trouble topping his stories with their own. These events appear to have triggered the transformation of Mohandas Gandhi, a mild-mannered lawyer, into Mahatma Gandhi, the civil rights leader. *Mahatma* is Sanskrit for "great soul."

IN THE 1780s, slavery was illegal in England, but British citizens were free to engage in the slave trade. In fact, Britain was the leading slave trader in the world, and because slave trading was so profitable, it played an important role in the British economy. Some British citizens participated directly in the slave trade, for example, as sailors on slave ships. Many more, including tradesmen, widows, and even clergy, participated in an indirect manner, by buying shares in those ships. These people weren't pro-slavery; they just accepted it as a fact of life.

Against this social backdrop, Thomas Clarkson experienced the moral aha moment I describe in the introduction to this book. He was at the time a student at Cambridge, preparing himself for a career in the church. In 1784, though, he entered an essay contest and won. He responded to this victory by setting for himself the goal of becoming the first Cambridge student to win two essay prizes. It was at this point that his life took the detour he later described in his *History of the Rise, Progress and Accomplishment of the Abolition of the African Slave Trade by the British Parliament.*

The second essay competition Clarkson entered had been devised by Cambridge vice chancellor Peter Peckard. Essay writers were to answer the question "Is it right to make slaves of others against their will?" Clarkson decided that a good essay-writing strategy would be to focus his attention on the African slave trade, inasmuch as he knew this would be of interest to Peckard, who had recently given a sermon on the subject.

In the course of doing research for his essay, Clarkson came across Anthony Benezet's *Historical Account of Guinea*, which described the slave trade in horrific detail. Clarkson hadn't realized the extent to which slaves suffered. Reading this book lifted a veil from his eyes and greatly distressed him. He later described this period of his life in the following terms: "In the day-time I was uneasy. In the night I had little rest. I sometimes never closed my eye-lids for grief." His essay-writing project, he said, "became now not so much a trial for academical reputation, as for the production of a work, which might be useful to injured Africa." This in turn caused him to redouble his effort in writing the essay: "I always slept with a candle in my room, that I might rise out of bed and put down such thoughts as might occur to me in the night, if I judged them valuable, conceiving that no arguments of any moment should be lost in so great a cause."[2] The effort he put into his essay must have been apparent to the competition judges. They awarded it first place.

Prize winners of such contests were expected to read their essays in public. In June of 1785, Clarkson traveled to London to do so. As he rode along, he tried to convince himself that the contents of his essay were not true, but to no avail. If they *were* true, though, slavery was clearly a moral abomination. And yet the people around him—even those who were educated and churchgoing—not only tolerated slavery but took steps to profit from it. How could this be? Near Wades Mill in Hertfordshire, he dismounted from his horse and sat down to think. He concluded that it was morally imperative that slavery be abolished.

Months after this epiphany, Clarkson remained in a state of moral turmoil: "I walked frequently into the woods, that I might think on the subject in solitude, and find relief to my mind there. But there the question still recurred, 'Are these things true?'—Still the answer followed as instantaneously 'They are.'" In the summer of 1786, these thoughts culminated in a second epiphany—that he should dedicate his life to bringing the slave trade to an end:

> My compassion for their sufferings were *at that moment* so great, so intense, so overwhelming, as to have overpowered me and compelled me to form the resolution, which I dared not resist, it was at my peril to resist, of attempting their deliverance. *Thus I was forced into* the great work...I have often indulged in the belief that this feeling might have come from God.[3]

Experiencing two connected aha moments, the way Clarkson did, is not unusual in the moral domain. In the first aha, a person realizes that something is morally wrong; in the second, he realizes that he has a duty to right that wrong. The first aha moment can transform the person who has it, but unless he goes on to have a second aha moment, the world will likely be unaffected by his original epiphany. Most of the people I examine in what follows have experienced a second aha moment; otherwise, it is unlikely that I would know of their existence.

Although Clarkson's first and second aha moments occurred a few months apart, Gandhi's realization that discrimination was wrong and his realization that he must fight it appear to have been simultaneous, or nearly so.

Once Clarkson took it upon himself to fight the moral evil of slavery, he had to decide what course of action to take. He was a relative nobody, so what, if anything, could he do to assist the cause of abolition? Then it dawned on him that by publishing his prize-winning essay he could influence public opinion. He found a publisher, and *Clarkson's Essay on the Slavery and Commerce of the Human Species* was subsequently favorably received by abolitionists.[4]

Thereafter, Clarkson continued his investigation of the slave trade. He discovered that British seamen were themselves victims of the trade: conditions on slave ships were so bad that a fifth of the seamen on them perished.[5] Revealing this and other facts, Clarkson thought, would sway British public opinion. To this end, he published pamphlets, books, and reports. He also sent petitions to Parliament. In the end, his efforts paid off: in 1807, the British slave trade was abolished, and in 1833—Clarkson was then in his seventies—slavery was abolished throughout the British Empire.

Clarkson is remembered, according to biographer Ellen Gibson Wilson, as "the architect and later the historian of the first national campaign for human rights that Britain had known. Hundreds share credit for the final victory but his contemporaries looked to Clarkson as the mastermind, the link 'by which it is all managed.' " She adds that Clarkson's "whole life was focused upon the slave question; indeed he was the only man in the movement who made it his career."[6] None of this would have happened, of course, if Clarkson hadn't, as a young man, been struck by a double moral epiphany.

THE NEXT MORAL EPIPHANY we'll consider may not be historically significant in the way those experienced by Gandhi and Clarkson are, but it is nevertheless worth considering, inasmuch as I have special insight into how it took place. This is because the epiphany in question was had by me.

I am a philosophy professor and as such am periodically called upon to encourage my students to explore their ethical beliefs. One of my favorite ways to do this is to ask them about their beliefs regarding cruelty to animals. They are, of course, opposed to it. I then inquire into their views regarding cockfighting, the "sport" in which birds known as gamecocks are put together in a cage to fight, often to the death. Sometimes their fighting ability is enhanced by attaching blades to the spurs on their legs. When they fight, people watch and bet on which gamecock will win. My students almost always find this activity to be morally abhorrent because of the cruelty it involves.

After querying my students about cockfighting, I ask them what they had for lunch. Invariably, some of them had chicken, in a salad, perhaps, or in a sandwich. I then ask whether it is morally permissible to eat chicken. Students typically reply that it is, as long as the chickens they eat weren't mistreated, so I ask them whether "broilers," the chickens they routinely eat, are raised in a humane manner. Usually they respond with silence. It is a question they have not seriously considered.

At this point, I share with them the likely life story of the broiler they had for lunch. It probably spent its life in a cage with several other chickens. It might never have gotten to spread its wings due to the cramped conditions, and its beak was cut off to keep it from pecking the other chickens in the cage to death. After about six weeks of this, while it was still tender, the broiler was removed from its cage and mechanically killed. A gamecock, by way of contrast, is typically raised outdoors. It might be tethered to a stake but has its own shelter. If it gets sick or injured, it might get medical attention, since its owner doesn't want his investment in the gamecock to be wasted. And after maybe two years of this existence, when it is in its fighting prime, the gamecock is given a chance to fight for its life.

I then present my students with a thought experiment. Suppose, I tell them, that reincarnation is true, and they are given the choice of coming back to life as either a gamecock or a broiler. Which would they choose? My students overwhelmingly pick the life of a gamecock. I respond with puzzlement at this choice: "You tell me that cruelty to animals is wrong. You also say that gamecocks are treated cruelly and therefore that cockfighting is immoral. But you apparently think that the way broilers are raised is even crueler, and yet you don't object to their being raised so you can eat them. Isn't this a double-standard?"

Students typically defend their beliefs by pointing to what they take to be an important difference between broilers and gamecocks: "You need to eat meat to live, but you don't need to fight cocks to live!" My response: "You *don't* need to eat meat to live, as the existence of hundreds of millions of vegetarians proves. Indeed, the medical consensus appears to be that the less meat you eat, the better your health will be." Another common student reaction to my thought experiment is to point out that not all broilers are raised in the conditions I describe. "Yes," I answer, "but you probably don't buy those chickens because they cost more. In other words, you don't mind cruelty to animals, as long as it saves you a few dollars at the grocery store."

When we become aware of an apparent inconsistency in our beliefs, three responses are possible. The first is to argue that the inconsistency in fact isn't an inconsistency at all. This is what my students do when they try to explain how making chickens fight is morally different from eating them. (It is also what many meat-loving readers of this book are now probably doing.) The second is to resolve the inconsistency by abandoning one of the beliefs in question. A student could, for example, react to my lecture by becoming a vegetarian; alternatively, the student could conclude that cockfighting isn't wrong! In my experience, though, it is pretty rare for students to instantly change their minds in response to this class discussion.

The third and most common way to respond to the discovery of an apparent inconsistency in our beliefs is to do nothing at all. We imagine that the inconsistency will, with the passage of time, resolve itself. My students might imagine, for example, that there *is* a morally significant difference between making chickens fight and eating them, but that they just haven't figured out what it is. Or they might hope that with the passage of time, they will simply forget about the inconsistency. They may also make a mental note to avoid vexatious philosophers in the future.

In many cases, students *will* succeed in forgetting about the inconsistency in their beliefs, but for others, awareness of the inconsistency will not go away. It will instead periodically make its presence known. Students in this second category will continue to eat meat. From time to time, though, a little voice in their mind will ask a troubling question: "What about the animals?" This voice apparently emanates from an unconscious component of their mind. This component has no problem with *false* beliefs—it will tolerate your believing that Bob is taller than Al, when the opposite is in fact the case—but it abhors *inconsistent* beliefs. If you believe, for example, that Al is taller than Bob, that Bob is taller than Charlie, but that Charlie is taller than Al, it will sound an alarm. Thereafter, it will pester you about this inconsistency.

What you are "hearing" when you find yourself in this predicament can best be described as the voice of reason (or more precisely as your *internal* voice of reason; if you are lucky, you have relatives and friends who play the role of *external* voices of reason for you). People can ignore the voice of reason, but when they do, they experience what psychologists refer to as a state of *cognitive dissonance*. It is the intellectual equivalent of having a pebble in your shoe: you are still able to walk, but the walking is uncomfortable and gets more so with the passage of time.

In saying this, I speak from personal experience. It was in the early 1980s that I first came up with the cockfighting thought experiment and started using it in the ethics classes I taught. Before I knew it, I had fallen victim to what is, for philosophers, a dreaded occupational hazard: I was persuaded by my own argument! For years after that, though, I continued to eat meat, all the while aware of the inconsistency in my beliefs. I discovered that Sigmund Freud was correct in his observation that "The voice of reason is small, but very persistent."[7]

In 1990, I finally conceded defeat to the voice of reason. There came a moment when I knew what I had to do to restore my mental equanimity: resolve the inconsistency in my beliefs by abandoning my belief that it was morally permissible to eat meat. It would be a mistake, by the way, to say that I *chose* to become a vegetarian; rather, I was browbeaten into doing so by the voice of reason. Furthermore, it would have been impossible for me to "fake" my way out of my predicament. Suppose, for example, that I tried to resolve my inconsistent beliefs by flipping a coin: "If it comes up heads, I will abandon my belief that cockfighting is morally wrong; if it comes up tails, I will abandon my belief that eating meat is morally permissible." My intellect would have seen through this ruse. Only by convincing myself that eating meat was morally impermissible—or, alternatively, that cockfighting was morally permissible—could I silence the voice of reason within me.

This episode was doubly transformative. Obviously, it changed the way I eat. But more significantly, it made me acutely aware of my capacity to harbor inconsistent beliefs. I have since devoted considerable effort to discovering other such beliefs so I can eradicate them. Some progress has been made, but much work remains to be done.

IN THE MORAL DOMAIN, there appear to be two ways in which aha moments happen. In some cases, they come quickly and without any "preparation" on the part of the person who experiences them. Instead, an event triggers them. This was the case with Gandhi's aha moment in South Africa. He doubtless knew about racial discrimination and disapproved of it, but it was only when he experienced it firsthand that he realized how wrong it was. This realization transformed him into a crusader. I shall refer to this sort of moral epiphany as a *Gandhi-style* aha moment, in his honor.

For another example of a Gandhi-style moment, consider Harriet Beecher Stowe, the daughter of religious leader Lyman Beecher. In the 1830s, she moved to Cincinnati. Across the Ohio river was Kentucky, a slave state. On visits there, Stowe saw with her own eyes how slaves lived and were treated. In 1839, she took on a former slave as a servant. Because Stowe lived in Ohio, the girl was considered free. Stowe heard, though, that the girl's master had come to Cincinnati, looking for what he regarded as his property. His plan was to get her back—by unlawful means, if necessary—to Kentucky, where she would again count as a slave. Stowe's husband took the girl into hiding till the danger had passed.[8]

The Fugitive Slave Act of 1850 allowed slaves who escaped to free states to be taken captive and returned to their masters. In the eyes of abolitionists, it was bad enough that those who had escaped slavery would be returned to it, but what made the Fugitive Slave Act morally noxious was its insistence that officials and citizens of free states assist in their capture. Stowe was disturbed by this state of affairs but not so much that she was willing to sacrifice personally for the abolitionist cause. She was, after all, a busy woman, with five children to look after.

This changed when her sister-in-law Isabella Porter (Jones) Beecher started sending her letters about the terrible things that were happening as a result of the Fugitive Slave Law— about the families broken up and the lives shattered. In one letter, she presented Stowe with a challenge: "Now, Hattie, if I could use a pen as you can, I would write something that would make this whole nation feel what an accursed thing slavery is." Stowe read the letter to her family, and when she came to the "I would write" passage, she stood up, crumpled the letter, and said, "I will write something. I will if I live."[9] She thereupon began work on her novel *Uncle Tom's Cabin*. Since she had a babe in arms at the time, working conditions were far from ideal. She complained in one letter that "As long as the baby sleeps with me nights I can't do much at anything," but went on to reaffirm her vow: "I will write that thing if I live."[10]

For yet another example of a Gandhi-style moment, consider the story of Ron Ridenhour. He grew up in Arizona and was raised by his white family to be a "good ol' boy." As a young man in the sixties, he was drafted and sent to fight in Vietnam. One night, lying in his bunk, he heard other soldiers making plans to attack a fellow soldier who happened to be the only black man in their unit. Ridenhour sat up in his bunk and, much to his surprise, heard himself say, "If you want to do that, you have to come through me."[11] It was enough to dissuade the other soldiers. Presumably, Ridenhour believed that racial hatred was wrong before he experienced this aha moment, but it took this incident to make him realize just how wrong it was and stand up for his belief.

After this moral awakening, Ridenhour became a crusader. He subsequently played a key role in exposing the massacre that had taken place in My Lai village in March of 1968. After his discharge from the military, he became an investigative journalist. The Ridenhour Prizes, which "recognize acts of truth-telling that protect the public interest, promote social justice or illuminate a more just vision of society,"[12] were inspired by his courage.

Ridenhour's moral transformation is by no means unique. Writer and contrarian Christopher Hitchens—about whom I have more to say in Chapter 6—interviewed many political dissenters. "Quite often," he says, "the 'baptism' of a future dissenter occurs in something unplanned, such as a spontaneous resistance to an episode of bullying or bigotry, or a challenge to some piece of pedagogical stupidity."[13]

BESIDES THESE GANDHI-STYLE AHA MOMENTS, there are what I shall call *Clarkson-style* moments. These aren't instantaneous, the way those experienced by Gandhi, Stowe, and Ridenhour were; they instead come at the end of a lengthy mental debate. In Clarkson's case, the debate lasted for months, and in my own case, it lasted for years.

It is important to realize that Clarkson and I could have arrived at our moral conclusions via Gandhi-style moments. Suppose Clarkson had been present at a Caribbean port when a slave ship was being unloaded. This horrific sight might have triggered an abrupt realization: without any mental debate, he might have decided that the slave trade is a moral abomination. Similarly, if I had somehow been forced to spend an afternoon in a commercial broiler-raising facility or a slaughterhouse, I might have felt such moral revulsion that on the spot I would have declared, "That's it; no more meat for me."

It would appear that Gandhi- and Clarkson-style aha moments have a different internal source. The former are triggered by our passions. We feel in our gut that something is wrong, and we therefore conclude that the thing in question *is* wrong. Our reason plays very little role, if any, in this process—although it might subsequently go to work coming up with plausible sounding reasons for our having drawn the conclusion that we did. Clarkson-style aha moments, however, are triggered by our reason, which becomes aware of an inconsistency in our beliefs and then works hard to resolve it. Because they have a different source, Gandhi-style moral epiphanies feel different from Clarkson-style epiphanies. In the former case, the feeling is one of moral indignation. In the latter, the feeling is likely one of relief: at last, the voice of reason will leave you alone.

The examples provided in this chapter help us understand how moral aha moments work, what they feel like, and the role they can play in human history. At the same time, they raise many new questions: Animals seem to lack a moral capacity, so why do we humans have one? What makes us special? And why are there two different ways in which we can experience a moral epiphany? It is to these questions that we will turn our attention in the next chapter.

CHAPTER 5

Moral Feelings and Moral Codes

WE ARE WIRED so that some things feel good and some things feel bad. It feels bad to go without eating for an extended period. It feels good to have sex. It feels bad to get burned by a fire. Such feelings are so woven into the fabric of our existence that it is easy to overlook the role they play in our lives.

In *On Desire: Why We Want What We Want*, I explore this wiring and the way it affects our lives. I argue that our wiring is a consequence of our evolutionary past. Our ancestors who were wired so that it felt good to have sex and felt bad to go without food or get burned were more likely to survive and reproduce than those who lacked this wiring. We have inherited the genes of these ancestors and thereby inherited their wiring along with the feelings to which it gives rise.

These feelings have a profound effect on how we live our lives. Think of how different your life would be if you weren't wired to enjoy sex. In other words, think of how different your life would be if, as you grew to adulthood, you had remained the psychologically asexual being that you were at, say, age four. You would never feel an urge to impress members of the opposite sex, date them, or mate with them. Similarly, think of how different your life would be if you weren't wired to want to be among other people and, when among them, to seek their admiration. You would probably be living in a different house, driving a different car, and wearing different clothes.

Besides being wired to have physical feelings, we are wired to have emotional feelings. We are able to feel anxious, fearful, angry, sad, proud, envious, and ashamed. Emotions can be triggered by inanimate objects—we might, for example, have a fear of ladders—as well as by nonhuman animals—we will likely be sad if our cat dies. But very often what gives rise to emotions are our relationships and interactions with other people.

This brings us to what, in our exploration of moral aha moments, is a very special group of feelings, which I will refer to as *moral feelings*. There are some things that we resist doing not because doing them would be physically painful and not because we are afraid to do them, but because it would feel *wrong* to do them. These feelings, as we shall see, can give rise to moral aha moments.

IN ORDER TO BETTER UNDERSTAND the nature of moral feelings, let us do a thought experiment. Consider the (imaginary) case of Mark and Julie, who are adult siblings vacationing together. One evening, when they are alone in the hotel room they are sharing, they start talking about what it would be like for them to have sex. They decide to give it a try but take multiple precautions: Julie is already using contraceptive pills, and Mark uses a condom. Although they enjoy their sexual encounter, they agree not to have another such encounter and not to tell others what they have done. Was it wrong for them to have sex?

You will probably find it easy to answer this question, and your answer will be that yes, it was wrong. This answer will be based on the "ick factor" that you probably experienced on hearing this story. But suppose someone asks you to explain *why* it was wrong. "Because of the dangers of inbreeding," you might reply. "If Julie had gotten pregnant, the resulting baby could be born with serious genetic disorders." The problem with this response is that since they used double birth control, it was highly unlikely that a pregnancy would result. And if this slim chance of pregnancy is bothersome to you, I can modify the story a bit: suppose Julie is a cancer survivor who no longer has ovaries.

After continuing this debate for a time, you might admit that you can't put into words why what Mark and Julie did was wrong. Chances are, though, that you will nevertheless continue to insist that it *was* wrong. Words will have failed you, for the simple reason that rational thought will have failed you. What motivates such behavior on your part? The presence in you of a powerful moral feeling with respect to incest.

Psychologists have explored moral feelings. Indeed, the thought experiment involving Mark and Julie is borrowed from one such study. In that study, led by psychologist Jonathan Haidt, people were asked to pass moral judgment on various hypothetical scenarios. Researchers found that subjects were able to quickly form judgments on the basis of gut feelings. It was only when they were asked to justify their judgments that their intellects played a role. They would attempt to come up with reasons for thinking that their judgments were correct. The reasons, however, tended not to be reasonable. Indeed, even the subjects seemed to realize as much: they would launch into defenses of their judgments only to come to a halt, realizing that their lines of argument didn't work. They were, as Haidt puts it, dumbfounded.[1]

It is important to realize that the moral *feelings* we experience can be disconnected from our moral *beliefs*. For example, I think it is morally permissible for someone to fight back when physically attacked. But if someone was physically attacking me, I would find it very difficult to punch him in the face in self-defense. It would be harder still for me to shoot him, if I had a gun handy, even though I think I would be within my moral (and legal) rights to do so, if I thought my life was in danger.

We ignore moral feelings at our peril. Suppose that, overcome by our desire for pleasure, we do something that feels wrong, such as cheating on a spouse. The pleasure we subsequently experience is likely to be contaminated by feelings of guilt, and those feelings might linger long after the moment of pleasure has passed. Similarly, even if we had a very good reason for doing something that felt wrong to do, we might subsequently pay a price: a person who kills someone in self-defense might years later have nightmares about the incident.

In what follows, I use the term *moral sense* to refer to our ability to have moral feelings—our ability, that is, to feel that something is wrong. When we examine the moral sense, we quickly conclude that in the same way that some people have more acute vision or hearing than others, some people have a more acute moral sense than others: they will be more likely to feel that things are wrong, or feel more intensely that particular things are wrong, than other people will. Furthermore, some people seem to have defective moral senses. Psychopaths, for example, can unhesitatingly do things that most people feel are wrong—indeed, so wrong that most people can't even conceive of doing them.

When we examine the moral sense, we also discover that among people who have fully functioning moral senses, there will be differences regarding what does and doesn't feel wrong. Indeed, although most readers, on hearing about Mark and Julie, probably felt that what they did was wrong, there were doubtless readers who failed to experience that feeling. Furthermore, it is possible for a person's moral sense to change. At one time in my life, the Mark and Julie story would have triggered the ick sensation within me. My exposure to philosophy, though, has undermined my susceptibility to the admonishments of my moral sense. I still experience moral feelings, but I no longer trust them to the extent that I once did.

WE HUMANS HAVE a limbic system. It is located in roughly the center of our brain and consists of numerous structures, including the hippocampus, amygdala, cingulate gyrus, and olfactory bulbs. Our limbic system appears to be the seat of our emotions. There is reason to think that it is also the seat of our moral feelings and therefore our moral sense.

Many nonhuman animals also have limbic systems. One function of the limbic system is to tag sensory input with an emotion. Thus, when animals see or hear a predator, their limbic systems cause them to experience fear; if they instead see or smell a member of the opposite sex, they experience lust. By causing animals to experience emotions, their limbic systems motivate them to behave in certain ways—to run, perhaps, or to mate, depending on the circumstances. Thus, an important part of the motivational wiring I have been talking about is found in the limbic system.

Although humans and other animals both have limbic systems, we have something they lack, namely, an oversized cerebrum, with its magnificent cerebral cortex. It is important to remember that the cerebrums of our hominid ancestors, as they grew, did not *supplant* their limbic system; they *supplemented* it. Thus, we modern humans still have a primitive brain, in the form of our limbic system, lurking within us. We can detect its presence by the emotions we experience and by the desires that "spontaneously" appear in our minds.[2]

It is also possible for us to encounter our primitive brain in a much more striking manner. One of these occasions is when we are in a rage. Under these circumstances, our reason deserts us, and we therefore have little control over what we do. Another occasion is in the late stages of a sexual act, when we enter, for a few seconds, a realm in which the rest of the universe has dropped away and nothing else matters but this moment, this act. Yet another time when we encounter our primitive brain, possibly with fatal consequences, is when we find ourselves underwater without any air in our lungs, perhaps as the result of getting submerged by an unexpected wave while swimming in the ocean. If we panic, we will stop making deliberate motions to get to the surface and instead, under the influence of our primitive brain, will start thrashing our arms and legs. Unless our reason regains control, we will likely drown.

If we humans had a limbic system but no cerebrum, our life would be simple: our limbic system would indicate, by means of the rewards and punishments it has to offer, what it wants us to do, and we would unthinkingly respond to its incentives. If we humans had a cerebrum but no limbic system, our life would also be simple: we would be utterly rational beings, with no lusts, fears, or spontaneous desires. (Life under these circumstances, I should add, would also probably not be worth living. We would, after all, never fall in love, never experience joy, and never feel the warm glow that comes from having helped another human being.) What we humans have instead is both a limbic system and a highly developed cerebrum. We are therefore, as the ancient Stoic philosophers observed, a hybrid creature, half god and half animal. Our cerebrum is the seat of our godly component and our limbic system is the seat of our animal component. As a result, we are often at cross purposes with ourselves. Such is the human condition.

Do nonhuman animals experience emotions? Probably. They have limbic systems, after all, and it is likely that these systems play a role similar to that played by ours. Since one primary function of our limbic system is to "color" our sensory input with emotional meaning, their limbic systems presumably also play this role, in which case they would experience emotions.

Besides this anatomical reason for thinking animals experience emotions, there are behavioral reasons. Cows presumably form herds because they experience anxiety when alone. When those herds stampede, it is presumably because cows experience fear. Anxiety and fear are, of course, basic emotions, but experiments suggest that some animals are capable of experiencing what we would think of as complex emotions. In one fascinating experiment, a capuchin monkey appeared to experience a profound sense of injustice on being paid less (in terms of a food reward) than another monkey for performing the same task.[3]

I would even go so far as to suggest that some animals have moral feelings and therefore have a moral sense as well. Consider, for example, a wolf. It will be happy to chase, kill, and dine on a mouse, rabbit, or deer. But even if it is famished, it will have no interest in killing and devouring a nearby wolf pup, even though it would be easy to do so. What is it, one wonders, that stops the wolf? Perhaps it is a strong internal feeling that doing this would be wrong. Stated differently, perhaps the thought of eating a cub provokes in a wolf an ick factor, the way eating a fellow human being would provoke an ick factor in you and me.

Some people will respond to the above claims by arguing that animals aren't smart enough to experience emotions. It is a mistake, though, to think that reasoning ability is required to experience emotions. It isn't. What is required is a limbic system, and this is something many animals possess.

In suggesting that animals have a moral sense, I am not suggesting that they are what philosophers would call *moral agents*. Being a moral agent requires reasoning ability that lets us weigh our options, taking into account the long-term consequences of the choices we make. It also allows us, if we have sufficient willpower, to overrule our wiring and do something that we know will feel bad or resist doing something that we know will feel good. It takes a highly developed cerebrum to have the requisite reasoning ability, and this is something that animals lack.

AS THEIR CEREBRUMS GREW IN SIZE, our hominid ancestors gained the ability to generalize about the world around them. They came to expect, for example, that if they let go of a rock, it would fall, and that a flash of lightning would be followed by thunder. Other generalizations involved their bodies. They came to understand, for example, that if the rock they dropped landed on their toe, they would subsequently experience pain, and that if they ate certain berries, they would subsequently vomit.

Yet other generalizations presumably involved their moral feelings. Our hominid ancestors might have kept track of what actions felt wrong and thought about whether these actions had common features. They might also have tried to figure out what sorts of actions were likely to give rise to guilt feelings or nightmares. They might then have made predictions on the basis of these generalizations: what sorts of things should or shouldn't they do to avoid triggering the disapprobation of their moral sense?

As a result of this investigation, they might have come up with a list of things that felt wrong, either as they did them or thereafter. Among the behavioral rules of thumb on this list might have been "Don't kill other people" and "Don't steal other people's food." These rules comprise what I shall call their *moral code*. Thus, a moral *code* is different from a moral *sense*. Our moral *sense*, as we have seen, is our ability to feel wrong about doing something. Our moral *code* is a set of rules of thumb regarding what we must do to avoid triggering our moral sense and thereby elicit a feeling that we are doing or have done something wrong.

It is possible for two people to develop different moral codes on the basis of the same moral sense. This is in part because of the logical leeway we have in forming generalizations on the basis of our experiences. Suppose someone eats the berries growing by a creek, washes them down with water from that creek, and subsequently gets sick. He might conclude that the berries caused the sickness and thereby adopt as a nutritional rule of thumb: "Don't eat the berries that grow by the creek." Another person who had the same experience might adopt a different rule of thumb: "Don't drink water from the creek." And yet another person who got sick might adopt yet another rule of thumb: "Don't eat berries and drink creek water at the same time." This same sort of thing can presumably happen when we deduce our moral code from the things we do that, instead of making us sick, feel wrong.

Before the acquisition of language, it would have been difficult for people to compare moral codes. You might have been able to guess, though, that your code was different from that of someone else when he hit you for doing something that was allowed by your moral code. You might thereupon have modified your moral code, not to avoid doing something that felt wrong—since it didn't feel wrong to you—but to avoid the pain that would result from getting hit by this person.

The advent of language allowed people to compare their moral codes. This in turn would likely have resulted in a standardization of those codes. Trouble would arise, after all, if you thought it was wrong to steal someone's wife and your neighbor thought it was right. You and your neighbor would either come to an agreement about what was acceptable behavior, or the stronger of the two of you would simply have done what he wanted without being concerned about the other person's disapproval.

The advent of language also allowed people to teach their moral codes to others. In particular, children no longer needed to figure out their own moral code. They could instead simply adopt their parents' moral code; indeed, they would likely be punished for failing to do so. Learning a moral code in this manner might alter a person's moral sense. Suppose, for example, that a girl's parents taught her that it is wrong to eat beef. It is entirely possible that as a result, the prospect of eating beef might trigger in her not just an ick sensation but outright nausea.

With the passage of time, people's moral codes became more complex. What started out as "Don't steal from others" might have evolved into "Don't steal from others unless you need something more than they do." What started out as "Don't kill people" might have been transformed into "Don't kill people unless they have killed your relatives and friends," which in turn might have transformed into "Don't kill people unless they are *likely* to kill your relatives and friends." Another thing that happened is that people's nonmoral beliefs about the world started interacting with their moral beliefs. Consider, for example, a mother whose moral sense tells her that it is wrong to inflict pain and suffering on her baby. Suppose this woman also believes that the gods will punish any baby who isn't circumcised. She might conclude that she has a moral duty to have her baby circumcised, even though she knows that it will be quite distressing to hear it cry during and after the procedure. In this case, she will struggle to suppress her moral sense.

THE ABOVE ACCOUNT of the genesis of human morality is, to be sure, highly speculative. Nevertheless, it is useful for our purposes, inasmuch as it invites us to think about our moral sense, our moral code, how they differ, and how they interact. It is possible, I think, for a moral sense to exist without a moral code: this is the case in many animals. I also think it is unlikely that we humans would have moral codes if we did not also have a moral sense to provide moral feelings on which—initially, at least—to base our code. Unless we had a capacity to feel that things were wrong, it simply would not have dawned on us to systemize our moral feelings, or even to come up with the concept of morality. And finally, I think that with the passage of time, our moral code has drifted away from the moral sense on which it is based.

For further insight into our moral sense, our moral code, and how they interact, let us do another thought experiment: let us consider what philosophers refer to as the *trolley problem*. The experiment in question involves not incestuous siblings but an out-of-control trolley.[4] Suppose you are standing next to the track on which this trolley is rolling. You look down the track and see five men working on the rails. You realize that because there are high walls on both sides of the track, there is no way for them to get off it before the trolley comes. Even if you yell to alert them, they will not be able to outrun the trolley. You also realize that if you throw the switch that is beside you, the train will be diverted onto another track. Unfortunately, one person—a rather corpulent individual named Bob—is working on that track, and because it is also surrounded by high walls, he likewise will not be able to get out of the way of the coming trolley. Should you throw the switch? If you don't, five innocent people will die. If you do, only one equally innocent person will die. You may not like throwing the switch, but would it be morally permissible for you to do so?

Judging from my classroom experience with this case, most people initially respond by trying desperately to figure out a way to save the lives of the workers without having to make a difficult moral choice. After that, they express a hope that they never find themselves in such circumstances. But if pressed, they will generally act on the basis of their gut feelings and conclude that they would be willing—reluctantly—to throw the switch.

Once you make up your mind about this case, here is another one to consider.[5] This case also involves a runaway trolley and a track on which five innocent people are working. This time, though, you are not standing beside the track; instead, you are standing on a footbridge over the track. And this time, there is no switch for you to pull; instead, Bob, the corpulent and perfectly innocent workman, is standing beside you. He is on his five-minute break. It dawns on you that if you bump against Bob, you can knock him off the bridge and onto the tracks—all it will take is a little bump of your body against his. Bob's impressive girth will then clog the wheels of the trolley, thereby bringing it to a halt and saving the lives of the five workers.

But wait a minute! Couldn't you yourself heroically jump off the bridge and thereby save the lives of the five workers? No. You are too skinny to stop the trolley. Your jumping would therefore end up costing six lives, compared to five if you did nothing, and only one if you bumped Bob off the bridge. It would be foolish for you to try to be a hero.

The moral question in this trolley case, of course, is the same as it was in the first case: is it morally permissible to sacrifice the life of one innocent person to save the lives of five equally innocent people? Students typically answer that they would find it much harder to bump Bob off the bridge to block the train than it would be to throw the switch to divert the train onto the track he is standing on, thereby killing him. When I ask students why it is more wrong to kill Bob by bumping him off the bridge than to kill him by pulling the switch, they are typically dumbfounded. "It just is," they say.

This raises a new question: given that these two cases involve the same moral choice—sacrificing one innocent life to save five equally innocent lives—why does our moral sense treat these cases differently? According to philosopher Peter Singer, it is because of how we humans acquired our moral sense. Our evolutionary ancestors were wired so it would feel wrong to commit acts of violence toward innocent people. But until about ten thousand years ago, violence could primarily be inflicted in what Singer describes as "an up-close and personal way—by hitting, pushing, strangling, or using a stick or stone as a club."[6] We therefore developed an aversion to doing such things; it got wired into our moral sense. But as Singer points out, our hominid ancestors never threw trolley switches. Consequently, we are not programmed by our evolutionary past to have moral feelings with respect to this action.[7] It therefore feels wrong for us to kill someone by bumping him off a bridge but does not feel wrong—or at least feels *less* wrong—to kill someone by throwing a switch. I am inclined to agree with Singer on this point.

Even though we have developed reasoning ability, and even though we have used this ability to develop a moral code, our limbic system still lurks within us, and we possess a moral sense as a result. Oftentimes, we can reason our way around the feeling that doing something is wrong. But in some cases, our moral sense prevents such circumvention. Our cerebrum capitulates to our limbic system.

We like to think our reason is in charge, but when we look at things more closely, we realize that in many cases, our reason plays the role of yes-man to our passions. It spends its time not controlling our passions but coming up with plausible-sounding justifications for the behavior they motivate. Our reason is also very good at devising complex strategies to get the passions whatever it is they want. And one last point: we use our reason to build impressive rational edifices, only to watch our passions knock them down. Unfortunately, our moral code can be among the razed edifices.

AS WE SAW IN THE PREVIOUS CHAPTER, there are two kinds of moral aha moments. Some are experienced in response to a morally traumatic event. This was the case with Mohandas Gandhi's moral epiphany. Other moral aha moments are experienced not in connection with a particular event but after an extended internal debate on how best to deal with an inconsistency someone has discovered in his moral beliefs. This was the case with British abolitionist Thomas Clarkson's moral epiphany.

Now that we understand the difference between the moral sense and a moral code, we are in a position to understand how Gandhi- and Clarkson-style moral aha moments arise and why they differ in the way they do. In a Gandhi-style moral epiphany, our moral sense rebels against our moral code. Thus, when Gandhi experienced the prejudice I described in the previous chapter, his moral sense elicited a strong feeling of injustice. This in turn made him realize that the moral code he had adopted radically underrated the moral significance of prejudice. He knew he had to modify his code, even though this would make him a moral outlier in British society. And as we have seen, he also concluded that he had a duty to change the moral codes of the people around him.

Although Gandhi was clearly a thoughtful person and although he put much thought into his subsequent reform efforts, it is remarkable how little thought seems to have been involved in his decision to become a reformer: on being morally provoked, he responded instantaneously—reflexively, almost. It was as if his moral sense simply shoved his intellect aside. This same thing probably happened to many readers when they considered the thought experiments presented above: they made their decisions not by consulting their intellect but by consulting their moral sense.

In a Clarkson-style moral epiphany, the intellect plays a prominent role, and the moral sense plays almost no role at all. In such an epiphany, we don't discover that our moral code is at odds with our moral sense; we instead discover that our moral code is at odds with itself and is therefore flawed. In other words, we discover an inconsistency in our moral code and, after much thought, decide to do something to resolve the inconsistency.

Like Gandhi, Clarkson had internalized the moral code of his society. This code said, in part, that it was morally impermissible to own slaves but morally permissible to enable their ownership by other people. But when he thought about this code more carefully, in conjunction with the research he did for his essay, he realized that to knowingly make it possible for someone else to do something morally wrong was itself morally wrong. He also realized that the act of transporting slaves could be more inhumane than the slavery they would experience on arriving at their destination. As a result, he found himself in the logical quandary I have described.

Although the moral sense does not play a direct role in the production of Clarkson-style aha moments, it arguably plays an indirect role. After all, if humans didn't possess a moral sense, it is, as I've said, unlikely that they would develop a moral code. Furthermore, although reason plays a role in laying the groundwork for a Clarkson-style aha moment, if reason were more thorough in its creation of moral codes, they wouldn't contain inconsistencies that could give rise to these moments. In conclusion, we are reasonable enough to have Clarkson-style aha moments, but if we were more reasonable still, there would be no need to have them.

What determines whether someone experiences a moral epiphany that resembles Clarkson's or one that resembles Gandhi's? My guess is that it depends primarily on how willing and able a person is to engage in analytical thinking. There are people who, even if led by the hand, as it were, to an inconsistency in their beliefs, will either not see it at all or will be indifferent to its existence. (I know this from having spent decades in the classroom.) For these individuals, the strategy of dealing with an inconsistency by forgetting its existence will be wonderfully effective.

There are other people who, because of their analytical nature, actively look for inconsistencies in their beliefs and feel perturbed when they find them. These individuals will be much more likely to reach their moral epiphanies slowly, after an internal debate, as Clarkson did, than quickly, in response to a moral challenge, as Gandhi did.

Another group of people who will be more likely to experience a Clarkson- rather than a Gandhi-style moral epiphany are those who understand that the feelings we experience are a consequence of how we are wired, which in turn is a consequence of the environment in which our evolutionary ancestors found themselves tens of thousands of years ago. These individuals will also understand that we were wired not so we could have happy and meaningful lives or be morally upstanding people, but so we could survive and reproduce on the savannas of Africa, perhaps in misery and perhaps by exploiting others.

People who understand this will be disinclined to trust their feelings. They won't trust their physical feelings: just because it feels good to glut ourselves on fattening foods doesn't mean we should spend our days doing it. They won't trust their emotional feelings: just because someone has insulted us doesn't mean we should allow ourselves to get angry. And they won't entirely trust their moral feelings: in particular, they will be disinclined to let their gut feelings bully their intellect. They will also acknowledge, though, that such bullying can lead to positive outcomes, as is demonstrated by the epiphanies experienced by Gandhi, Stowe, and Ridenhour.

I mentioned above that my views on nonreproductive incestuous sex between consenting adults have changed. This happened because I started taking—and eventually teaching—philosophy courses and as a result became a more analytical person than I used to be. Consequently, my cerebrum is better able to win debates with my limbic system than it formerly was. More generally, when I cannot give reasons for the moral beliefs I hold, I take it as compelling evidence that I need to take a closer look at those beliefs.

MANY OF THE READERS who opened this book presumably did so in the hope that by reading it, they could experience more aha moments of their own. I couldn't offer much advice in Part 1 on how to experience more religious revelations. This is because whether or not you experience them—if they are genuine—is in the hands of God. History seems to show that you can pray all day long and not experience a revelation, or hardly pray at all and be the recipient of repeated revelations.

I can, however, offer advice on how to increase the number of moral aha moments you experience. As we have seen, there are two primary ways to trigger such moments. You can, to begin with, explore the world around you in search of experiences that, because of the moral feelings they elicit, will cause you to re-evaluate your moral code. This might involve doing research in books or on the Internet, or for the more adventurous, going on field trips. What you learn about, say, living conditions in third-world countries, the sex trade, or factory farms might cause you to experience a moral gut feeling that will leave you no choice but to alter your moral code. Aha! Most people, I should add, not only don't attempt this sort of moral self-education but take steps to avoid finding out things that might make them rethink their moral views. There are lots of questions that they are careful not to ask.

Alternatively, you can explore your moral code. You can look for inconsistencies in it and then think about how best to resolve them. To aid you in this process, you can take steps to improve your analytical skills—perhaps by taking a philosophy course or two.

There is also another, rather easier way to trigger personal moral epiphanies: you can seek out people who have experienced them and listen to what they say. This will mean exposing yourself to people who have different moral beliefs than you do. After all, someone with the same beliefs as you will not help you see anything within your own moral landscape that you weren't already aware of; you will simply confirm one another's beliefs. Doing your moral homework by engaging with people who have different moral views will also mean exposing yourself to the ideas of moral reformers.

Most people, however, are reluctant to take these steps. It is a reluctance that has unfortunate consequences, inasmuch as it impedes their moral growth.

CHAPTER 6

The Problem with Moral Reformers

EXPERIENCE ONE MORAL EPIPHANY, and you might try to change yourself; experience a second, and you might try to change the world. In your first aha moment, you realize that your moral beliefs are mistaken—that something you thought was morally permissible is in fact morally objectionable. In response to this epiphany, you might alter your moral code, which will likely entail changing the way you live. In your second aha moment—if you have it—it will dawn on you that you have a moral obligation to convince other people to change their moral code the way you are changing yours. As a result, you might reveal your moral insights to the world. Judging from history, the world won't be very receptive to them.

Encountering a moral reformer puts people in a bind. According to the reformer, they are doing something morally wrong, a state of affairs they won't want to admit. Even worse, if they do admit it, they will probably have to change important aspects of their lifestyle, something they will be reluctant to do. Consequently, they will feel compelled to defend their current moral beliefs, but they will likely find this difficult to do, for the simple reason that they don't know why they believe what they do. This is because people normally acquire their moral beliefs not by means of careful thought and analysis, but through a process of indoctrination: they believe what their parents, teachers, or religious leaders have told them, either explicitly or implicitly, to believe.

When someone's moral views are constantly challenged, he is forced to think about why he believes the things he does, a process that will give him a deeper understanding of his beliefs. In most cases, though, the moral views people are taught are widely held in the community in which they live, meaning that it is entirely possible for them to go through their lives without ever having had their moral code challenged. Consequently, when they finally do encounter a moral reformer, it is a novel experience—and one that is likely to discomfit them.

In some of the classes I teach, I have the task (and honor!) of being the first person to seriously challenge my students' moral beliefs. In doing this, though, I am not playing the role of moral reformer: there is no particular change I want them to make in their moral code. I am better characterized as a moral provocateur. It is my job to challenge my students' moral beliefs, whatever they may be. (Put me in front of a classroom full of moral vegetarians, and I will respond by challenging their vegetarianism.) I proceed by finding out what my students believe and then asking them why they believe it. In almost every case, they don't really know. Indeed, I think even they are astonished by their inability to defend their moral beliefs.

If you know why you believe something, you will not be upset by having that belief challenged. If, for example, someone asks you to defend your belief that 2 + 3 = 5, you might do so by getting some coins out of your pocket and doing a simple demonstration. You would put down two coins, put down three more coins, and then invite him to count the coins with you. (This demonstration will have the look and feel of an episode of *Sesame Street*.) Rather than getting mad at him, you will pity him for his ignorance of math. If, on the other hand, someone asks you to defend your moral beliefs, you are unlikely to have a similarly convenient explanation at hand. You might find yourself dumbfounded (as psychologist Jonathan Haidt puts it) and you will likely get angry at the person who challenged your beliefs, because her challenge reveals that you don't really know why you believe what you do. Philosopher Bertrand Russell summed the situation up nicely: "If an opinion contrary to your own makes you angry, that is a sign that you are subconsciously aware of having no good reason for thinking as you do."[1]

It is never pleasant to have your views challenged, but it is particularly annoying to have your moral beliefs challenged. If Thomas Clarkson convinced one of his fellow Brits, who happened to be involved in the slave trade, that her belief about the location of Paris was wrong—that it was in France rather than Spain—that person would feel the sting of having been mistaken: nobody likes to be wrong. But if Clarkson convinced this person that her views about the morality of the slave trade were wrong, she will not only feel the sting of having been mistaken but will also have to admit that she had been behaving immorally before Clarkson came along to enlighten her. And on top of that, she will have to give up her lucrative investments in the slave trade. To her, this will seem like a lot to ask. Why couldn't Clarkson simply have left her alone?

THIS IS WHY PEOPLE typically avoid moral reformers. If they encounter one against their will, they will politely decline to discuss the issue that obsesses him. And if forced to defend their own views, they will likely, for reasons I have described, find it hard to do. In many cases, they will have little choice but to resort to arguments that have a certain initial plausibility but that won't stand up to closer logical scrutiny.

Thus, the person whose views have been challenged might respond to the moral reformer by appealing to popular opinion: "Everyone knows that what you are saying is wrong." If the reformer is holding an unpopular view—as will generally be the case—it means that for him to be right, lots of people will have to be wrong. And what is the chance of this happening? Pretty small.

This sounds logical, but this line of reasoning assumes that other people have given the issue in question serious thought, and this is by no means certain. Indeed, history is full of instances in which large groups of people jointly held mistaken beliefs, moral or otherwise. Consider the hypothetical British woman just described. She might have responded to Clarkson by pointing out that "nobody" shared his belief on the immorality of the slave trade. And in the society in which she lived, this claim would have been pretty much true. But we in the twenty-first century look back on Clarkson's fellow Brits and shake our heads in amazement: how could they all have been so wrong? There is, by the way, every reason to think that in two hundred years, our descendants will be asking similar questions about us.

Alternatively, people might defend their beliefs by appealing to expert rather than popular opinion. They may not know why the reformer's claims are mistaken, but they know someone who claims to know why, and that is good enough for them. The problem with this line of argument is that there are rival experts on almost any topic; indeed, Clarkson himself would presumably have counted as an expert on the slave trade. This leaves the non-expert the challenge of choosing among experts, and we can reasonably question whether she has the expertise to do so.

What if a person has given a moral issue so little thought that she can't even think of an expert to appeal to? She might then respond to the moral reformer in what can most charitably be described as a nonlogical manner. She might deflect the reformer's comments by rolling her eyeballs. She might call him stupid or even crazy. She might try to find evidence that he is a hypocrite or that he is getting paid to say the things he is saying. Or she might seize on one mistake he has made somewhere in his writings as an excuse to dismiss everything he has said: "If he could make *that* mistake, just think of the other mistakes he must have made."

People, including even highly educated individuals, are remarkably averse to thinking about moral issues. They seem to be the product of not one but two indoctrinations. In the first, they were indoctrinated by their parents, teachers, and religious leaders. In the second, they maintain their first indoctrination via an ongoing program of self-indoctrination. They refuse to entertain challenges to their beliefs; indeed, they avoid exposing themselves to such challenges. Inasmuch as a mind is a terrible thing to waste, it is a sad thing to witness in someone else—and even sadder to discover in oneself.

When a moral reformer confronts us, we are doing ourselves a disservice if we dismiss his arguments out of hand. Indeed, if we take an inventory of our current moral beliefs, we will find that many of them were initially proposed by moral reformers like the one who is challenging us. Perhaps we owe it to ourselves to devote *some* thought to his claims— at least if our goal is to become a better human being.

Along these lines, before having my moral epiphany regarding vegetarianism, I used to mock the moral vegetarians I encountered. How frightfully stupid I was! And yet at the time I thought I was being quite clever.

Before moving on, let me add that you don't have to openly challenge people's moral beliefs to make them behave in a defensive manner. All you need to do is change the way you live, perhaps in response to a personal moral epiphany. Even though you don't breathe a word to others about the reason for your change, they might infer from it that you have altered your moral values and thereby abandoned some of the values that they hold dear. They might therefore construe your new lifestyle as an (unstated) challenge to their moral beliefs, which will displease them. They might respond by mocking you or making jokes at your expense. It is easy for you to bring this behavior to a halt: you need only repudiate your moral epiphany and return to living like they do. They will then praise you for your wisdom. It is, after all, a socially acceptable way to praise themselves.

MOST MORAL REFORMERS, as we have seen, have two moral epiphanies. In the first, they realize that their moral code is mistaken, and in the second, they realize that they have a moral obligation to change the moral codes of the people around them. Many people have the first moral aha without subsequently having the second: although they might be personally transformed, they will not go around trying to change other people's minds. It turns out, though, that it is also possible to have a "second" moral aha moment without having a first. It is possible, in other words, to feel compelled to transform the society in which you live, but not about any particular moral issue. Instead, you will feel compelled to transform the way the people around you think about *all* moral issues. Do this, and you will significantly increase their chances of engaging in the kind of moral self-education that I described in the previous chapter.

Consider the Greek philosopher Socrates. He was born in Athens in 469 BC. Early in his life, being the thoughtful, analytical person that he was, he presumably had his share of moral aha moments. In some cases, these were apparently followed by second aha moments and attempts at specific moral reforms. But then he experienced a moral epiphany of a rather different kind: it dawned on him that he had a duty to play the role of gadfly to Athens. Allow me to explain how this epiphany came about and describe the consequences it had for him.

Socrates had a resident "voice." It began, he says, "in my early childhood—a sort of voice which comes to me; and when it comes it always dissuades me from what I am proposing to do, and never urges me on."[2] He describes it as "my constant companion, opposing me even in quite trivial things if I was going to take the wrong course."[3] The voice, he thought, came from the gods.

In conjunction with this voice, he appears to have been subject to spells. One story about him can be found in the *Symposium:*

> One morning he was thinking about something which he could not resolve; he would not give it up, but continued thinking from early dawn until noon—there he stood fixed in thought; and at noon attention was drawn to him, and the rumour ran through the wondering crowd that Socrates had been standing and thinking about something ever since the break of day. At last, in the evening after supper, some Ionians out of curiosity (I should explain that this was not in winter but in summer), brought out their mats and slept in the open air that they might watch him and see whether he would stand all night. There he stood until the following morning; and with the return of light he offered up a prayer to the sun, and went his way.[4]

It sounds like Socrates was engaged in a mental debate that ended at dawn; we are not told, though, of the substance of the debate or of what insight, if any, he thereby gained.

Socrates's life-altering epiphany did not come via the voice in his head but instead from a human voice, that of the Oracle of Delphi. According to the story told in Plato's *Apology* (and in a slightly different form in Xenophon's *Apology*), Socrates's friend Chaerophon asked the Oracle whether there was anyone wiser than Socrates. She replied that there wasn't. Socrates was puzzled to hear this: "What is the god [on whose behalf the Oracle spoke] saying, and what is his hidden meaning? I am only too conscious that I have no claim to wisdom, great or small; so what can he mean by asserting that I am the wisest man in the world?"[5]

He thereupon set about trying to disprove the Oracle. He tried to find someone wiser than himself but kept discovering that supposedly wise people were not as wise as reputed. After one such encounter, Socrates reflected, as he walked away, "Well, I am certainly wiser than this man. It is only too likely that neither of us has any knowledge to boast of; but he thinks that he knows something which he does not know, whereas I am quite conscious of my ignorance. At any rate it seems that I am wiser than he is to this small extent, that I do not think that I know what I do not know."[6] This was for him an important realization. His encounters with other "wise" men only served to reinforce this conclusion.

This was the aha moment that launched Socrates on what became his mission in life—to "go about seeking and searching in obedience to the divine command, if I think that anyone is wise, whether citizen or stranger; and when I decide that he is not wise, I try to assist the god by proving that he is not."[7] Elsewhere, he describes his mission as playing the role of intellectual gadfly to Athens: "God has assigned me to this city, as if to a large thoroughbred horse which because of its great size is inclined to be lazy and needs the stimulation of some stinging fly. It seems to me that God has attached me to this city to perform the office of such a fly; and all day long I never cease to settle here, there, and everywhere, rousing, persuading, reproving every one of you."[8] Socrates felt duty-bound to carry out this mission; indeed, he did so with such passion that he had little time for practical affairs and was therefore reduced to extreme poverty.[9]

There were times when it would have benefited him to go along with the crowd, but he refused to do so. In one such case, he was the only person on the Athenian Council to vote against a proposal that certain commanders be tried *en bloc*, an action which he thought was illegal. Because of this, "the public speakers were all ready to denounce and arrest me, and you were all urging them on at the top of your voices." But, says Socrates, "I thought that it was my duty to face it out on the side of law and justice rather than support you, through fear of prison or death, in your wrong decision."[10] He also refused to participate in the arrest of Leon of Salamis, even though this defiance might have cost him his life.[11]

Some people loved Socrates. Many more did not. Some of those he encountered refused to talk to him. Others mocked him or even physically attacked him. Yet, for Socrates, this sort of ill usage was to be expected. In fact, it indicated that he was successfully playing the role of gadfly.

In 404 BC, late in Socrates's life, the defeat of Athens in the Peloponnesian War changed the political environment. As a result, it became more dangerous to challenge popular beliefs. Also, the people whose ignorance Socrates had revealed—in some cases publicly—had a score to settle with him. As a result, Socrates was accused of having committed certain crimes, including corrupting the youth of Athens (by, perhaps, encouraging them to think for themselves?). He was convicted by a jury of his peers and sentenced to death. He was then imprisoned and could easily have escaped but chose not to. He ended up, rather famously, drinking the poison hemlock that was brought to him as the instrument of his execution.

SOCRATES PLAYED THE ROLE of gadfly for ancient Athens. Journalist Christopher Hitchens played a similar role in the modern English-speaking world. Hitchens's style was rather different from that of Socrates, though, and the beliefs he challenged were rather less esoteric. Thus, rather than examining the meaning of justice, as Socrates had done, Hitchens asked whether it was just for then-governor of Arkansas Bill Clinton to have permitted the execution of a mentally retarded individual. And rather than examining the meaning of piety, as again Socrates had done, Hitchens asked whether Mother Teresa was in fact pious. Hitchens characterized himself as a contrarian: present him with a wide variety of generally accepted viewpoints, and he would take apparent delight in opposing them.

So far in this chapter, we have focused our attention on how things look from the point of view of someone whose beliefs are being challenged. What makes Hitchens worthy of our attention in this, a discussion of moral reformers, is the insight he gives us into how such challenges look from the point of view of the challenger. In his book *Advice to a Young Contrarian*, Hitchens describes strategies that can be used to sway public opinion. He also describes the obstacles that will confront anyone wishing to challenge popular beliefs, as well as the emotional ups and downs the person will experience in doing so. Perhaps learning more about contrarians will make us more receptive to their educational efforts and— who knows?—maybe even lead us to admire their courage and tenacity.

Hitchens was born in 1949 and died in 2011, from cancer. In college at the University of Oxford in the late 1960s, he was a devout leftist. This makes him sound like a rebel, but in that environment, to be a leftist was to be a conformist. In 1968, while in Cuba to attend a work camp for young revolutionaries, he got a chance to meet Cuban filmmaker Santiago Alvarez. Hitchens asked him what it was like to work in a country that had official policies regarding what artists could and couldn't do. Alvarez replied that in Cuba artistic and intellectual liberty were "untrammeled." When Hitchens asked whether this meant that they could say whatever they wanted, Alvarez admitted, with a laugh, that it would be unwise to say anything critical or satirical about Castro, but that otherwise, freedom of conscience and creativity was "absolute."

"I do not know," says Hitchens, "if what I next said came from the 'Left' or 'Right' part of my brain, but I like to think I anticipated at least some of the huge cultural and literary defection that later cost Castro the allegiance of [many] writers....I made the mere observation that if the most salient figure in the state and society was immune from critical comment, then all the rest was detail." He adds, "I don't think I have ever been so richly rewarded merely for saying the self-evident."[12] It marked, for him, an important turning point in his life and launched him on his career as a contrarian.

ACCORDING TO HITCHENS, "most people, most of the time, prefer to seek approval or security."[13] He adds that "those who need or want to think for themselves will always be a minority; the human race may be inherently individualistic and even narcissistic but in the mass it is quite easy to control. People have a need for reassurance and belonging."[14] This is why contrarians, by their efforts to get people to rethink popular beliefs, make many people unhappy and even incur their anger.

Those confronted by a contrarian might respond by challenging his moral authority: "Who appointed you?," they will ask. Their logic is that unless some authority appoints a person to the role of dissenter, his dissent will not be legitimate. This logic is peculiar, though, inasmuch as an obvious target for a contrarian's dissent would be the authority whose stamp of approval, according to this line of thinking, he needs. Hitchens's response to this criticism is to admit, proudly, that he is self-appointed. He adds, "Nobody asked me to do this and it would not be the same thing I do if they had asked me. I can't be fired any more than I can be promoted. I am happy in the ranks of the self-employed. If I am stupid or on poor form, nobody suffers but me."[15]

Given that becoming a contrarian makes you the target of animosity, why would anyone choose to become one? As it turns out, most people don't set out to become a contrarian. What they choose to do is take an unpopular stand on a particular issue, perhaps as the result of a moral epiphany. Most of the people who do this don't go on to become contrarians. Indeed, they might vow never again to back an unpopular cause, because the social cost of doing so is simply too high.

Other people, though, find the challenges associated with taking contrary views to be stimulating. Yes, it is a bit scary to stand alone before a crowd and tell its members why they are mistaken. But if you do so successfully, you will be rewarded with a big boost to your self-confidence. This in turn will make you more willing to stand alone again, ideally before an even bigger crowd. You are also likely to explore new topics about which to be contrary.

And these aren't the only rewards for playing the role of contrarian. If he knows his stuff, the contrarian can have the pleasure of confounding the people he debates. This pleasure, I should add, is significant. It is the intellectual equivalent of serving an ace in tennis or throwing a strike in baseball. Contrarians are also motivated by altruistic impulses. They believe that by affecting what people think or, more important, *how* people think, they can make the world a better place. They are, Hitchens says, "actuated by concern for others, and for causes and movements larger than themselves."[16] Being a contrarian, says Hitchens, "is something you are, not something you do."[17]

According to Hitchens, for a certain kind of person, the life of the contrarian is "worth living on its own account."[18] Stated differently, what the contrarian concludes is, "Dammit, I have only one life to live and I won't spend a moment of it on some dismal compromise."[19] Alternatively, a contrarian might regard it as a waste of his talents to defend consensus views. As mathematician G. H. Hardy put it, "it is never worth a first class man's time to express a majority opinion. By definition, there are plenty of others to do that."[20]

Those who embark on the contrarian path might wonder whether there is a way to make it their "day job." This is hard to do, since people are generally unwilling to pay to be intellectually spanked, as it were. Hitchens's own life, however, demonstrates that it is possible to make one's living as a writer of contrarian literature. One can also express a contrarian bent by becoming a university professor. To pursue this path, though, a person will have to suppress his contrarian tendencies until he acquires tenure. At that point, he will become one of the intellectually freest people ever to walk the globe—if, at any rate, his university is in a country that protects free speech. Indeed, one justification for granting professors tenure is so they will be free to challenge the beliefs of those around them. For the most part, though, professors do nothing at all with the intellectual freedom they have been granted; instead, they take it to their grave with them. What a waste!

ON ASSUMING THE ROLE OF CONTRARIAN, a person might seek job performance feedback. Most of it, of course, will be negative: the people he is trying to change will tell him to stop bothering them. But from his point of view, this negative feedback will count as positive. If people liked what he was telling them, it would be a sign that he wasn't sufficiently contrary, which for him would be a bad thing.

A contrarian might try to measure his effectiveness by checking to see whether he is indeed changing the minds of the people he encounters, but this will be hard to do. For one thing, the people he deals with will likely be slow to change their thoughts or manner of thinking. A contrarian therefore needs to keep in mind that, as Hitchens explains, "it is very seldom...that in debate any one of two evenly matched antagonists will succeed in actually convincing or 'converting' the other. But it is equally seldom that in a properly conducted argument either antagonist will end up holding exactly the same position as that with which he began. Concessions, refinements and adjustments will occur, and each initial position will have undergone modification even if it remains ostensibly the 'same.'"[21]

In other words, under most circumstances, a debate, either formal or informal, will cause at best a slight deflection in the intellectual trajectory of the debaters. It is only through a cumulative series of such "nudges" that these trajectories are substantially altered. This means that for a contrarian to have an impact on the world, he needs to keep repeating his message and thereby run the risk of boring other people. But, says Hitchens, "if you really care about a serious cause or a deep subject, you may have to be prepared to be boring about it."[22]

Suppose the contrarian's efforts bear fruit. After a period of time, the people around him start changing their minds along the lines he suggests. If at this point the contrarian goes up to these individuals and says, "I'm glad to see that you've come around to my way of thinking," they will likely reject the implication that his efforts had any impact on them. Indeed, they might claim not even to remember his efforts. The contrarian will be left wondering whether he should take them at their word—in which case he will question his effectiveness as a contrarian—or assume that this behavior is simply a reflection of human pride. People hate to admit that they have had their minds changed. Many contrarians, thanks to their highly developed self-confidence, will be happy to make this assumption.

A contrarian will keep in mind that at some deeper level, his goal is not to change people's minds but to make them question the things they believe. In other words, his goal is to deprive them of their feeling of certainty with respect to their beliefs. He will know that some of the biggest tragedies in human history were the result not of people holding false beliefs but of people being certain that their false beliefs were true. Their confidence gave them license to do extreme things. Reduce people's confidence in their beliefs, and you can reduce the size of the mistakes they make on the basis of those beliefs.

A contrarian will have great faith in a single dissenting voice's ability, not to change the views of those in the crowd, but to plant a seed of doubt in their mind. It is a seed that, even if it doesn't grow, can dramatically reduce the chance that the crowd will run amok on the basis of its beliefs. In the previous chapter, we saw the role our internal voice of reason can play in shaping our moral views. A lone contrarian can play a similar role in shaping the moral views of a crowd.

To be an effective contrarian, it is helpful to know your stuff and be able to express yourself in an articulate manner. Hitchens possessed both these characteristics in spades. You can, however, play an important contrarian role without being brilliant and articulate. In many circumstances, all you have to do to challenge the thinking of a crowd is to state the obvious or ask the obvious question. You can, in other words, play the role of the little boy in Hans Christian Andersen's story about the emperor's new clothes: "But the emperor is naked!"

The thing to remember about crowds, though, is that they have the power to silence the lone voices among them. They can do so through intimidation or by enacting laws to restrict the expression of ideas. This brings us to the topic of free speech. Ask people whether they believe in free speech, and they will almost unanimously tell you that they do. Probe their beliefs, though, and you are likely to find that they make some exceptions. There is the obvious one: you should not be allowed to shout "fire!" in a crowded theater. But probe deeper and you will likely find cases in which they think it appropriate to suppress people's speech. In particular, they might argue that in the same way as you shouldn't be allowed to disturb the peace by banging pots and pans at midnight, you shouldn't be allowed to disturb the peace by challenging people's beliefs. In short, you shouldn't be allowed to go around telling people things they don't want to hear.

In response to this sort of thinking, Hitchens points out that although disputes can be socially unpleasant, they are also socially beneficial: "In life we make progress by conflict and in mental life by argument and disputation.... There must be confrontation and opposition, in order that sparks may be kindled."[23] Nineteenth-century British philosopher John Stuart Mill goes even further in his essay *On Liberty*, in which he gives a powerful argument for free speech. Mill is sufficiently convinced of the social value of people who question common beliefs that he recommends that in the unlikely event that mankind ever does come into possession of the truth, someone should go around and (insincerely) challenge people's beliefs, just to give them a chance to remember why those beliefs ought to be held.[24] Doing this would keep the beliefs in question alive instead of allowing them to lapse into what Mill refers to as *dead dogma*.[25]

Socrates was similarly convinced of the value of contrary thinkers like himself. In the sentencing portion of his trial, he boldly asserts that he is the best thing that ever happened to Athens. He also tells jurors that although they have it in their power to finish him off "in a single slap," the way they would eliminate a gadfly, they would live to regret doing so. They would, after all, have trouble finding someone willing to play the role Socrates played for the city "unless God in his care for you sends someone to take my place."[26] And until they found such a person, they would have little choice but to spend their lives with heads full of mistaken beliefs.

Fortunately for Athens—and for humanity as well—Socrates's prophecy was wrong. Indeed, his death triggered a gadfly outbreak in Athens, as many of his followers started their own schools of philosophy. And of course, even today the intellectual heirs of Socrates walk among us. If we care about our well-being, we owe it to ourselves to seek them out and give them a listen.

PART THREE

The Aha Moment in Science

CHAPTER 7

The Joy of Discovery

ONE OF THE MOST SIGNIFICANT aha moments of the twentieth century was Einstein's realization that time is not absolute. As we saw in the Introduction, he had become fixated on what looked like an inconsistency in his fellow physicists' views regarding space and time. Try as he might, he couldn't find a way to resolve the inconsistency until, during a conversation with his friend Michele Besso, "a storm broke loose" in his mind and he gained the insight that allowed him to formulate his special theory of relativity.[1]

The special theory was, as its name suggests, special. It dealt only with frames of reference that were moving at a constant velocity with respect to one another. What if they were instead accelerating? Einstein set about trying to develop a *general* theory of relativity that would deal with such cases. Two years later, he had a breakthrough insight: "I was sitting on a chair in my patent office in Bern. Suddenly a thought struck me: If a man falls freely, he would not feel his weight. I was taken aback. This simple thought experiment made a deep impression on me. This led me to the theory of gravity."[2] Einstein later described this insight as "the happiest thought in my life."[3] It took Einstein another eight years of work to complete his development of the theory. It would have taken only six if he hadn't made some math errors.[4]

After formulating his general theory of relativity, Einstein went on to consider its consequences. He turned his attention, for example, to a peculiarity in the orbit of Mercury. Each time Mercury revolves around the sun, the lowest point of its orbit (its *perihelion*, as astronomers say) moves (more correctly, it *precesses*) in a manner that Newtonian physics cannot explain. When Einstein realized that his theory could account for this orbital behavior, he was so excited that he experienced heart palpitations. "I was," he said, "beside myself with ecstasy for days."[5]

EINSTEIN WAS THE FIRST OF MANY scientists to have important aha moments regarding relativity. According to his theory, it is possible to transform matter directly into energy. Intrigued by this possibility, physicist Leo Szilard started contemplating whether it was possible to liberate the energy of the atom; the greatest minds of his time said it was not. But then, on the morning of September 12, 1933, he went out for a walk in London. He stood at an intersection. When the streetlight turned green, he stepped from the curb and, in a flash, had the solution to his problem: he realized the possibility of a neutron chain reaction.[6]

In the early 1960s, mathematical physicist Roger Penrose had devoted considerable intellectual effort to trying to prove the singularity theorems of general relativity theory. One day in 1965, he was walking through London with a friend.

As they crossed a street, a thought flashed through Penrose's mind but vanished before he could fully comprehend it. He resumed the conversation. That evening, Penrose found himself inexplicably elated. He started reviewing the day's events, trying to figure out the reason for his happiness. It was then that the idea he had while crossing the street came back to him.[7] He realized that it was a major breakthrough, just the insight he needed to finish the proof he had been working on. This proof was subsequently instrumental in making scientists accept the possibility of stars collapsing into what we now call black holes.

Another important aha moment struck theoretical physicist Alan Guth in December of 1979.[8] He sat down at his desk to ponder a difficulty that had stymied his efforts to describe how the universe had behaved in the first moments after the Big Bang. At one o'clock in the morning, he pulled out a piece of paper, wrote down the words *SPECTACULAR REALIZATION*, and set about working out the details of what has since become known as the *inflationary universe theory*.[9] According to this theory, the Big Bang, rather than involving an "explosion" of matter *into space*, involved an incredibly fast expansion—Guth referred to it as "inflation"—*of space itself.*

Guth's aha moment came as the result not just of brilliance and hard work, but luck as well. He would not have started thinking about cosmic inflation had he not, on November 13, 1978, attended a lecture by physicist Robert Dicke. He later reflected on how close he came to not attending that lecture. He was, at that time, recovering from bronchitis; had his doctor scheduled Guth's appointment a day earlier, he would not have been able to attend. His wife was recovering from an injured toe; had she injured it a few days later than she did, he again would not have been able to attend. Indeed, if his week had simply been a bit more hectic than it was, he would not have been able to attend.[10] But because the stars lined up for him, he did attend, and as a result, we have the inflationary universe theory.

Scientific aha moments, it would appear, are highly contingent things: change ever so slightly the life of the person who experiences such a moment, and it can easily fail to materialize. There is, of course, no way to know in advance whether a lecture, or some other event, will yield a first-rate aha moment. Given that this is so, what should a scientist do? Come up with a sensible research strategy, cross his fingers, and hope for the best.

PHYSICIST RICHARD FEYNMAN made several important discoveries. One of them involved working out what he refers to as "the theory of helium." Doing so provided him with a delightful aha moment: "I had been struggling and struggling for two years and suddenly saw everything. I can remember everything about it, by the way. It's psychologically funny— you can remember the color of the paper you were writing on and the room and everything else." And what, after two years of effort, finally triggered this aha moment? "I simply looked up and I said, 'Wait a minute—it can't be quite that difficult. It must be very easy. I'll just stand back, and I'll treat it very lightly. I'll just tap it, boomp-boomp.' And there it was."

Feynman knew that if he could figure out how aha moments worked, he could dramatically improve his productivity. The obvious thing to do was to repeat the circumstances that triggered his helium discovery. He tried this, but to no avail: "How many times since then I am walking on the beach and I say, 'Now look, it can't be so complicated.' And I'll tap-tap—and nothing happens."[11] Feynman was one of the most brilliant human beings ever to live, but even he couldn't fathom aha moments.

Theoretical physicist Lee Smolin had an aha moment that was strikingly similar to Feynman's. Smolin had gone to a café to work on a problem that had long perplexed him. He was ready to call it quits. "This is boring," he said in despair. "This is frustrating. I want to have a new idea about quantum mechanics."[12] But instead of quitting, he opened a new notebook, took out a pen, and sipped his coffee. In less than a minute, the insight he needed popped into his head.

Smolin, by the way, admits to experiencing another, radically different sort of aha moment. In conventional aha moments, a person suddenly gains insight into the truth. In this other sort of aha moment—I will refer to it as an *anti-aha moment*—a person suddenly realizes that he has made a mistake. There is every reason to think that anti-aha moments contribute as much to the advance of science as aha moments do.

THE GREAT AHA MOMENTS OF SCIENCE tend to come about as the result of a collaboration between the conscious and unconscious mind. The conscious mind tends to be rule-bound: provide it with rules, and it will happily apply them to the world. It will also attempt to derive new rules from old rules. The unconscious mind, by way of contrast, is "unruly." Consequently, as our conscious mind slumbers, our unconscious mind is capable of producing dreams in which we break the rules that bind us in daily life: we might fly by flapping our arms, thereby violating the laws of nature, or we might do things that violate cultural norms. The unconscious mind is also capable of exploring solutions to scientific problems that a scientist's conscious mind is reluctant to consider. And as we shall see in the remainder of this book, science isn't the only domain in which the unconscious mind plays an important role in the production of significant aha moments.

It is important to realize that the unconscious mind will yield meaningful scientific insights only if it has first been "primed" by the conscious mind. More precisely, a scientist's unconscious mind will turn its attention to a scientific problem only if the scientist has spent hours, days, or even years pondering that problem, unsuccessfully, with his conscious mind. This is why significant scientific discoveries are rarely made by people who, despite having vivid imaginations, lack scientific training. It is also why scientific problems are rarely solved by those who, despite having scientific training, lack the fortitude necessary to spend months or years trying, unsuccessfully, to solve them.

It is also important to realize that although training and conscious effort are a *necessary* condition for having an aha moment, they are by no means a *sufficient* condition. It is, sad to say, possible to spend one's entire scientific career doggedly trying to solve some problem and never have the requisite aha moment. Indeed, most scientists go through their careers without having an aha moment significant enough to win them a place in history. Furthermore, just because a scientist has one notable aha moment doesn't mean he will have another; indeed, the history of science is filled with one-hit wonders.

Often, a scientist's unconscious mind will hand him the insight he sought on a silver platter, as it were. This is what happened to Leo Szilard. As he stepped into the street, the idea of a neutron chain reaction came to him. In other cases, though, a scientist's unconscious mind will be coy: it will whisper to the scientist that it has the insight he seeks but won't tell him the exact nature of that insight. This is what happened to Roger Penrose. While crossing the street, he suddenly felt elated without knowing why. It was as if Penrose's unconscious mind had handed his conscious mind a wrapped present. Penrose was confident that the present was valuable, but until his conscious mind had a chance to unwrap it, Penrose didn't know what, exactly, it contained.

Because of the role played by his unconscious mind, a scientist who has a flash of insight might, besides feeling elated, experience a degree of puzzlement. "Where did *that* come from?" he will ask. He will know that the insight had to have come from himself. Scientists are loathe to attribute their insights—or anything else, for that matter—to divine or supernatural sources. At the same time, he will know that he does not have direct access to the unconscious mind that provided him with the insight.

In most cases, a scientist's feeling of elation will soon overcome his feeling of puzzlement, and his conscious mind will proudly take full ownership of the insight his unconscious mind has so kindly given him: "I just had a great idea!" he will announce to those around him, and by "I" he will mean his conscious mind.

EXPERIENCING AN AHA MOMENT can be the source of intense delight. Those having such a moment, says sociologist Robert K. Merton, experience an "ecstatic joy in discovery."[13] Nineteenth-century physiologist (and later physicist) Herman von Helmholtz characterized his own moments of discovery as "happy ideas."[14] Sigmund Freud spoke of "the incomparable pleasure of gaining first insight."[15] And physicist Richard Feynman, on winning the Nobel Prize in Physics, reported that what motivated him was not winning prizes but "the kick in the discovery."[16] In a conversation with astronomer Fred Hoyle, Feynman described the delight of having a good idea as "absolute ecstasy. You just go absolutely wild."[17]

The joy scientists experience in making discoveries is rarely expressed in the scientific literature, though. Consider James Watson and Francis Crick's discovery of the structure of DNA, one of the greatest aha moments in the history of science. At lunch that day, they reportedly marched into the nearby Eagle pub and announced to those present that they had just "discovered the secret of life." In the journal article in which they reported their find, though, they are rather more subdued. They conclude their one-page article by observing, "It has not escaped our notice that the specific pairing we have postulated immediately suggests a possible copying mechanism for the genetic material."[18] This sort of restraint, although understandable, is unfortunate: it makes scientific research seem like a joyless enterprise, when in fact it is the source of some of the greatest joys a person can experience.

Besides experiencing joy on making a discovery, a scientist might experience aesthetic delight: the truth he discovers can be remarkably beautiful. In many cases, says physicist Steven Weinberg, scientists are "guided by their sense of beauty not only in developing new theories but even in judging the validity of physical theories once they are developed."[19] Along similar lines, physicist Hermann Weyl noted that his work "always tried to unite the true with the beautiful" but added that "when I had to choose one or the other, I usually chose the beautiful."[20] This bias in favor of beauty served Weyl quite nicely on one occasion. He had become convinced that his "gauge theory of gravitation" was not true. The theory was so beautiful, though, that he could not bring himself to discard it altogether. This was a good thing, since the theory later played an important role in quantum electrodynamics.[21]

Besides being struck by the beauty of a discovery, scientists might be struck by the feeling that the discovery was inevitable. It isn't that scientists think it was inevitable that *they* would have the requisite aha moment; rather, they are convinced that the universe could not have been otherwise than they discovered it to be. "Surely someday," writes physicist John Archibald Wheeler, "...we will grasp the central idea of it all as so simple, so beautiful, so compelling, that we will all say to each other, Oh how could it have been otherwise!

How could we all have been so blind for so long!"[22] It is, to be sure, paradoxical that a truth we take to be inevitable once we reveal it should have been so hard to reveal, but such is the nature of science.

On experiencing an aha moment, scientists often feel that they have been made privy to an important secret: Gerard Edelman, winner of the Nobel Prize in Medicine, describes the "almost lustful feeling of excitement when a secret of nature is revealed."[23] And with this feeling can come a curious sensation of power: chemist Linus Pauling, on making an important discovery, was capable of boasting that "I know something that no one else in the whole world knows—and they won't know it until I tell them."[24]

THE INTENSITY WITH WHICH someone experiences the rush of discovery depends, presumably, on the personality of the discoverer and the circumstances of the discovery. In particular, it is possible for two individuals to have the same aha moment but to respond to it differently. Consider, for example, the independent discovery of the theory of evolution by Charles Darwin and Alfred Russel Wallace. Darwin's aha moment concerning evolution doesn't appear to have excited him very much. He never described what, exactly, it felt like to have what many take to be one of the most significant scientific breakthroughs ever. All we have is the brief notation—"I think"—on the page of the notebook on which he has sketched what appears to be the tree of life theorized by evolution—the diagram, that is, showing how one species can evolve from another. Ho hum!

Wallace appears to have been rather more animated about his epiphany. While recovering from a bout of fever, he experienced the "sudden flash of insight" that allowed him to discover "the long-sought-for law of nature that solved the problem of the origin of species."[25] That evening, he started writing down his ideas and a few days later sent them off in a letter to Charles Darwin, who was stunned to receive them.

Sometimes scientists are subdued in their response to an aha moment for the simple reason that they fail to recognize its significance. In the early 1960s, for example, Bell Labs asked Arno Penzias and Robert Wilson to make improvements on a microwave receiver so it could be used for transatlantic satellite communications. They weren't terribly excited by this project but agreed to undertake it after Bell told them that they would eventually be allowed to use the receiver to make astronomical observations.[26]

The receiver, they quickly realized, was plagued by background noise. At first they assumed that the noise had an outside source, but after eliminating all known external sources of static and laboriously cleaning the giant hornlike antenna of the receiver (pigeons and their droppings were an ongoing problem), the static remained. No matter where they pointed the antenna, they could detect a low hiss. This discovery annoyed them. They thought it was evidence that their receiver was defective. They then faced a quandary: how would they address the noise issue in the paper they were writing that described their efforts at calibrating the antenna? The best plan, they concluded, was to give the noise only a passing mention.[27]

Unbeknown to Penzias and Wilson, other scientists had deduced that if our universe had started in a Big Bang, as many astronomers thought, an echo of that bang would still be reverberating. This echo, they calculated, would take the form of cosmic background radiation that could be detected by a microwave receiver—like the one Penzias and Wilson were working on. Penzias and Wilson were also unaware that physicist Robert Dicke—the person who triggered Alan Guth's interest in cosmic inflation—was about to start his own search for the noise they had already detected.[28] Had the story ended there, Penzias and Wilson would have gone down in the history of science as the poor guys who uncovered smoking-gun evidence for the Big Bang theory but failed to recognize the significance of their discovery.

But the story didn't end there; Penzias and Wilson got lucky. While flying home from a scientific conference, Penzias happened to sit next to a scientist, who on hearing of the trouble he and Wilson were having with their receiver, put him in touch with Dicke, who explained to them the scientific significance of the noise that had been plaguing them. Even then, though, Penzias and Wilson appear to have been a bit in the dark regarding the importance of their discovery. Wilson later reported that it was only when he read a story about their research on the front page of the *New York Times* that he truly appreciated the magnitude of their discovery.[29] In 1978, Penzias and Wilson were awarded the Nobel Prize in Physics.

PENZIAS AND WILSON may have been slow to appreciate the significance of their discovery, but at least they worked hard to make it and therefore—perhaps—deserve credit for having done so. In other cases, scientists don't so much make a discovery as have one thrust on them by nature.

Consider, by way of illustration, the "discovery" of X-rays. In the mid-1880s, William Crookes put two metal plates inside a glass tube, connected these plates to a voltage source, and pumped all the air out of the tube. Crookes noticed that such tubes had the power to fog photographic film. The only conclusion he drew from this, however, was that it is unwise to leave undeveloped film near a Crookes tube.[30] A decade later, Wilhelm Conrad Roentgen, while experimenting with a Crookes tube, found that when the mystery rays produced by the tube fogged film, they captured the "shadows" cast by whatever was between the Crookes tube and the film, thus producing what we now call X-ray images. For his ability to appreciate the discovery that had fallen into his lap, Roentgen was, in 1901, awarded the very first Nobel Prize in Physics.

In 1928, a streak of lucky accidents enabled Alexander Fleming to discover something he hadn't really been looking for, namely, penicillin. Some penicillium spores got into Fleming's laboratory by accident: they apparently drifted in from the lab of another researcher and found a home on one of Fleming's culture dishes.[31] Had Fleming cleaned these dishes before leaving on a summer vacation, the spores wouldn't have had time to grow and display their antibiotic characteristics, and had the summer been warm, the mold would not have thrived. Not only that, but if, when he finally got around to cleaning his dishes by putting them into a tub of disinfectant, Fleming had stacked the dishes in a different order, the dish with the penicillium would have been submerged and destroyed before Fleming could notice its effect on other microorganisms.[32] But Fleming did notice, and as Louis Pasteur observed, "chance favors the prepared mind." In 1945, Fleming was awarded the Nobel Prize in Medicine for his discovery.

Even horseplay can give rise to scientific discoveries. In 1976, an important find was made when two paleoanthropologists were having a friendly fight, in which they pelted each other with dried elephant dung. While looking for "ammunition," one of them came across the 3.6-million-year-old fossilized footprints of an early ancestor of man. The footprints turned out to belong to a double trail of footprints that was eighty feet long, and because there were no impressions of knuckles on the trail, it was striking evidence that the hominids in question were walking upright.[33] Before this find, scientists had relied on less-conclusive anatomical arguments to support the claim that the hominids of that period had walked upright.

IN SOME CASES, scientific aha moments are triggered not by scientists finding something but by their failure to find what they are looking for. Suppose, for example, currently accepted theory tells scientists that if they do a certain experiment, something specific will happen. Suppose they do the experiment only to have nothing happen. If they have been trained properly, they will assume that their experiment is somehow flawed—that maybe their experimental apparatus is malfunctioning. Suppose, though, that after much investigation they can find nothing wrong with it. What should they do now?

This is what happened to Albert Michelson and Edward Morley. In the late nineteenth century, it was thought that light moves through a substance known as *luminiferous aether*, the way ocean waves move through water and sound waves move through air. In 1881, Michelson tried to detect the aether with an instrument known as an interferometer, but the instrument was not sufficiently sensitive to accomplish the task. In 1885, he and Morley repeated the experiment, using an improved interferometer. Try as they might, though, Michelson and Morley couldn't detect any aether.

What is significant about this episode is that Michelson and Morley didn't shy away from publishing results that weren't what the scientific world expected. They didn't, in other words, assume that an experiment that fails to yield expected results is necessarily flawed and should therefore be ignored. If we examine the great discoveries of science, we find that in many cases what is most remarkable is not the discovery itself but the courage one or more scientists displayed in defending that discovery. We will return to this topic in Chapter 9.

In the meantime, though, let us explore the psychology of scientific aha moments. What motivates scientists to do all the work necessary to have a chance at making an important scientific discovery? The short answer: curiosity, a lust for scientific fame, or both. More importantly, what, if anything, can scientists do to increase their chances of making an important discovery? They can work very hard to acquire what is called a *scientific paradigm* and then work almost as hard to avoid becoming enslaved by it.

CHAPTER 8

On Keeping an Open Mind

AFTER GRADUATING FROM HIGH SCHOOL, Stuart Firestein became a professional stage manager and director. After more than a decade in the theater, he went to college, took an interest in biology, and subsequently began a career in science. He is currently a professor of neuroscience at Columbia University. People who hear his story sometimes ask him to compare the two careers. In particular, they want to know whether he misses theater. He responds, "As for excitement and creativity, I don't think that science has any less of that than the theater, or any of the arts."[1]

A nonscientist, on hearing this kind of talk, will probably be surprised. For many people, science is anything but exciting. They remember the classes they were forced to take and perhaps hated. And yet here is someone who argues that if what you are looking for is excitement, a life in science compares favorably with a life in the theater. How could this be?

The obvious answer to this question is that by doing science, one can enjoy the delights that come with making a major discovery. Such discoveries are rare, and scientists start their careers knowing full well that the odds are stacked against them. Are they, perhaps, like gamblers placing long-shot bets? This is unlikely, inasmuch as scientists are highly rational individuals. We are therefore left to wonder what, other than the off chance of making a significant discovery, motivates scientists. What induces them to go through years of education, followed by years of arduous research, so they can spend decades in the lab, out in the field, or—in the case of theoretical science—sitting at a desk?

The primary driving force would appear to be curiosity. Scientists are invariably curious people, and as driving forces go, curiosity is doubly motivating: it provides both a stick to push a person forward and a carrot with which she can subsequently be rewarded. When scientists realize that they don't know something, they are irritated: they experience what social scientist Herbert Simon calls "the itch of curiosity."[2] If they successfully scratch this itch, they are rewarded with a pleasurable aha moment.

Consider, then, a scientist who goes through her entire career never making a breakthrough discovery. Her career will not be joyless. As a student learning basic science, she will experience many personally significant aha moments: "So *that's* why the sky is blue!" As a researcher, she will periodically make discoveries that, although they don't count as scientific breakthroughs, will nevertheless give her delight. And even if her scientific career is unproductive, she will, if she is curious, enjoy learning about the discoveries being made by others in her field.

Another thing to keep in mind about curiosity is that it is potentially insatiable. In satisfying your curiosity about one thing, what you learn will likely make you aware of something else that you don't know, and your curiosity will thereby be re-stimulated. To some people, this sounds like a recipe for a hellish existence; indeed, it sounds very much like being addicted to a drug. To a scientist, though, it is a heavenly state of affairs. What would be hellish would be a world in which there was nothing left to find out.

Curious people, psychologists have found, tend to be happy people.[3] This means that a scientist might be happy in her work, even if her efforts don't produce breakthrough discoveries. Indeed, she will find that her job, rather than being oppressively boring, as many people find theirs to be, is endlessly entertaining and worthy of obsessive dedication.

CURIOSITY IS FIRST EXPERIENCED in early childhood; indeed, children are profoundly curious about nearly everything, and a bright three-year-old, on learning how to ask "why" questions, will ask them incessantly. By the time they are teenagers, though, children's curiosity typically will have subsided. They are no longer eager to learn about everything; they are instead somewhat anxious to learn about some things. And by the time they are adults, their curiosity will be directed, for the most part, toward trivial and personal things. They will watch the entertainment news so they can keep up to date on the dysfunctional life of some movie star. They will spend their free time looking up obscure sports statistics. They will have become part of the public that, as Oscar Wilde quipped, has "an insatiable curiosity to know everything, except what is worth knowing."[4]

Why do people become less curious as they age? In part because they have found out what they need to know in order to function in everyday life: they have learned, for example, how to drive a car and how to microwave macaroni and cheese. It is also likely, though, that social forces have curbed their inquisitive tendencies. A three year old might innocently ask his parents a simple question—"Why is the sky blue?"—only to discover, much to his astonishment, that they can't answer it! And if this child continues to ask why-questions, in the belief that surely his parents know *something*, he will quickly make another discovery: why-questions irritate adults. Such questions force adults to confront their profound ignorance regarding the world around them.

Put yourself, for a moment, inside the mind of a precocious three-year-old. He asks the adults around him obvious questions that they are unable to answer time and time again. And yet these adults have been put in charge of things. It must be some ghastly mistake! It is therefore not surprising that children stop asking why-questions: adults not only can't answer them but get mad at you for asking them. In such an environment, we can expect children's curiosity to atrophy, the way their muscles would atrophy if their mother got mad whenever they tried to exercise.

Scientists somehow manage to escape childhood with their curiosity intact. It could be that when they were children, scientists had the good luck to be surrounded by adults who could answer many of their why-questions, or who, when stumped by a question, honestly admitted as much and then set off in search of an answer. It could also be that as children, scientists were simply more curious than other youngsters, and their curiosity was harder for the adult world to extinguish. At any rate, by the time future scientists reach high school, they are delighted to discover that there is a career that will not only let them spend their days satisfying their curiosity but will provide them with a good living. They realize, as physicist Murray Gell-Mann put it, that "if a child grows up to be a scientist, he finds that he is paid to play all day the most exciting game ever devised by mankind."[5] And so they begin their scientific training.

When they are in the grip of curiosity, scientists lose themselves in their research and as a result might lose interest in the business of daily living. They become "absent-minded professors," which is a misnomer. Their mind isn't absent; it is present but profoundly focused. For an example of this kind of single-mindedness, consider Isaac Newton. When he was fixated on a problem, he ignored the meals brought to him; his cat did not.[6] Newton's bedtime was determined not by the clock but by when he reached the point of utter exhaustion.

While doing research, a scientist can experience what psychologist Mihaly Csikszentmihalyi calls *flow*.[7] During a flow experience, a person lives, as Zen Buddhists put it, "in the moment." He might become so involved in what he is doing that he becomes indifferent to what other people think of his activities. The rest of the world falls away. He loses track of time. To experience flow, says Csikszentmihalyi, a person must undertake a challenging activity that involves an element of novelty and discovery. Among those who experience flow are athletes, artists, religious mystics, and scientists.

For one delightful example of a scientist in the grip of curiosity, consider entomologist and evolutionary biologist Edward O. Wilson, who has spent much of his life studying ants. When asked in an interview to explain his fascination with them, Wilson launched into an encomium to the humble ant: "They're so abundant, they're easy to find, and they're easy to study, and they're so interesting. They have social habits that differ from one kind of ant to the next. You know, each kind of ant has almost the equivalent of a different human culture. So each species is a wonderful object to study in itself." He then turned the tables on the interviewer: given how incredible ants are, he said, the real question isn't why *he* studies them but why other people *don't* study them.[8]

Nonscientists might pity scientists for being driven by curiosity. Those doing the pitying, however, might be astonished to discover that scientists pity *them* in return: how boring the world must be if you don't share their hunger for knowledge! We live in an astonishing world, but if you are incurious, you are unlikely ever to realize as much.

CURIOSITY, THOUGH, isn't the only thing that motivates a scientist. If it were, scientists wouldn't feel particularly driven to share their discoveries with others. They wouldn't, metaphorically speaking, feel the need to kiss and tell; the kiss would be enough. A scientist would privately savor any discovery he made and then move on to new investigations. Yet scientists not only share their discoveries with others but are quite eager to do so. In some cases, this is because they want to benefit mankind. If you come up with a cure for ulcers, for example, you will want to share your discovery. In many more cases, though, what motivates scientists to share their discoveries isn't so much altruism as a desire to improve their standing on the scientific hierarchy.

This last desire manifests itself in a number of ways. To begin with, there is the matter of scientific one-upmanship. If you are an athlete, you want other athletes to acknowledge your athletic prowess. If you are a scientist, you have a similar need for recognition. To win it, you triumph over your peers not on fields of play, but in your laboratory, at professional meetings, or in journals. Neuroscientist (and former theater director) Stuart Firestein observes, "One of the more gratifying, if slightly indulgent, pleasures of actually doing science is proving someone wrong."[9]

One delightful example of this phenomenon took place at a scientific meeting in 1862. Biologist Richard Owen had just claimed, as many other scientists had before him, that no animal other than man has the brain structure known as a hippocampus. Biologist Thomas Huxley replied that English zoologist William Flower had found the hippocampus in other primates. The men argued the point until Flower, who was in the audience, stood up and announced, "I happen to have in my pocket a monkey's brain." Huxley and Owen took a look, and the debate was settled.[10] Touché!

If it is fun to show another scientist is wrong, it is more fun still to show that a scientist was wrong in saying that *you* were wrong. Scientists, it turns out, are perfectly capable of bearing grudges against those who, they feel, have slighted them. Biochemist Peter Mitchell was interested in how substances are transported across cell membranes and in the early 1960s proposed a theory regarding such transport. His views were at first ridiculed. Slowly, though, his colleagues came around to his way of thinking, and when they did, Mitchell celebrated the event by recording it on a chart that showed when those who rejected his theory finally admitted he was right.[11] In 1978, Mitchell was awarded the Nobel Prize for Chemistry.

Philosopher of science David L. Hull, who has investigated the behavior of scientists, reports, "Time and again, the scientists whom I have been studying have told stories of confrontations with other scientists that roused them from routine work to massive effort. No matter what the cost, they were going to get even." Thus, in the same way that an athlete might intensify his training regimen so he will have the opportunity to avenge, on the field of play, what he views as a past humiliation by a rival athlete, a scientist might be driven to redouble his research efforts so that he might someday, as Hull puts it, "get that son of a bitch."[12]

Some would argue that scientists should overcome these petty, vengeful tendencies and instead cooperate with one another. Although doing this might make science more pleasant, it would almost certainly make it less productive. Grudges can, after all, be powerful motivators.

Besides being driven by curiosity and a desire to show up their colleagues, scientists are driven by a desire for fame. They want to win awards, prizes, and best of all, immortality through eponymy. If we are surprised that highly rational individuals—as scientists invariably are—would be fame seekers, we would do well to keep in mind Roman historian

Tacitus's observation that "the lust of fame is the last that a wise man shakes off."[13]

SCIENCE ISN'T DONE in a vacuum; instead, scientists work within a *paradigm*. Students acquire this paradigm during their scientific education. To begin with, they learn how the scientific method works—that is, how to do experiments and make observations, and how to assess the quality of other people's experiments and observations. They learn how to reason in a scientific manner. Quite significantly, they are exposed to the consensus views held in various scientific disciplines. These views comprise the paradigms of the disciplines in question. Thus, geology students learn how to interpret stratigraphic layering and learn about the theory of plate tectonics. Physics students learn about Newton's laws of motion and Einstein's theory of relativity.

By acquiring a paradigm, students will develop a feel for what experiments are worth doing and what observations are worth making. If you tell someone who has acquired the current physics paradigm that you have invented a perpetual motion machine, she will likely dismiss your claim out of hand: her paradigm tells her that it can't be done. Tell her that you have detected subatomic particles traveling faster than the speed of light, and she will likewise be dismissive.

Initially, science students may form the impression that science is dogmatic: they are handed a paradigm to internalize and graded down if they depart from it. As they continue their scientific education, however, they will be made aware of the ongoing disputes within their discipline. Thus, paleontology students, instead of simply being taught that the dinosaurs were killed by an asteroid that struck the earth sixty-five million years ago, will be exposed to other theories about how they perished. (There are, by one count, at least ninety such theories.)[14] They will also be taught that the disappearance of the dinosaurs is a complex event best explained by invoking multiple theories. Finally, and perhaps most importantly, they will be taught that scientists do not vote—not as a group, at any rate—to determine which theory is correct. Each scientist assesses theories separately, with different scientists drawing different conclusions. Thus, in a randomly chosen group of ten paleontologists, it is entirely possible that no two will hold precisely the same views regarding the fate of the dinosaurs.

Students will also be exposed to the history of science and will come to realize that it is possible for paradigms to be overturned. They will learn that at one time, astronomers thought the earth was at the center of the universe, then that the sun was, and finally that the universe doesn't have a center. They will learn that before 1905, physicists thought space and time were absolute; by 1930, they believed them to be relative. They will learn that before 1960, geologists thought the position of the continents was fixed; by 1970, they believed that the continents were attached to tectonic plates that moved with respect to each other. Thoughtful students will conclude that similar abandonment will likely be the fate of some currently favored scientific paradigms. They will also realize that, judging from the history of science, the best way to gain fame within a scientific discipline is to successfully challenge the paradigm of that discipline.

Ideally, students will emerge from their scientific education with a curiously schizophrenic mindset. In their research, they will proceed on the basis of numerous assumptions—those that constitute the paradigm of the discipline in which they are working—while simultaneously entertaining the possibility that one or more of those assumptions is mistaken. This mindset is essential if a scientist is to have any chance of experiencing the kind of aha moment that will win him enduring fame.

PARADIGMS CREATE EXPECTATIONS in those who acquire them. A paradigm will, for example, enable scientists to make very precise predictions about what will happen if they perform a certain experiment. But suppose they perform the experiment and fail to obtain the predicted results. There are three possible explanations for this outcome: their experiment is flawed, their prediction is flawed, or the paradigm under which they labor is mistaken. The first of these possibilities is the most probable: they simply blew the experiment. Even though scientists take great care in doing experiments, this can happen. The second possibility is that their prediction is flawed, possibly as the result of a math error. Or maybe they neglected to take certain factors into account when they made their prediction. The third possibility—that their paradigm is mistaken—is least likely to be the case. The paradigm in question will, after all, have been extensively tested; otherwise, it wouldn't be the paradigm. Then again, if the paradigm is mistaken and they are the first to reveal that mistake, they will gain scientific immortality.

Suppose a scientist does an experiment on the basis of a certain prediction, only to obtain an anomalous result. If she is sensible, she won't rush to tell the world about her discovery. After all, if she makes such an announcement, only to have it turn out that her experiment or prediction were flawed, she will be humiliated. She will therefore recheck her prediction, recheck her equipment, and redo the experiment—not once but many times—before concluding that the anomalous result is real.

What if she can't find a mistake in her research? Will she announce her discovery to the world? Not necessarily. Even then, after all, there is a chance that she has indeed made a mistake. She might announce her results if she is confident and courageous; otherwise, she will be tempted to suppress them.

Along these lines, allergy researcher Erika von Mutius did an epidemiological study comparing asthma rates of children living in Munich with those living in small towns. She found that the small-town children had asthma at the same rate as the city children, except for one thing: kids who lived in homes with "dirty" coal- or wood-burning furnaces seemed to be protected against asthma. This result was so counterintuitive, though, that she couldn't bring herself to publish it.[15] Subsequent research by von Mutius and others yielded a body of evidence for what has become known as the hygiene hypothesis, according to which exposure to a hygienic environment in early childhood increases susceptibility to allergic diseases later in life.

How often do scientists fail to publish out of a fear that their results are mistaken? It is hard to say, since the only way such cases come to light is if a scientist is subsequently willing to admit to a failure of courage. Von Mutius is unusual for her willingness to make such an admission.

Another example of reluctance to publish involves physicist Gerald Guralnik, who in 1962 predicted the existence of what became known as the Higgs boson. The particle is named after Peter Higgs who, along with François Englert, predicted its existence two years after Guralnik did. Why, then, isn't it called the Guralnik boson? Because Guralnik lacked the confidence necessary to publish his prediction.

Guralnik had included the prediction in his doctoral dissertation but took it out when his adviser challenged it: "I don't know what's the matter with it," the adviser said, "but it's not right." Guralnik subsequently wrote a paper in which he made his prediction, but he was slow to send it off for publication, for fear that it contained one or more mistakes. When he finally did submit it, he had lost priority: on the same day that he mailed his manuscript to *Physical Review Letters*, he received a reprint of the article in which Englert announced his own version of the theory.[16] In 2012, Englert and Higgs were awarded the Nobel Prize in Physics; Guralnik was not.

So what is the Nobel Prize in Physics awarded for? Obviously, it recognizes breakthrough discoveries in physics. And less obviously, it is, in many cases, an award for scientific courage.

IF IT IS HARD FOR MEN to publish and subsequently defend controversial results, it can be even harder for women. When it comes to getting their scientific work accepted, women face challenges that men don't. Consider the career of astronomer Vera Rubin. In the late 1940s, as a high school student, Rubin wanted to study astronomy at Swarthmore, but when the admissions officer there suggested that she should learn to paint the stars rather than learn to observe them, Rubin decided to attend Vassar instead. She graduated in three years and was the school's only female astronomy major that year. Rubin set her sights on Princeton for graduate school, only to discover that it didn't accept women. She ended up at a lower-ranked astronomy program at Cornell. One upside of attending Cornell, though, was that it let her take classes from Hans Bethe and Richard Feynman, who at that time were on its physics faculty.[17]

For her master's thesis, Rubin did work on the motion of galaxies and got results that went against the then-current scientific consensus that galaxies exhibit only straight-line motion. Shortly after the birth of her first child, she announced these results at a meeting of the American Astronomical Society, only to encounter skepticism.[18] She subsequently tried, unsuccessfully, to get her thesis published. After that, she was too busy taking care of her children and working on her doctorate to defend her results.[19] Of course, even if she had the time and energy to undertake such a defense, it probably would have been foolhardy for someone possessing only a master's degree to take on the scientific establishment.

The eminent astronomer W. W. Morgan was one of the journal editors who had rejected her thesis; indeed, he had done so in an insulting manner. Many years later, Rubin encountered Morgan at a party. He asked why she had never published her master's thesis—apparently having forgotten that she would have done so, had he not rejected it. At that same party, Morgan made a sexual overture to her.[20]

In her doctoral dissertation—written while her children were sleeping—Rubin considered the distribution of the galaxies: were they spread smoothly throughout the universe or was their distribution "clumpy"? She argued for a clumpy distribution. This result, which again was contrary to consensus views, was ignored, and again, Rubin did not rise to its defense.

At age thirty-six, Rubin got her first real job in astronomy, at the Department of Terrestrial Magnetism at the Carnegie Institute in Washington, DC. There, she entered into a collaboration with W. Kent Ford, a physicist and designer of astronomical instruments. They started doing research on the motions of galaxies and found that galaxies moved as Rubin had claimed they did in her master's thesis. These results—which have become known as the Rubin-Ford effect—were again rejected by the scientific community.

Rubin and Ford then turned their attention to the rotation of galaxies. The rate at which galaxies rotate is proportional to how massive they are. Rubin and Ford discovered that galaxies are spinning too fast, given the amount of matter they seem to contain. They concluded that galaxies contain vast amounts of matter that is essentially invisible to astronomers.

Indeed, there is far more of this "dark" matter, as it subsequently came to be known, than there is ordinary matter. In the 1930s, astronomers Fritz Zwicky and Sinclair Smith had speculated that the universe contained invisible matter, but they lacked the necessary supporting observational data. Rubin and Ford provided that data. Not only that, but Rubin labored on, adding galaxy after galaxy to her database. Largely as the result of her efforts, the scientific community came to accept the existence of dark matter. Rubin was subsequently showered with scientific awards.

WHEN SCIENTISTS HAVE what looks like a brilliant idea, there are two big mistakes they can make. The first is to publish the idea only to discover that it is mistaken; the second is to fail to publish the idea out of fear that it is mistaken, only to see a peer publish the same results and have the idea turn out to be correct. Some scientists, on finding themselves faced with this predicament, resort to what might be called stealth publishing: they publish their possibly breakthrough article in an obscure journal. That way, it won't get much attention, and if their idea is mistaken, few people will notice. If it turns out, however, that their idea is correct, they will be able to prove that they were the first person to have it.

One example of this phenomenon took place in conjunction with the Snowball Earth hypothesis, according to which the earth froze solid about 650 million years ago. The possibility of a frozen earth was first proposed in 1948 by explorer Douglas Mawson, who found evidence of glaciation in Australia.[21] There was a problem with the hypothesis, though: an earth frozen solid would be so reflective of sunlight that it could never again free itself of ice. Thus, the fact that the earth isn't now completely covered with ice is compelling evidence that it never has been completely covered.

In the late 1980s, geologist Joe Kirschvink hit on a way that a frozen earth could subsequently thaw. Volcanic activity, he reasoned, would not be deterred by ice. Volcanoes would continue to spew carbon dioxide and other greenhouse gasses into the atmosphere. This would trigger an episode of extreme global warming, which would subsequently melt the ice. Kirschvink did not try to publish his theory in a prestigious journal; instead, it became a chapter in an obscure scholarly monograph, which took four years to appear.[22] Few would have read it, and those who did might have overlooked his theory, since he devoted only one sentence to it: "Escape from the 'ice house' would presumably be through the gradual buildup of the greenhouse gas, CO_2, contributed to the air through volcanic emissions."[23]

The Snowball Earth hypothesis, although still the subject of scientific controversy, seems headed toward general acceptance. Although Kirschvink played a role in its rise, the hypothesis is much more strongly linked, in scientists' minds, with Paul Hoffman, who for years was its chief proponent. Kirschvink has subsequently expressed chagrin at not having been bolder in his statement and subsequent defense of Snowball Earth.[24]

SUPPOSE A SCIENTIST performs an experiment, only to get results that are at odds with the paradigm. If she publishes these anomalous results, she will make her colleagues aware of what might be an inconsistency in their beliefs. They won't be happy to hear this and will likely respond by attacking the obvious targets: the scientist's experiment and quite possibly the scientist herself. Thus, a scientist who reports anomalous results has something in common with the moral reformers we investigated in Chapter 6. Those individuals make people aware of the inconsistencies in their moral beliefs and thereby succeed, in many cases, in annoying them.

There is also a chance that her colleagues will respond to news of the anomaly by doing nothing at all. They will be so sure that a mistake has been made that they won't even bother to look for it. They will assume that at some point, somebody will explain away the anomaly. For some of these scientists, though, a curious thing will happen. The anomaly will take up residence in a back corner of their minds. From this hideout, it will periodically remind the scientists of its existence and demand to be dealt with. These scientists will find themselves in a state of cognitive dissonance: they will be uncomfortably aware of a seeming inconsistency in their beliefs.

In the same way that a state of cognitive dissonance can trigger a moral epiphany—remember Thomas Clarkson's aha moment?—it can trigger a scientific epiphany. This is what happened to Albert Einstein in the spring of 1905. After spending a period agonizing about an apparent contradiction in Newtonian physics, he hit upon a brilliant solution, which he bravely defended. As a result, he was able to effect a paradigm shift, from Newtonian physics to relativistic physics, and thereby gained scientific immortality.

REALIZE THAT PARADIGM SHIFTS, when they happen, take place one scientist at a time. Scientists don't vote on whether an old paradigm should be replaced by a new one. Instead, paradigms shift when so many scientists have changed their minds about the issues involved that those who don't change their minds start seeming out of touch with ongoing research and thereby run the risk of being regarded as dinosaurs, intellectually speaking.

We have already encountered Edward O. Wilson, notable for his intense interest in ants. In his autobiography, we can find a description of a paradigm shift, seen from the point of view of an individual scientist. The shift in question involved the theory of kin selection, which is an attempt to reconcile the theory of evolution with the existence of altruistic behavior. According to the theory of evolution, animals that successfully reproduce will thrive. And yet, when we look at the animal world, we can find lots of examples of animals that seem more concerned with helping other animals reproduce than with their own reproductive efforts. Consider ants, for example. If you are a worker ant, you have no chance of reproducing. Instead you spend your life working hard so the queen ant can reproduce. How are we to explain this altruistic behavior?

Darwin suggested an answer to this question. Yes, natural selection favors creatures that propagate their genes, but there are two ways in which a creature can do this. One is by reproducing; the other is by aiding the reproductive efforts of another creature who shares many (or ideally, all) of its genes. Ants and other social insects employ the latter strategy. The queen ant is the mother of the worker ants, and as such, shares many (and in the case of some species, all) of their genes. Thus, by helping her reproduce, they are indirectly helping propagate their own genes.

This is the theory of kin selection. Besides explaining the bio-logic of social insects, it explains why we are more inclined to do things for our children, brothers, and sisters than we are for nonrelatives. Kin selection got a boost when statistician and evolutionary biologist Ronald Fisher gave it a mathematical treatment in 1930. A further boost came when evolutionary biologist William D. Hamilton refined this treatment in the early 1960s. After that, it was up to individual biologists to decide whether or not to adopt the theory.

Wilson was one of these biologists. Since he specialized in ants, he had given considerable thought to how these and other social insects could have evolved. In conjunction with his research, he brought Hamilton's article on kin selection on a train trip from Boston to Miami in 1965. He was initially unimpressed by Hamilton's argument:

> Impossible, I thought, this can't be right. Too simple. [Hamilton] must not know much about social insects. But the idea kept gnawing at me...By dinnertime, as the train rumbled on into Virginia, I was growing frustrated and angry. Hamilton, whoever he was, could not have cut the Gordian knot....And because I modestly thought of myself as the world authority on social insects, I also

thought it unlikely that anyone else could explain their origin, certainly not in one clean stroke...By the time we reached Miami, in the early afternoon, I gave up. I was a convert and put myself in Hamilton's hands. I had undergone what historians of science call a paradigm shift.[25]

What Wilson experienced was an episode of cognitive dissonance of the scientific variety, compressed into a few hours of mental anguish. Before this episode, he was not an advocate of kin selection; after this episode, he was.

Although each scientist must make up his own mind in ongoing debates, some will do so by waiting for other scientists to make up their minds. As part of my research for this book, I interviewed Paul Hoffman, the leading proponent of the Snowball Earth hypothesis. He said that as far as he could tell, most scientists weren't actively taking part in the Snowball Earth debate: because it didn't affect their area of research, they had better things to think about. He characterized them as fence-sitters: they were waiting until the leading paleoclimatologists made up their minds, at which point, they would fall into line behind them.[26] This behavior, I should add, is perfectly understandable.

WE HAVE SEEN THAT the paradigm under which a scientist operates will affect what he expects to see when he makes observations or does experiments. Strangely enough, it can also affect what he *does* see and thereby prevent him from experiencing an aha moment that in all fairness ought to be his. Allow me to explain how this can happen.

In the early 1960s, astronomers struggled to understand the astronomical objects known as quasars. These objects, which had been detected by radio telescopes, were surprisingly "bright." Later, astronomers succeeded in locating quasars with optical telescopes and obtained their spectra. Stated simply, these spectra are the "rainbows" created by the light an object emits. Under certain circumstances, the rainbows in question will have dark lines across them. These spectral lines give scientists information about what chemical elements are present at the light source, whether that source is moving toward or away from them, and how fast it is moving.

On February 5, 1963, Maarten Schmidt was examining a quasar spectrum when it dawned on him that the spectral lines he saw made perfect sense if he assumed that they had been radically shifted toward the red end of the spectrum. Schmidt knew that such shifting implied that quasars were at a very great distance from us. But if quasars were able to look incredibly bright despite being incredibly far from us, they had to be enormously powerful—more powerful than seemed physically possible. In other words, the paradigm under which he was operating seemed to rule out radical red-shifting of a quasar's spectral lines.

Schmidt decided to try out the red-shift explanation on his colleague Jesse Greenstein, who reflexively rejected it: "Impossible!" Greenstein then recalled that this wasn't the first time someone had suggested to him that quasar spectra were radically red-shifted, and that on the previous occasion, he had likewise rejected the suggestion. It was at this point that it dawned on Schmidt and Greenstein that perhaps the red-shift explanation made sense after all, and they experienced a simultaneous epiphany. They briefly celebrated their discovery and then, being meticulous scientists, went to work trying to find a mistake or alternative explanation for what they had observed. When Schmidt got home that evening, he reported to his wife that "something horrible happened at the office today." He went on to explain that by "something horrible," he meant something wonderful.[27]

This case is instructive. Many astronomers had examined quasar spectra without being able to see what later was obvious, namely, that the spectra were radically red-shifted. Not only that, but the astronomers who did suspect radical red-shifting managed to talk themselves out of this explanation or let themselves be talked out of it. They did this because they "knew"—according to the paradigm under which they operated—that quasar spectra *couldn't* be radically red-shifted. Their scientific preconceptions distorted their assessment of the evidence that lay before their very eyes! Historians of science refer to this phenomenon as paradigm blindness.

AT THIS POINT, readers might wonder whether it is a good idea for scientists to operate under a paradigm. Doing so, after all, can blind them to physical phenomena. More generally, it prevents them from doing science with an open mind: they will, as we have seen, tend to cling to their paradigm, even when there is evidence that it is mistaken.

These concerns are legitimate, but realize that someone who attempted to do science outside of a paradigm would have nothing to "build on," meaning that her contribution to scientific progress would be negligible. Such a person wouldn't be able to assume that chemicals had the properties they had in the past, that Newton's laws of motion were still true, or even that two rabbits, when they mated, would give birth to a rabbit rather than a frog. The scientist-sans-paradigm would be in the position of reinventing the wheel every day. By operating on the assumption that past discoveries are still valid and that a range of thoroughly tested theories are correct, a scientist can build on the work of his scientific forebears. The resulting progress can be—and has been—spectacular.

A scientist who wishes to avoid becoming enslaved by a paradigm would do well to make full use of his unconscious mind. The paradigm under which he operates resides in his conscious mind, and its forte is in mastering rules and deducing the consequences of those rules. His unconscious mind, however, has the ability to flout the rules of science—and society. The conscious mind is fastidious and wants to sort things into nice, neat categories: there is space and there is time; there is matter and there is energy. The unconscious mind, though, is untidy and is therefore perfectly willing to blur these categories.

In the words of biologist and Nobel laureate Peter Medawar, "All advances of scientific understanding, at every level, begin with a speculative adventure, an imaginative preconception *of what might be true*—a preconception that always, and necessarily, goes a little way (sometimes a long way) beyond anything which we have logical or factual authority to believe in.... Scientific reasoning is therefore ... a dialogue between two voices, the one imaginative and the other critical."[28] In science, as in many fields, inspiration is the result of a curious interaction between the odd couple consisting of the conscious and unconscious mind.

For more evidence of the role the unconscious mind plays in scientific discoveries, we can turn our attention back to the aha moments described in the previous chapter. Many of those moments were experienced not while scientists were sitting at their desk, trying desperately to answer a scientific question, but while they were attempting to recover from those labors. Thus, the aha moments experienced by Penrose and Szilard occurred while they were out for a walk. Along similar lines, Helmholtz reported that his own "happy ideas" never came to him at his desk. They instead waited until he had left his desk and, as the result of relaxing, had achieved a state of "complete physical freshness."[29]

Given the role the unconscious mind plays in scientific discovery, scientists will want to take steps to enlist its cooperation. Since we don't have direct access to our unconscious mind, though, the steps in question will have to be indirect. More precisely, by controlling what goes on in his conscious mind, a scientist can attempt to influence what goes on in his unconscious mind. Allow me to explain.

If a scientist never thinks about a scientific question, there is zero chance that his unconscious mind will one day reward him with an aha moment. If he spends his waking hours thinking about that question, though, there is a good chance that his unconscious mind will take an interest and start working on it as well. And what a splendid worker the unconscious mind will be! It will continue its labors long after the scientist's conscious mind has quit for the day. We will consider this "incubation" phenomenon in detail in Part 4 of this book, when we explore the aha moments that take place in mathematics.

The conscious mind is, to be sure, unaware of what is going on in the unconscious mind until the latter sees fit to communicate. At that moment, the conscious mind will have the sensation of "having an idea." A better description of this event, of course, is that the conscious mind has been given an idea by the unconscious mind. Ideas may seem to come to us "out of the blue," but they don't; they instead come to us from the apparent blackness of our unconscious mind.

Although the unconscious mind is wonderful at coming up with ideas, they won't all be good. This is because the unconscious mind is both unruly and untidy. The conscious mind is therefore faced with the task of sorting through the ideas the unconscious mind presents to it, and this is messy work. The danger is that, because it is both rule-bound and tidy, the conscious mind will be quick to reject those ideas. A scientist must guard against this danger if he wants to maximize his chances of achieving the breakthrough that he hopes for. When a seemingly outlandish idea pops into his head, he won't simply discard it; he will instead inspect it carefully. When asked how he got his ideas, chemist Linus Pauling replied, "If you want to have good ideas you must have many ideas. Most of them will be wrong, and what you have to learn is which ones to throw away."[30]

ANOTHER WAY SCIENTISTS can maximize their chance of experiencing a significant aha moment is by performing what Charles Darwin referred to as a *fool's experiment*. In one such experiment, he put an unfertilized female flower into a bell jar along with, a short distance away, some pollen from a male flower. He wanted to see if the flower would be fertilized under these conditions. Since "everybody knew" that it wouldn't, it was an experiment that only a fool would do. Darwin was nevertheless happy to do the experiment. It was easy enough to do, and if the flower had gotten fertilized, it would have been a significant result.[31]

Despite their name, fools' experiments have yielded important results. In the late 1960s, for example, "everyone knew" that microorganisms couldn't survive in the hot sulfur springs of Yellowstone National Park. Microbiologists Thomas Brock and Hudson Freeze decided to look for them there anyway, and thereby discovered the first example of what became known as extremophiles. These are organisms that thrive where most organisms can't survive—in, for example, extremely hot or cold environments, extremely acidic environments, or highly radioactive environments. The discovery of these organisms forced scientists to reassess the possibility of life existing elsewhere in the universe: if life is possible in the earth's most inhospitable locations, then why not on planets with less than ideal environments?

Given how easy they are to do, you would think scientists would be eager to perform fools' experiments, but this is not the case. For one thing, some scientists are so paradigm-bound that they lack the imagination necessary to think up these experiments. In other cases, pride makes scientists reluctant to carry them out: if such an experiment fails to produce surprising results, they will look like fools for having tried it. Their (less imaginative) fellow scientists might, under these circumstances, ridicule them for having wasted their time doing an experiment that everyone knew would fail.

The striking thing about fools' experiments is that when one of them does reveal something new, these same scientists might be unimpressed. They will point out that *anyone* could have done the experiment. This is true, of course, but few scientists were open-minded and courageous enough to have done it. Perhaps the scientific community can learn something important from the "fools" in their midst.

ONE WAY A SCIENTIST can increase his chances of making a paradigm-challenging discovery is to wander outside the boundaries of his discipline and become what I'll refer to as a *scientific interloper*. He can, that is, take an interest in a discipline other than the one in which he was trained. As a scientist, he will have mastered the scientific method. He will also have acquired the paradigm of his own discipline. He will not, however, be imbued with the paradigm of the discipline into which he intrudes, and this can be an advantage. It might enable him to see things that scientists in that discipline fail to see. He might also be more likely to try experiments that they regard as misguided or to give serious consideration to theories that they dismiss out of hand.

With these advantages comes one big disadvantage: the scientists in the intruded-upon discipline will resent the intrusion. They might express this resentment indirectly, by refusing to take the interloper's research seriously. Thus, because Helmholtz was a physiology professor when he proposed his theory of the conservation of energy, he had a hard time getting physicists to pay attention to it. Likewise, Louis Pasteur, a chemist, had a hard time getting physicians to pay attention to his discoveries regarding the germ theory of disease.

In other cases, rather than ignore an interloper, scientists will openly ridicule him. One of the great interlopers in the history of science was Alfred Wegener, a meteorologist who proposed the theory of continental drift, a precursor to plate tectonics. Some scientists, including physicist W. Lawrence Bragg, were intrigued by this theory. Geologists were not. Indeed, according to Bragg, when he arranged in 1922 to have the Manchester Literary and Philosophical Society hear a paper Wegener had written, "the local geologists were furious; words cannot describe their utter scorn of anything so ridiculous as this theory."[32]

Flashing forward to the early 1980s, gastroenterologists were convinced that ulcers were caused primarily by stress or perhaps by spicy food. Barry Marshall and Robin Warren challenged this assumption. They noticed that people with ulcers tended to have *Helicobacter pylori* in their stomachs and started wondering whether this bacteria was in fact the cause of the ulcers. At that time, though, the field of ulcer research was "owned" by gastroenterologists, meaning that Warren and Marshal were interlopers: Marshall was a physician in training, and Warren was a pathologist. Then again, if they had been gastroenterologists, they probably wouldn't even have considered the possibility that ulcers would have a bacterial cause. Such views were contrary to the paradigm under which gastroenterologists operated.

Faced with the challenge of convincing the medical community that their theory was correct, Marshall resorted to a fool's experiment: he drank a solution containing *H. pylori* and soon thereafter developed an ulcer, which he cured by taking an antibiotic. This sounds pretty convincing, but after publishing the results, Marshall says that he was "met with constant criticism that my conclusions were premature and not well supported. When the work was presented, my results were disputed and disbelieved, not on the basis of science but because they simply could not be true."[33] In other words, the theory proposed by Marshall and Warren had to be wrong because the paradigm under which gastroenterologists operated said that it couldn't be right. One suspects that gastroenterologists had another reason for their hostility toward Marshall and Warren: they didn't appreciate these interlopers revealing that for the last several decades, gastroenterologists had been seriously misguided in their treatment of ulcers.

Scientists, as I've said, are remarkable for their rationality. As this chapter shows, though, they remain susceptible to all the usual emotions. They crave recognition. They fear ridicule. And they are perfectly capable of petty and self-serving behavior. It is a curious mix but one that nevertheless has yielded some of the greatest intellectual accomplishments of human history.

CHAPTER 9

Dealing with Rejection

IN THE TIME IT TAKES YOU to read this sentence, your body will have been penetrated by trillions of neutrinos. Most of them come from the sun, which creates them in the process of fusing together hydrogen atoms to make helium. Even if you are reading this at night, you will be subject to this bombardment. The neutrinos in question will have penetrated the entire earth in order to penetrate you. But not to worry: when they penetrate you, they won't interact with any of the atoms that comprise you. You will be no worse for the wear.

Neutrinos, it should be clear, are ghostly particles. Their behavior is the result of their being almost massless, electrically neutral, and unaffected by the strong nuclear force. This means that they can travel through an atom without being affected by its electrons, protons, or neutrons—unless they run right into the nucleus of an atom, which is hard to do, since atoms consist mostly of empty space. And just how empty is an atom? If you built a scale model of a hydrogen atom, consisting of a proton orbited by an electron, and if you used a golf ball to represent your proton, the electron would orbit nearly a mile away.[1] Atoms, in other words, are composed mostly of nothing at all, meaning that you, dear reader, are also composed mostly of empty space. If this thought doesn't utterly astonish you, you have my sympathy.

In the 1950s, theoretical physicists knew enough about subatomic particles to be able to predict how many neutrinos the sun would emit each second and how many of these neutrinos would pass through a given area on the surface of the earth. Physicist Raymond Davis did an experiment to test this prediction. He built a neutrino detector, consisting of a 100,000-gallon tank of dry-cleaning fluid situated in an unused tunnel a mile underground in a lead mine. The mile of rock would block the cosmic rays that might otherwise interfere with his measurements, and all that dry-cleaning fluid would provide a big target for neutrinos to hit and react with, thereby producing a detectable residue. Davis ran his detector and got about one-third as many neutrinos as theory predicted. He checked his apparatus, ran it again, and got the same results.

When he finally reported his findings to his fellow scientists, they did not like what they heard. It was, Davis said in a later interview, a "socially unacceptable result."[2] The scientific community assumed that his apparatus was malfunctioning, but Davis stood fast. Over the next two decades, other neutrino detectors were built to find the neutrinos Davis seemed unable to detect, but they couldn't find them either.

In the end, neutrinos turned out to be more complicated than physicists had thought. It was already known that neutrinos came in what physicists playfully refer to as three different "flavors." Subsequent experiments showed that as they travel through space, individual neutrinos cycle through these three flavors, spending one-third of their time in each. Davis's detector was capable of detecting only one of the flavors. In other words, he was able to count only one-third of the neutrinos that came his way. Had it not been for Davis's experiment and his refusal to back away from its results, scientists would have been slower to discover the transient nature of neutrino flavors.

In 2002, Davis received the Nobel Prize for Physics. He was eighty-eight years old, the oldest person to have won the prize. He had Alzheimer's disease by then, so one wonders whether he could fully appreciate this vindication of his "socially unacceptable result."

ALTHOUGH SCIENTISTS' ATTACKS on their colleagues can be withering, the attacks in question are child's play compared to those that are sometimes directed against scientists by political and religious authorities. Consider Nicholas Copernicus's claim that the sun, not the earth, is at the center of the solar system. Copernicus was not attacked for his views, in large part because he had the good sense to wait until he was on his death bed before publishing them (in 1543, in his *On the Revolutions of the Celestial Spheres*). But in 1600, Giordano Bruno was not so lucky: he was burned at the stake for suggesting, among other things, that the sun is at the center of the solar system. Three decades after that, Galileo was put under house arrest for his assertion that the earth orbits the sun. (In all fairness, the Catholic Church did subsequently apologize for its treatment of Galileo—in 1992, three-and-a-half centuries after he had died.)

In other places, at other times, scientists have lived in fear of not religious but political authorities. In the early twentieth century, for example, Soviet leaders attempted to reform society by transforming people from greedy, competitive individuals into altruistic individuals who valued cooperation. Such a transformation would be difficult to accomplish if people, rather than being "blank slates" at birth, were born with a "nature" that had to be overcome. Furthermore, the transformation process would be greatly accelerated if the traits acquired by one generation could be passed on to the next.

Mendelian genetics, however, suggested that humans were in a sense held captive by their genetic ancestry and that the transformation of people into ideal Marxist men and women would take many generations, if it could be accomplished at all. Soviet leaders therefore found this theory to be inconvenient. If it were true, it meant that it would be very difficult for them to accomplish their goals. Their solution was to suppress Mendelian genetics in favor of Lamarckism, according to which traits acquired by parents can be directly transmitted to children.

Soviet dictator Joseph Stalin therefore appointed agronomist Trofim Denisovich Lysenko as head of Soviet agriculture. Part of his job was to disseminate agricultural views consistent with Marxist doctrines and to suppress dissenting views. It was a job he carried out with considerable zeal, and many Soviet scientists ended up in prison as a result. In Stalin's Russia, being sent to prison could be a death sentence; indeed,

Soviet botanist Nikolai Ivanovich Vavilov, who had made the mistake of arguing against Lysenko, died in prison of malnutrition. Stalin also wanted to suppress quantum mechanics and Einstein's theory of relativity because of the challenge they posed to Marxist-Leninist ideology.[3] He changed his mind, though, when it was explained to him that such suppression would hinder Russia's ability to develop an atomic bomb.

Even when scientists live in societies in which they don't have to fear imprisonment by church or government for the views they hold, they might fear what their fellow citizens will think of them. Such appears to have been the case with Charles Darwin. He had his aha moment with respect to evolution in July of 1837 but waited for more than two decades to share it with the public. Historians of science speculate on the reasons for this dilatory behavior. Some argue that his work was slowed by illness; others claim that it was because he wanted to accumulate an impressive body of supporting evidence before publishing his theory. It is quite reasonable, however, to think that Darwin's reluctance to publish was also motivated by a concern over how the general public would respond to his theories. Darwin was an unusually retiring individual and as such would have been quite sensitive to public attacks. Not only that, but such attacks could have distressed his relatives, including his devout wife.

It is also important to realize that when Darwin presented the theory of evolution to the general public in *On the Origin of Species*, published in 1859, he did not argue that humans were the result of evolution. Indeed, it is only in the closing paragraphs of the book that this topic is broached, ever so gingerly: the theory of evolution, Darwin comments, will throw "much light" on the origin of man and his history.

BESIDES WORRYING ABOUT attacks from state authorities, religious authorities, or the public at large, a scientist will have to worry about attacks from his colleagues. Scientists in particular resist challenges to the paradigm under which they work. Part of this resistance can be characterized as intellectual. They know that their paradigm has been extensively tested and passed those tests, and so they conclude, quite sensibly, that an anomalous experimental result is likely to be mistaken. The other reason for scientific resistance to significant aha moments is best characterized as emotional: scientists have selfish reasons for clinging to their paradigm. Allow me to explain.

Consider a scientist who, early in his career, had a significant aha moment and thereafter spent decades enjoying the fruits of that moment. Now suppose this moment is supplanted by an aha moment experienced by a scientist fresh out of grad school. It will be emotionally difficult for the older scientist to see this happen. The discovery he made is, after all, his baby, and no one likes to see his offspring attacked. His bitterness might cause him to bully the younger scientist.

Even when a discovery doesn't supplant a discovery made by an older scientist, it can threaten his world. Older scientists are often intellectually and emotionally attached to the science of their youth. It is the science they grew up with and the science they understand. This means that if someone comes along to challenge their paradigm, they will, says astronomer Halton Arp, feel insecure[4] and will likely become angry at the scientist responsible for disturbing their intellectual tranquility.

Older scientists therefore tend to be scientifically conservative: they are reluctant to accept new theories. Not only that, but because of their seniority and accumulated accomplishments, these scientists wield considerable power within their field. Displease them, and a scientist might find that it is difficult to get published, get a job, or get funding for a research project. Consequently, younger scientists, unless they are very brave, will be reluctant to champion a theory that older, respected scientists oppose. The progress of science is thereby hindered.

Max Planck, the physicist who originated quantum theory, was frustrated by the conservatism of older scientists. He concluded that "a new scientific truth does not triumph by convincing its opponents and making them see the light, but rather because its opponents eventually die, and a new generation grows up that is familiar with it."[5] When asked how often science changes, Planck responded, "With every funeral."[6] Biologist Lynn Margulis echoed this sentiment, late in the twentieth century: "The only way behavior changes in science is that certain people die and differently behaving people take their places."[7] As we shall see below, Margulis had good reason to be frustrated by scientists' reluctance to change their views.

IF A SCIENTIST'S EMOTIONS can affect his scientific views, so can his political beliefs. In the previous chapter, we discussed the theory of kin selection, the role William Hamilton played in popularizing it, and Edward Wilson's reluctant acceptance of it. At about that same time, biologists J. B. S. Haldane and John Maynard Smith understood kin selection and could have played an important role in promoting it, but chose not to. According to Smith, it was because of their political views. They were Marxists and consequently were reluctant to admit that genes could influence human behavior.[8] Hamilton's biological thinking was not similarly colored by his political views, leaving him open to champion kin selection. (Haldane, by the way, also sided publicly with Lysenko, whose suppression of Mendelian genetics was described above.[9])

When Edward Wilson published his groundbreaking *Sociobiology: The New Synthesis* in 1975, he encountered fierce attacks, voiced by biologists Richard Lewontin and Stephen Jay Gould. In his book, Wilson argued that the human mind, and therefore human behavior, is very much a result of our genetic inheritance. This is unwelcome news to anyone who believes, as Lewontin and Gould did, that the human mind is affected primarily by culture.

Lewontin and Gould published their attack not in a scientific journal but in the *New York Review of Books*, and the bulk of the attack was directed not at the science behind sociobiology but at the social and political consequences of expressing sociobiological views. In particular, they argued that theories like those proposed by Wilson "tend to provide a genetic justification of the *status quo* and of existing privileges for certain groups according to class, race, or sex,"[10] which in turn can lead to sterilization law, eugenic policies, or even the Nazi gas chambers.[11] Other scientists joined the attack. The American Anthropological Association considered a motion to censure sociobiology and probably would have passed the motion had Margaret Mead not condemned the proposal as tantamount to book burning.[12]

Besides being affected by his political beliefs, a person's scientific views can be affected by his religious beliefs—or even, somewhat surprisingly, by his aversion to religion. In the first half of the twentieth century, scientists found themselves in an ongoing debate with creationists. Since creationists tended to invoke historical catastrophes—most notably, Noah's flood—to explain how the world came to be the way it is, scientists were taught to reject such explanations. This training, however, arguably impeded scientific progress in geology and astronomy.

Consider the channeled scablands of eastern Washington State. The area has some truly remarkable geological features, including what look like the ripples and potholes that are found on the bottom of a river, except that these are ripples and potholes on a truly grand scale. In the 1920s, when geologist J. Harlen Bretz suggested a great flood as the cause of the scablands, the geological community hooted him down: to them, it sounded like creationism. Bretz continued to fight for acceptance of his theory, though, and it helped his cause considerably when geologist James Pardee found evidence that at the end of the most recent ice age, a giant lake had formed in Montana. Its glacier-fed water was held back by an ice dam, and when that dam collapsed, a great flood resulted. This discovery handily answered the question that Bretz's critics were fond of raising: "And just where did the water for this supposed flood come from?" In 1979, the geological community acknowledged Bretz's insights by awarding him the prestigious Penrose Medal. He was then ninety-six years old.

Scientific anti-catastrophism was arguably still a factor in 1970, when paleontologist Digby McLaren suggested that dinosaurs had gone extinct because an asteroid had slammed into the earth some sixty-five million years ago. This theory drew little attention and even less support. The tide started to turn in 1980, when physicist Luis Alvarez and his son, geologist Walter Alvarez, together with chemists Frank Asaro and Helen Michel, found important evidence for such an impact: they discovered an unusual amount of the element iridium (which is rare in the earth's crust but common in asteroids) in the geographical sediments laid down just above those that were formed when dinosaurs ruled the planet. By the end of the 1980s, most scientists thought that a meteorite impact had played a significant role in the demise of the dinosaurs.

In 1994, a cosmic event simultaneously bolstered support for the Digby theory and dealt a blow to scientific anti-catastrophism: the comet Shoemaker-Levy 9 collided with Jupiter, dramatically affecting the planet's atmosphere. It created dark spots that were visible from the earth. It was irrefutable evidence that such impacts could be planet-altering events, and in the face of this evidence, scientists not only abandoned anti-catastrophism but embraced what has been termed *neo-catastrophism*[13]—that is, they became eager to offer catastrophic theories in their efforts to explain earth's features and history. Scientists had at last freed themselves of creationism's subtle influence on their theories.

YOU MIGHT THINK scientists would be genteel individuals and that this trait, combined with their innate rationality, would lead them, when it was necessary to point out the mistakes of their colleagues, to do so in a circumspect manner. Regrettably, this is not the case.

Consider, by way of illustration, the tribulations of Indian astrophysicist Subrahmanyan Chandrasekhar—Chandra for short. In the summer of 1930, Chandra was twenty years old and a scientific nobody. He had recently received a bachelor's degree in physics from India's Presidency College and was traveling to England to pursue graduate studies at Cambridge. During the voyage across the Arabian Sea, Chandra sat on a deck chair, pondering the death of stars. Stars die when they exhaust the fuel required for fusion reactions. Without these reactions to create thermal pressure to counterbalance the inward pull of gravity, stars collapse to become super-dense bodies.

Chandra wondered whether the mass of a star could affect its ultimate fate. He did some calculations and within a few minutes deduced that if a star had more than a certain mass, it would not, when it underwent its final death throes, collapse into what is known as a white dwarf. Instead, the process of collapse would take it past the gravitational point of no return, and it would become what we today call a *black hole*.[14]

In 1935, Chandra was asked to present a paper on white dwarfs at a meeting of the Royal Astronomical Society in

London. Sir Arthur Stanley Eddington, the preeminent astro-physicist of the time, was scheduled to present a paper just after Chandra. Before their presentations, Eddington visited Chandra and asked questions about what he would be saying in his paper.[15] Eddington used the information he obtained in that conversation to viciously attack Chandra in his own presentation. He not only declared that Chandra was wrong but also that his conclusions were absurd.[16] Chandra rose to defend himself but was rebuffed by the Society's president. He ended up feeling like a fool.[17] And this wasn't the end of the bad blood between Eddington and Chandra. A few years later, when Chandra published a scholarly monograph in which he expressed his views on white dwarfs, Eddington reacted by commenting, "How nice to have all the wrong things in one place."[18]

Although many scientists, including physicists Léon Rosenfeld and Wolfgang Pauli, were unconvinced by Eddington's theories, few were willing to attack him in pub-lic.[19] Likewise, there were scientists—including Niels Bohr, Paul Dirac, Henry Norris Russell, and John Von Neumann—who let Chandra know of their support for his views but were unwilling to declare this support in public.[20] As a result of Eddington's bullying and the scientific community's apparent complicity, Chandra decided to redirect his research efforts. He reasoned, "Adhering to my point of view would only make more of a Don Quixote of me than I already appeared to be among the astronomical community."[21] But Chandra later admitted that some good came out of his dealings with Eddington. He enjoyed his exploration of other areas and made important discoveries in them. He later summed up his multifaceted career in these terms: "I owe all this to Eddington!"[22]

Chandra's story does not end there. Although he abandoned his research on collapsing stars, other scientists took an interest in them.[23] The development of computers enabled scientists, in the early 1950s, to run programs that modeled the physics of a collapsing star. One such program, written by Stirling Colgate and Richard White, showed that it was possible for stars to not only collapse but to collapse endlessly, to a point of infinite density.[24] Colgate and White wrote an article describing their findings and submitted it to *Reviews of Modern Physics*, where it spent two years in limbo. They then submitted the article to the *Astrophysical Journal*, which happened at that time to be edited by Chandra. He immediately realized that their findings provided important evidence in support of his own work on collapsing stars. Chandra, after editing the article to make it more accessible to astrophysicists, published it. Sweet vindication!

One might expect Chandra to respond to the rough treatment he received from his fellow scientists by refusing to emulate them, but this was not the case. To the contrary, Chandra subsequently became known for his rudeness. He was likely to interrupt when others were talking—or even when they were delivering a lecture—in order to criticize their line of argument. In one case, after a scientist had finished presenting a paper, Chandra, who had been in the audience, made a single brusque remark and walked out of the room. The scientist in question found this behavior to be quite disconcerting until his colleagues explained that, coming from Chandra, this counted as a compliment: if Chandra had *disliked* the lecture, he would have walked out during the presentation itself, not during the discussion period.[25]

SOMETIMES, THE SCIENTIFIC COMMUNITY responds to unortho- dox theories with silence instead of verbal attacks. In some ways, being ignored is worse than being attacked. If you are attacked, people who witness the attacks might end up siding with you, and your cause will be advanced; this can't happen if you aren't even attacked. And of course, being ignored is deeply insulting since it implies that one's ideas are so mis- taken that they don't even deserve a reply.

Gregor Mendel, who discovered the laws of inheritance and published his results in 1866, was a recipient of the scien- tific silent treatment. We have seen how dismissive scientists are of interlopers—people from one scientific field who pro- pose theories in another. Mendel, however, can't be catego- rized as a scientific interloper, for the simple reason that he wasn't even a scientist: he was a monk. Scientists therefore found it easy to dismiss his work. Partly as a result of being ignored, he stopped doing research.[26] It was only in the early twentieth century that biologists recognized the significance of his findings. This recognition was lost on Mendel, how- ever; he had died in 1884.

Scientists are also capable of ignoring the work of fellow sci- entists, especially when that work challenges their paradigm. This was the fate of biophysicist Carl Woese, who made one of the most important discoveries in twentieth-century biology. Until the late 1970s, biologists divided living things into two domains, bacteria and eucarya. As the result of painstaking research, Woese came to the conclusion that there was in fact a third domain, archaea. The microbes in this last domain look like bacteria, which is why microbiologists had lumped them together with bacteria, but the molecules in their ribosomes told a different story.

At the time he made this discovery, Woese would have counted as a bit of an interloper. His undergraduate education had been in physics and mathematics, and his doctorate was in biophysics. But here he was, telling microbiologists that they had made a fundamental mistake in their grouping of living things. Furthermore, Woese supported his claim of the existence of a third domain by using a research technique that microbiologists had trouble comprehending. The technique, known as *oligonucleotide cataloging*, involved breaking up ribosomal RNA strands and then painstakingly analyzing the results in order to determine the order of the nucleotides they contained.

He ended up, one researcher said, with a reputation as "a crank, who was using a crazy technique to answer an impossible question." And leading biologists thought it wasn't just Woese's techniques that were crazy, but Woese himself. They therefore tried to talk Woese's few allies into abandoning him. One of these allies was microbiologist Ralph Wolfe, who got a call from a Nobel-Prize-winning microbiologist who warned him, "Ralph, you're going to ruin your career. You've got to dissociate yourself from this nonsense!"[27]

When Woese published his results, the scientific community responded with silence. They didn't tell him he was wrong, and they didn't publish papers critical of his claims; they simply ignored him. In retrospect, Woese regretted *not* being attacked. "It would," he says, "be helpful to have that record."[28] Helpful, perhaps, as a public reminder of the close-mindedness of his fellow scientists?

Woese understood why the scientific community behaved the way it did: "That's what happens when you break a paradigm; people scoff and they don't treat you seriously." Even though biologists now universally recognize the importance of his discovery, and even though they have showered him with accolades, colleagues say Woese seems to have trouble forgiving and forgetting. Says Norman Pace, an early ally, "Even now [in 1997], he sometimes lashes out at the people on whose shoulders he stood and who, he thinks, failed him."[29]

IT IS ONE THING TO PUBLISH an article only to have it ignored; it is quite another not even to be able to publish it. When we look at the history of science, we find that this was the fate of many articles reporting what we now recognize as breakthroughs.

Articles submitted to scientific journals are subject to peer review. This makes it sound like articles will be accepted or rejected solely on the basis of their scientific merit, but this isn't necessarily so. The journal's editor, who herself is a scientist, can simply reject an article as not being of interest to her journal's readers or as not even being worthy of review. And if she does send it to reviewers, she gets to decide which reviewers to use. She knows that some reviewers have lower standards for acceptance than others; thus, in her choice of reviewers, she can stack the deck for or against a submission.

In the early 1970s, paleontologist Leigh Van Valen came up with the Red Queen hypothesis, which holds that competition between species in a specific environment can lead to an unending chain of adaptive responses. (The Red Queen is a character in Lewis Carrol's *Through the Looking Glass*; it was she who explained to Alice that in her country, "it takes all the running you can do, to keep in the same place.") Consider, for example, the relationship between predator and prey. In a given environment, a species that is preyed upon will evolve to resist predation, at which point the species that prey upon it will evolve so as to overcome those adaptations. The resulting arms race between predator and prey can result in dramatic changes in a short period of time. Van Valen wrote an article explaining and defending the Red Queen hypothesis. After having it repeatedly rejected, he took matters into his own hands and started a journal, *Evolutionary Theory*, in which he published the article. It has since become one of the most cited articles in evolutionary biology.[30]

Biologist Lynn Margulis overcame scientific rejection not by starting a journal but by becoming an outspoken advocate of her views. In 1967, she wrote an article defending endosymbiotic theory, according to which the mitochondria that power our cells are in fact the descendants of bacteria that were engulfed by other cells. The article was rejected fifteen times[31] and on finally being published did not win many converts.

Some scientists, as we have seen, are reluctant to fight for the theories they propose. This was not the case with Margulis. She clearly reveled in the role of defender of unpopular theories. It was a role she first played with respect to endosymbiotic theory and subsequently with respect to the Gaia hypothesis, according to which the earth and the living things on it form what is, in essence, a single organism. According to physicist Lee Smolin, Margulis was a force to contend with. At one dinner party, he watched as she cornered a biologist who had attacked the Gaia hypothesis, quoted to him word for word what he had said in his attack, and demanded an explanation. "She was," Smolin reports, "very intent on having him see why it was wrong."[32] This doubtless was an unpleasant experience for the cornered scientist. And yet, this kind of aggressive promotion of radical new theories is apparently necessary if science is to advance. The problem is that not all scientists are confident and courageous enough to play the role of promoter.

I mentioned in the previous chapter that I interviewed Paul Hoffman, the leading proponent of the Snowball Earth hypothesis. I asked him what it is like to defend an unpopular scientific viewpoint: did he notice anything about the way other scientists were treating him? He said that he in no way felt like an outcast and that his employer, Harvard University, had been quite supportive of him, despite his unorthodox views. He added, though, that it sometimes seemed like other scientists were avoiding him at parties. He surmised that they were afraid that he would buttonhole them and ask which side of the Snowball Earth debate they were on. Although

Hoffman would be unlikely to do such a thing, the above story about Lynn Margulis shows that not all scientists are similarly reserved.

FOR AN IDEA TO TRANSFORM SCIENCE, several things have to happen. First, someone must have the idea—that is, someone must experience an aha moment. Second, she must decide to share that moment with the scientific world; otherwise, the idea will be stillborn. Such stillbirth is likely common, but it is hard to know how common, inasmuch as scientists are loathe to admit a reluctance to publish.

If a scientist does decide to share her aha moment, she will have to decide where to publish it. If she sends it to an obscure journal, acceptance is likely. She will thereby have created the evidence she needs to establish priority. The problem is that the scientific world will be unlikely to read the journal, meaning that it will be unchanged by her "publication" of her idea. If, however, she sends it to a prominent journal, there is a very good chance that it will be rejected; indeed, the more profound the aha moment is, the more likely rejection will be. And if her article is rejected, she has to decide how to respond. Should she give up? The rejecting referees, after all, might be right. And if she keeps trying, how many times before she quits?

Suppose a scientist succeeds—perhaps after many attempts—in getting her breakthrough idea published. When other scientists read her article, there is a chance that they will instantly recognize its brilliance and be converted to her way of thinking, but there is a much greater chance that they will take issue with it. In some cases, this resistance will be intellectual, but in other cases, as we have seen, it can best be described as emotional. To overcome this resistance, the scientist will have to work very hard to promote her views and might have to do so for years or even decades.

So what does it take for a scientist to make a discovery that transforms science? It takes hard work and intelligence, of course, to trigger a significant aha moment—although it is entirely possible for a brilliant scientist to work hard for her entire career without being rewarded with such a moment. But when we look at the scientific aha moments that have changed the world, what is most notable is not, in many cases, the brilliance or diligence of the scientists who experienced those moments but the character traits they exhibited in fighting for acceptance of their research or theory. At the top of the list of such traits I would place courage and perseverance. Raymond Davis, Harlen Bretz, Carl Woese, Paul Hoffman, and Lynn Margulis clearly exhibit these traits, and these are only a few profiles in scientific courage. Many more can be found in the history of science. This suggests, perhaps, that the training of scientists, besides focusing on such things as scientific method and theories, should concern itself with character building, particularly the development of courage and perseverance.

PART FOUR

The Aha Moment in Mathematics

CHAPTER 10

Moments of Pure Insight

SUPPOSE YOU HAD one night to live. How would you spend it? If you were a mathematician, you might spend it doing math.

At age twenty, Frenchman Évarista Galois (1811–1832) had an affair with Stéphanie-Félicie Poterine du Motel. Unfortunately for Galois, she was engaged to Pescheux d'Herbinville, one of the finest shots in France.[1] Galois was challenged to a duel at dawn and decided to spend what would probably be his last night on earth writing out his most important mathematical thoughts. He requested that if he died, they should be distributed to the greatest mathematicians in Europe. "In my life I have often dared to advance propositions about which I was not sure. But all I have written down here has been clear in my head for over a year, and it would not be in my interest to leave myself open to the suspicion that I announce theorems of which I do not have a complete proof."[2] The next morning, Galois died from a shot to the gut. His papers were distributed, and his genius was recognized.[3]

German industrialist Paul Wolfskehl (1856–1906) fell in love with a woman and, on being rejected, concluded that life was not worth living. He decided to commit suicide at midnight on a certain day. He started putting his affairs in order but did so with such efficiency that he found himself with a few hours to kill before killing himself. He therefore turned his attention to Ernst Kummer's critique of the attempts by Gabriel Lamé and Augustin-Louis Cauchy to prove Fermat's last theorem, and—lo and behold!—he spotted a gap in the logic of that critique. By morning, he had filled it and thereupon realized that he had missed his self-imposed suicide deadline. Pleased with the mathematical breakthrough he made, he figured that perhaps life was worth living after all, particularly if one could spend it studying math.[4]

Suppose that instead of having one night to live, you learned that you had a year. How would you spend it? Some people would live riotously: they would max out their credit cards financing days and nights of debauchery. Other, more sensible people would quit their jobs so they could spend more time with family members and maybe take a trip they had always dreamed of taking. A mathematician, though, would quite possibly want to spend his final days doing what he had always done—namely, math.

In April 2003, mathematician David Robbins was told by doctors that he had only two years, maybe less, to live. Faced with this information, he chose to spend his last days of life doing math. Those who knew Robbins weren't surprised by this choice. His wife understood and accepted it. Likewise, his boss at the Princeton center where Robbins worked wasn't surprised: "That's what mathematicians do," he said.[5] Robbins passed away in September of that year.

These stories will come as a surprise to those who either hate math or are indifferent to it. Why, they will wonder, would any sensible person want to spend time—even more strangely, spend their dying days—doing math? In large part because it gives them the prospect of experiencing one of the greatest delights life has to offer, a mathematical aha moment.

And it isn't just the moment that is enjoyable; the pursuit of it can also be enormously rewarding. Mathematician and philosopher Bertrand Russell was exposed to Euclidean geometry at age eleven. It was, he says, "as dazzling as first love. I had not imagined there was anything so delicious in the world. From that moment until I was thirty-eight, mathematics was my chief interest and my chief source of happiness."[6] Mathematician G. H. Hardy describes his own mathematical endeavors as "the one great permanent happiness" in his life.[7] He adds that "there is nothing in the world which pleases even famous men (and men who have used disparaging language about mathematics) quite so much as to discover, or rediscover, a genuine mathematical theorem."[8] This last comment, by the way, raises an interesting point: you can experience a perfectly delightful mathematical aha moment even though many other people have already discovered what you discover.

Mathematician Gian-Carlo Rota says that when considered in retrospect, moments of mathematical insight seem "as if they had been perceived in a moment of bliss, in a sudden flash like a light bulb suddenly being lit."[9] He adds that "of all escapes from reality, mathematics is the most successful ever. It is a fantasy that becomes all the more addictive because it works back to improve the same reality we are trying to evade. All other escapes—sex, drugs, hobbies, whatever—are ephemeral by comparison."[10]

Rota isn't alone in comparing the rush of mathematical discovery to the rush of drugs. On one website, for example, an anonymous mathematician, who presumably had extensive experience of the rushes life has to offer, wrote this: "Sex and drugs? They're nothing compared with a good proof!"[11] People who spend their days partying might pity the poor mathematicians who are sitting at home doing proofs. At the same time, those mathematicians might be pitying the poor people who, because they are not smart or patient enough to solve math problems, must resort to lesser means of gratification.

We saw that one of the things that makes scientific aha moments so delightful is their incredible beauty. The same claim, says Russell, can be made regarding mathematical aha moments:

> Mathematics, rightly viewed, possesses not only truth but supreme beauty—a beauty cold and austere, like that of a sculpture, without appeal to any part of our weaker nature, without the gorgeous trapping of painting or music, yet sublimely pure, and capable of a stern perfection such as only the greatest art can show. The true spirit of delight, the exaltation, the sense of being more than man, which is the touchstone of the highest excellence, is to be found in mathematics as surely as in poetry.[12]

MANY NEWSPAPERS CARRY the Jumble puzzle, in which the letters of words are scrambled. To solve the puzzle, you have to put the letters back in the right order. Consider, then, the scrambled word "PIOHP." It is the jumbled version of an English word, but what word?

The puzzle can be solved by randomly rearranging the letters until they result in a legitimate word, but this process is likely to be slow. A better strategy is to use enlightened trial and error. Based on her knowledge of English, a person will assess the likelihood of various combinations of letters. She will then try the combinations that are most likely to work. Thus, she might think it unlikely that she would find the letter combination HP in the original word, although the letter combination PH wouldn't be surprising. She also might think it unlikely that the two vowels would be neighbors in a word only five letters long. By reasoning in this fashion, she will dramatically reduce the number of letter combinations to try. And after trying for a few seconds, the answer will probably come to her.

Mathematicians go through a similar process to trigger an aha moment. They begin solving a problem by trying strategies that experience tells them are most likely to work. When an attempt fails, they don't give up; they instead learn from the failure and thereby educate themselves about the problem. The solutions they try will become increasingly exotic, until finally they find one that works.

I am assuming, dear reader, that you felt a little rush of delight on your realization that "hippo" is the answer to the above Jumble puzzle. The rush was small because you invested only a few seconds of conscious effort trying to trigger it. Imagine, though, that you had spent a day, a month, a year, or a decade trying to trigger it. And suppose that hundreds of incredibly smart people had spent substantial amounts of time trying, unsuccessfully, to trigger it. These are the circumstances under which a mathematician might experience an aha moment. The resulting moment will be breathtaking; indeed, it might move him to tears.

If this last claim seems an exaggeration, consider mathematician Andrew Wiles's personal campaign to prove Fermat's last theorem. To square a number (or "raise it to the second power") is to multiply it by itself; thus, $3^2 = 3 \times 3 = 9$. To cube a number (or "raise it to the third power") is to multiply it by itself three times; thus, $2^3 = 2 \times 2 \times 2 = 8$. It is sometimes the case that the square of an integer is equal to the sum of two other integers that have been squared. Notice, in particular, that $3^2 + 4^2 = 5^2$ (since $9 + 16 = 25$). One might wonder, though, whether the same thing can be done with cubed integers—whether, in other words, we can find integers x, y, and z such that $x^3 + y^3 = z^3$. When Pierre de Fermat considered this question in 1637, no such integers were known. He thought he could prove that such integers could not be found; indeed, he thought he could prove that the equation $x^n + y^n = z^n$ has no whole-number solutions for $n > 2$. This claim has become known as Fermat's last theorem.

It is one thing to think something is provable; it is quite another to prove it. Unfortunately, Fermat did not leave us a proof. All we have is his comment, written in the margin of a book, that "I have a truly marvelous demonstration of this proposition which this margin is too narrow to contain."[13] Over the next three and a half centuries, mathematicians struggled to come up with the proof. None succeeded.

When mathematician Andrew Wiles took on the problem in the late 1980s, he knew the odds were against him. He therefore worked on it in secret: if people knew what he was doing, it would not only put needless pressure on him but also cause most of his colleagues to think he had gone mad. Wiles also knew that if his mathematical output dried up while he was working on Fermat's theorem, colleagues would have gotten suspicious about what he was up to or might even have worried about his intellectual well-being. He was able to forestall such suspicions and concerns by slowly dribbling out a stream of papers describing an important discovery he had made before turning his efforts to Fermat.[14]

In a subsequent interview, he had this to say about his seven-year campaign to prove the theorem: "When doing math there's this great feeling. You start with a problem that just mystifies you. You can't understand it, it's so complicated, you just can't make head nor tail of it. But then, when you finally resolve it, you have this incredible feeling of how beautiful it is, how it all fits together so elegantly."[15] When the interviewer asks for more detail regarding the aha moment itself, speech fails Wiles: "I was sitting here at this desk, when suddenly, totally unexpectedly, I had this incredible revelation. [pause] It was the most [pause] the most important moment of my working life. [pause] Nothing I ever do again will... Sorry." At this point he turns from the camera, apparently on the verge of tears.[16]

Why should mathematical aha moments be so grand? Because they are in a sense the purest moments of insight a person can have. A prophet can think it was God who appeared before him but cannot prove this to be the case; indeed, most people will think he is mistaken. A scientist can point to a huge body of evidence in support of the theory he has developed, but he cannot prove the theory to be true; indeed, a subsequent observation might be its undoing. Mathematicians have the luxury of being able to *prove* that their insights are correct. And as Gian-Carlo Rota reminds us, "once solved, a mathematical problem is forever finished: no later event will disprove a correct solution."[17] Many aha moments are accompanied by a feeling of certainty, but in the case of mathematics, it is possible to prove that the feelings of certainty are justified. This, I think, is what heightens the rush of delight that accompanies mathematical aha moments.

To forestall any confusion, I should add that "mathematical" aha moments can be experienced outside of mathematics, proper. Logicians can have them. So can physicists like Roger Penrose, whose aha moment was described in Chapter 7. By trying to prove the singularity theorems of general relativity theory, he was essentially doing math. So can a computer scientist who is not so much writing programs as making discoveries regarding computability. In each of these cases, the person can *prove* that his insight is correct.

SCIENTISTS, AS WE HAVE SEEN, aren't motivated solely by the prospect of experiencing an aha moment; they also have worldly motivations. The same can be said of mathematicians.

They seek, in particular, the recognition of their colleagues. Rota demonstrated this with an experiment. In a bibliography at the end of a long paper he had written, he cited some math papers that in fact had nothing to do with his own. The authors of some of those papers, he says, sent letters in which they "warmly congratulated me for being the first to acknowledge their contribution to the field."[18]

Another telling piece of evidence for mathematicians' craving for recognition is the fights for priority that have occasionally arisen within the discipline. The most famous of these was the fight between Isaac Newton and Gottfried Wilhelm von Leibniz regarding which of them discovered calculus. The fight was surprisingly acrimonious. At one point, Newton called upon the Royal Society to settle the matter. This was easy for him to do, since he was the president of that august body. He appointed an investigative committee, packed with supporters. He also wrote a draft of the preface for the committee's second report on the dispute, in which he cited the legal adage that "no one is a proper witness for himself."[19] Most likely, Newton and Leibniz independently discovered calculus, an outcome neither of them was willing to admit. Furthermore, evidence has recently come to light suggesting that neither of them was in fact the original discoverer of calculus, but that Archimedes beat them by two thousand years.[20]

Besides seeking the recognition of their colleagues, mathematicians seek immortality. They might even go so far as to argue that mathematical immortality is better than scientific immortality, inasmuch as it cannot be "revoked," the way scientific immortality can. In defense of this claim, they might point to the fates of the scientist Ptolemy and the mathematician Euclid. Although both individuals were at one time immortalized for their discoveries, only Euclid still is. This is because it turned out that Ptolemy made some mistakes. Euclid's proofs, on the other hand, are unimpeachable. Likewise, a mathematician might argue that artistic immortality can "die" in a manner that mathematical immortality can't and is therefore an inferior kind of immortality.[21]

Because they value priority, mathematicians are quick to publish their discoveries. Carl Friedrich Gauss was a notable exception to this rule. He would publish only those discoveries he regarded as complete. As a result, many mathematicians needlessly duplicated his efforts. They would excitedly report their discoveries to Gauss, only to have him reply that he had already made those discoveries, sometimes decades earlier, but had not bothered to publish his results. This news could be emotionally devastating to the mathematician who heard it.[22] When Gauss's notebooks came to light after his death, they were found to contain many proofs which, had they been published when he conceived of them, would have advanced the progress of mathematics by decades.

Other mathematicians have shown greater sensitivity to the egos of their colleagues. Hyper-productive mathematician Paul Erdős was happy to act as a sounding board for other mathematicians and happy to help them develop their ideas by throwing them insights. As a result, many mathematicians shared with him their work and discoveries. In some cases, Erdős would already have made but not yet published a discovery they revealed to him; rather than telling them as much, Erdős would simply encourage them to publish their results[23] and thereby take credit for the discovery. Such intellectual generosity is rare.

TO EXPERIENCE AN AHA MOMENT, a mathematician has to solve a problem. The question is, what problem should he try to solve? We can think of this as the mathematician's pre-problem problem. The problem he works on should be chosen with care. It should be a significant problem, one that can potentially lead to advances in mathematics or in other sciences. At the same time, though, it should be a problem that he has a reasonable chance of solving.

Many mathematicians set for themselves the task of finding a new way to solve a problem that has already been solved. This might sound like a redundant activity, but it is in fact what most mathematicians spend their days doing. According to Rota, "the overwhelming majority of research papers in mathematics is concerned not with proving, but with reproving; not with axiomatizing, but with re-axiomatizing; not with inventing, but with unifying and streamlining."[24] Thus, although the Pythagorean theorem (which holds that the sum of the squares of the sides of a right triangle equals the square of its hypotenuse) was first proved in around 500 BC, it had, by the middle of the twentieth century, been re-proved in at least 370 different ways.[25] Some of these proofs are shorter and more intuitive than others.

Re-solving a problem that has already been solved has one important advantage: a mathematician knows that what he is trying to do can be done. He thereby avoids the danger, which we will explore below, of embarking on the task of trying to prove a claim that is impossible to prove, for the simple reason that it isn't true.

The alternative to re-solving a problem is solving one that hasn't yet been solved. For example, a scientist might work on a problem that someone else has publicly identified. There are lists of such problems, including, most famously, the list of twenty-three unsolved problems that mathematician David Hilbert published in 1900. (Fewer than half of these problems have subsequently been completely solved.)

In other cases, mathematicians stumble upon a problem to solve. In particular, in the process of trying to solve one problem, they encounter a difficulty—that is, a problem that needs to be solved in order to solve the original problem. It was for this reason that F. S. Macauley, who taught math at Cambridge, instructed his students, "Try a hard problem. You may not solve it, but you will prove something else."[26] One of the students who heard this advice and used it to good effect was mathematician John Edensor Littlewood. We will encounter him again later in the next chapter.

Another way to come up with an unsolved problem to work on is to *create* one. Taking this approach requires a mathematician to be doubly inventive: it takes creativity to come up with a problem and additional creativity to solve that problem. The upside is that doing this can yield two aha moments rather than one. Another upside is that it is unlikely that someone else is working on the same problem and could therefore frustrate the mathematician's efforts to be the first to solve it.

The problem-creation process typically involves a mathematician sitting with a sheet of paper before him, on which he writes fragmentary bits of math. This is what famed Indian mathematician Srinivasa Ramanujan did for hours on end.[27] Even simple doodling can give rise to profound theories. While listening to a boring presentation at a conference in 1963, mathematician Stan Ulam started writing down the numbers, first 1, then 2 to the right of it, then 3 above the 2, 4 to the left of the 3 (and above the 1), and so on. The resulting "Ulam spiral" gave mathematicians a visual means to discover patterns in the distribution of prime numbers.[28]

This sort of brainstorming gives free rein to the unconscious mind, inviting it to come up with bold conjectures. Most of these conjectures will be misguided, and it is up to the conscious mind to sort through them. It would be wonderful if mathematicians could find a way to come up with only good ideas; it would do much to improve their productivity. But in mathematics, as in science, the best way to have good ideas is to have *lots* of ideas, most of which will be bad. Indeed, according to Rota, "there is a ratio by which you can measure how good a mathematician is, and that is how many crackpot ideas he must have in order to have one good one. If this ratio equals ten to one then he is a genius. For the average mathematician, it may be one hundred to one."[29]

SUPPOSE THAT AS THE RESULT of brainstorming, a mathematician comes up with a likely looking mathematical conjecture. His next step, if he is sensible, will be to test the conjecture: he will make mathematical predictions on the basis of it and then check to see whether those predictions are correct. By way of illustration, suppose that a mathematician starts exploring integers that begin with one or more 3s and end with 1— numbers like 31, 331, and 3331. He notices that these are all prime numbers: they are evenly divisible only by themselves and 1. His interest will be piqued. He might test additional numbers: 33331, 333331, 3333331, and 33333331, which also turn out to be prime. He might now suspect that *all* integers that begin with 3s and end with 1 are prime.[30]

At this point, clarification is in order. The logic of science differs from that of mathematics. Suppose an ornithologist starts examining swans around the world. Suppose the first thousand he sees are white. On the basis of this evidence, he might conclude that all swans are white and report this conclusion to the world. As he does so, though, he will have to admit that despite his extensive research, it is possible that there are non-white swans that he has overlooked. They might live in some remote jungle, or they might have been recently born in places that he investigated with great care in the past. Inductive reasoning, like that used by this ornithologist, can tell us what is probably true, but it can never provide us with certainty.

Mathematicians use inductive reasoning when they test conjectures in the manner described above. When a conjecture passes numerous tests, though, a mathematician's labors are not over, the way an ornithologist's are; to the contrary, they are just beginning. This is because a mathematician worth his salt will not be satisfied with having shown that a statement is *probably* true. He will instead attempt to show that it is *necessarily* true, and the only way to do this is by giving a deductive proof of the statement.

To see how deductive proofs work, consider the squares of integers. Some squares will be odd; for example, 3^2 is equal to 9, an odd number. But when we examine the squares of even numbers, we find that they are even: for example, $2^2 = 4$, $4^2 = 16$, $6^2 = 36$, and $8^2 = 64$. If we continue our investigation, we will get similar results: $10^2 = 100$, $12^2 = 144$, and $14^2 = 196$. On the basis of this sort of inductive reasoning, we might become confident that squares of even numbers are always even. It is always possible, though, that the next even number we square will yield an odd number. To go from confidence to certainty regarding the squares of even numbers, we will need to come up with a deductive proof.

The proof in question is straightforward. Let N be any even integer. Then by the definition of *even*, there will be an integer M such that $N = 2M$. (If this weren't the case, N wouldn't be evenly divisible by 2 and therefore wouldn't be an even number.) Thus, N^2 will be equal to $(2M)^2$, which in turn is equal to $4M^2$. This last number, though, will be evenly divisible by 2 and will therefore be even. (Indeed, multiply any integer, even or odd, by 4, and the resulting product will be evenly divisible by 2; this is because 4 is evenly divisible by 2.) Conclusion: squares of even numbers will themselves necessarily be even numbers. It is amazing that with a few well-chosen deductive assertions, we can conclusively prove something that no amount of inductive testing could prove. This is part of the magic of mathematics.

If deductive proofs are the gold standard of mathematics, then why bother to test conjectures inductively? Because it is a very efficient way to detect false conjectures. Indeed, a computer can easily be programmed to check numbers that start with 3s and end with 1 to see whether they are prime. It is important to detect false conjectures, inasmuch as they are impossible to prove!

Any mathematician who creates problems to solve or who attempts to solve already-known unsolved problems is in danger of spending time and energy on the fool's errand of trying to prove an unprovable claim. His attempts at proving the claim will repeatedly fail, and when they do, he won't know why. Perhaps the claim in question is false. Then again, the claim might be true and he simply hasn't tried hard enough to prove it, meaning that he should redouble his effort. And all this time, lurking in the back of his mind, will be the fear that although the claim in question is provable, he simply isn't smart, inspired, or lucky enough to prove it.

To avoid this predicament, mathematicians will spend time testing claims before spending time trying to prove them. Indeed, if they test only a bit further the claim about numbers that start with 3s and end with 1, they would realize that it is false: the very next number in the series—namely, 333333331—is not prime, since it is the product of 17 and 19607843.

Even extensive testing, however, leaves mathematicians vulnerable to wasting their time trying to prove the unprovable. Consider, for example, Goldbach's conjecture, according to which every even integer greater than 2 can be expressed as the sum of two prime numbers. (Thus, $3 = 1 + 2$, $4 = 2 + 2$, $5 = 2 + 3$, and jumping ahead, $58 = 11 + 47$.) This conjecture has been tested, by computers, for numbers up to 4×10^{18}—in other words, 4 followed by eighteen zeroes. Despite 250 years of effort, though, mathematicians have been unable to come up with a proof of the conjecture. Is it because the conjecture is false? Or are mathematicians simply not clever enough to prove it? No one knows.

Back in Chapter 7, we encountered anti-aha moments, in which a scientist suddenly realizes that he has made a mistake. Mathematicians are susceptible to this same phenomenon. Indeed, it is possible for a mathematician, in the process of trying to prove some claim, to gain the insight necessary to prove that the claim *can't* be proved. This is what happened to mathematician Louis Antoine, when he was trying to prove a three-dimensional analog of the Jordan-Schönflies theorem.[31] By the way, Antoine is blind—more about him in the next chapter.

Since mathematical proofs are deductive in nature, one might think that their creation would fall squarely in the domain of the conscious mind, which specializes in rule-bound deductive thought, but this is not the case. In the same way as a scientist must rely on a collaboration between his conscious and unconscious mind to come up with new theories, a mathematician must rely on a collaboration between his conscious and unconscious mind to come up with proofs. It is to this collaboration that, in the following chapter, we turn our attention.

CHAPTER 11

The Magic of Incubation

MATHEMATICIAN JOHN EDENSOR LITTLEWOOD was working on a problem that had a certain variable r: "One day I was playing round with this, and a ghost of an idea entered my mind of making r, the number of differentiations, *large*."[1] At this moment, people came to clean his room, so he went out for a walk—for two hours, in pouring rain. "The problem seethed violently in my mind: the material was disordered and cluttered up with irrelevant complications cleared away in the final version, and the 'idea' was vague and elusive. Finally I stopped, in the rain, gazing blankly for minutes on end over a little bridge into a stream...and presently a flooding certainty came into my mind that the thing was done."[2]

Even lesser mathematicians can experience this phenomenon. One of my undergraduate majors was in mathematics. As a result, I found myself, on most afternoons, confronted with a set of problems to solve. I would quickly dispatch the easier problems and turn my attention to the hardest one. After spending a few hours of fruitless effort trying to solve it, I would take a nap. I would often awake knowing the solution to that problem. It was like magic: while I had slept, my unconscious mind had solved it, and when I awoke, my unconscious mind was waiting there to hand the solution to me—to my conscious mind, that is. (For the record, I tried this napping technique in other classes, but with little success. In history, for example, napping is no substitute for reading the course material.)

The feeling that you have the solution to a problem without knowing the details of that solution is quite reliable but not infallible. Because Littlewood knew this, he felt anxious during the forty minutes it took him to get back to his room to verify the result.[3] He was worried that the seeming insight would turn out to be an illusion—that he had experienced a false aha moment.

Sometimes the fruits of a false aha get incorporated into a proof before a mathematician realizes that his logic is flawed, in which case the resulting proof will be defective. As we shall see later in this chapter, spurious proofs of this sort are not uncommon, and mathematicians live in fear of producing them.

Curiously, even false aha moments can trigger genuine insights. Littlewood describes one such event. In the course of trying to prove a theorem, he says, he tried an approach that looked quite promising only to realize that it didn't work. Later, in the middle of a three-week vacation in which mathematics was "completely below the horizon," it again occurred to him to try that same promising approach—he had forgotten that it didn't work. Once again, using it didn't enable him to prove his theorem directly but, to his delight, let him prove something else that could be used to prove that theorem.[4]

THE PROCESS THAT GIVES RISE to mathematical discovery, according to Littlewood, has four phases: preparation, incubation, illumination, and verification.[5]

Preparation. This phase is carried out in the conscious mind. In this phase, Littlewood says, "the essential problem has to be stripped of accidentals and brought clearly into view; all relevant knowledge surveyed; possible analogues pondered. It should be kept constantly before the mind during intervals of other work."[6]

Readers went through this preparation phase when doing the Jumble puzzle presented in the previous chapter. They tried various unscramblings, in hopes of finding a genuine word. Because there are only a finite number of possible solutions to Jumble problems (there are, for example, only 120 ways to unscramble the five letters of PIOHP), and because these solutions are easy to list, a computer can be used to sort through them.

In the mathematical preparation phase, however, there are many more possible solutions to try—so many, in most problems, that you couldn't try them all in one lifetime.[7] It is therefore important that mathematicians carry out the preparation phase in a systematic manner. They start out by trying things that experience shows are likely to work. When they don't work—as will generally be the case, if the problem is difficult—they will learn from their failures and go on to try more exotic possible solutions.

It is through this process of trying, failing, and learning that mathematicians gain a deep understanding of the problem, one that will hopefully make them smart enough to solve it. In this respect, says George Pólya, "mathematics in the making resembles any other human knowledge in the making. You have to guess a mathematical theorem before you prove it; you have to have the idea of a proof before you can carry through the details. You have to combine observations and follow analogies; you have to try and try again."[8]

Preparation is the most difficult of the four phases of mathematical discovery, inasmuch as it involves what Littlewood describes as "hopeless muddle and floundering, sustained on the 'smell' that something is there."[9] This phase of mathematical research can be quite disheartening. Indeed, says Littlewood, because preparation is so demanding, "most of a mathematician's life is spent in frustration, punctuated with rare inspirations. A beginner can't expect quick results; if they are quick they are pretty sure to be poor."[10] Along similar lines, mathematician Paul Cohen—about whom I will have more to say in the next chapter—says that he felt "a deep sense of frustration" when doing his work on the continuum hypothesis. "I remember one day, shaving and looking at myself in the mirror. I said, 'You poor fellow. You're driving yourself nuts. You'll never be able to do this. You think your ideas are correct, you're just never going to get anywhere with it.' So I felt rather depressed." Nevertheless, he continued to work on the problem.[11]

Published mathematics, says mathematician Reuben Hersh, is like the dining room of a restaurant. Everything is orderly, precise, and elegant. The process that gives rise to published mathematics, though, resembles the restaurant's chaotic kitchen. In the same way as you cannot get an idea of what is going on in a restaurant's kitchen by visiting its dining room, you will be completely misled about how math is done if all you ever look at is published articles. You won't realize, says Hersh, the extent to which the process of mathematical discovery is "fragmentary, informal, intuitive, tentative. We try this or that. We say 'maybe,' or 'it looks like.' "[12]

During the preparation phase, a mathematician's primary investigative tools are paper and a pen or pencil. Littlewood made a point of restricting himself, in this phase, to a single page of paper that he filled with equations and drawings. It would look like a disconnected mess, but he felt that to have it present before him was the best way to get his unconscious mind involved in the problem.[13] Other mathematicians are profligate in their use of paper. According to one story, the maid of a famous mathematician asked him what he did at work. His reply: "I spend the day writing on pieces of paper, crumpling them up, and throwing them into the wastebasket."[14]

It is, however, possible to do math without paper. This is what blind mathematicians, who are not nearly as rare as one might think, are forced to do. Interestingly, many blind mathematicians specialize in geometry or its related field, topology. Louis Antoine, mentioned in the previous chapter, is one of them. This seems paradoxical, inasmuch as geometry is perhaps the most visual branch of mathematics. But as blind (since age eleven) geometer Emmanuel Giroux points out, in analytical mathematics, one must keep track of long strings of equations, which is difficult to do without paper. In geometry, "the information is very concentrated" and is therefore something you can "keep in your mind."[15]

The preparation phase, although exhausting and frustrating, is absolutely necessary, for it is in consciously trying to solve a problem that a mathematician can enlist the cooperation of his unconscious mind. If the problem is a difficult one, it can't be solved "mechanically," the way one might add up a column of numbers; that sort of problem can be solved by the conscious mind going solo. Doing proofs, though, will typically require a mathematician to have one or more insights, and the best—and maybe only?—place to get them is his unconscious mind.

Mathematical inspirations, writes Henri Poincaré, will generally take place only "after several days of voluntary effort, which have appeared fruitless and which one believed were of no value, where it appeared that we have taken a totally false path." He adds that these conscious efforts are nevertheless crucial, inasmuch as they "put our subconscious into motion, and without these, it would not have been set in motion and would not have produced anything."[16]

Stated differently, in its collaborations with the unconscious mind, the conscious mind can't issue orders. A mathematician cannot wake up in the morning, and think, in his most authoritative mental voice, "Unconscious mind, today I want you to prove Goldbach's conjecture" (according to which every even integer greater than 2 can be expressed as the sum of two prime numbers). His unconscious mind will utterly ignore him and might even, for all he knows, laugh at him. If, however, the mathematician spends the morning trying to prove Goldbach's conjecture, his unconscious mind might take an interest and start looking over his shoulder, as it were. "Oh, look at that," it will say. "He is trying to prove Goldbach's conjecture." After a while, it might start making suggestions; it might, in other words, behave like a chess kibitzer. With luck, it will eventually come up with a winning move.

In another respect, the collaboration between a mathematician and his unconscious mind resembles the relationship between a celebrity and his ghostwriter. The latter labors long and hard out of public view, and the former is happy to take the book that results, claim authorship of it, and sign copies of it for an adoring public.

Incubation. If the mathematician successfully gains the cooperation of his unconscious mind, he will enter the second phase of mathematical discovery, incubation. The problem he is working on will take up residence in his unconscious mind, which will ponder it even when the mathematician's conscious mind has turned its attention elsewhere—when, for example, he is dining, playing tennis, or even sleeping. From the point of view of neuroscience, this phase of mathematical discovery is mysterious; from the point of view of the mathematician, it is a magical, wonderful gift.

Illumination. After hours, days, or even years of incubation, an aha moment might emerge from the mathematician's unconscious mind, and as a result, he will experience what Littlewood calls illumination and what I have been calling a mathematical aha moment. According to Littlewood, "illumination implies some mysterious rapport between the subconscious and the conscious, otherwise emergence could not happen."[17] It also implies that a mathematician's unconscious mind is better at math than his conscious mind!

The insight a mathematician's unconscious mind provides him with might be the solution to the problem he is working on. In many cases, though, it will be something less than this: it will be an insight into what technique he should use in trying to solve that problem.

Verification. After the moment of illumination comes the process of verification, in which the rule-bound conscious mind checks to see whether the insight that it was given breaks any of the rules by which the conscious mind lives. And if the insight came in the form of a new strategy to try, the mathematician might spend considerable time and effort applying it to the problem at hand. If the verification is successful, the mathematician will be ready to write up his results for publication.

Verification, I should add, wouldn't be necessary if the moment of illumination were invariably trustworthy, but as we have seen, this isn't the case. Mathematicians not only have false aha moments but periodically publish proofs based on them. Sometimes their mistake subsequently comes to light, causing them considerable embarrassment.

MATH TEACHERS, if they are worthy of their job, ask their students to do lots of homework. This raises an obvious question: what is the point of doing homework? It is, I think, a question that math teachers rarely ask. They give their students homework because their teachers gave *them* homework. They are simply doing what tradition dictates that they do.

Fair enough, but a more complete answer to this question is possible. To begin with, doing homework problems forces students to practice certain mathematical techniques and thereby increases the chance that students will master those techniques. By doing problems, students also develop a feel for which techniques are appropriate to use with different sorts of problems. This information will come in handy when, in their subsequent mathematical endeavors, they use an enlightened form of trial-and-error reasoning to solve a problem.

But there is another, very important benefit to be derived from doing math homework: it allows students to develop their ability to withstand frustration. Such frustration, after all, is an inevitable component of the preparation stage, in which a mathematician tries very hard to do something and repeatedly fails to do it. Doing math homework, in other words, teaches students that in the same way that sore muscles come with being a weightlifter, frustration comes with doing math. If you experience frustration, it doesn't mean that you are bad at math; it means that you are taking your mathematical endeavors seriously.

By exposing students to frustration-inducing problems, teachers show them what they are in for if they become mathematicians. Some students will quickly decide that math is not for them. Those who remain will benefit from being exposed to difficult problems, inasmuch as the exposure will allow them to develop techniques for dealing with frustration. In short, doing difficult homework problems toughens students mentally so they will be able to succeed as mathematicians.

The frustration math students experience is somewhat assuaged by the knowledge that the problem they are working on has a solution and that they can get this solution by accessing a book, the Internet, or their teacher. Mathematicians working on an as-yet-unsolved problem, however, have no such assurances. Perhaps the problem they have been unable to solve cannot be solved. Or perhaps it has a solution, but one that they, because of their mathematical shortcomings, will never hit upon. They are left with a very important question: how much time should they spend trying to solve a problem before they give up? In this sense, they are like a miner who must decide whether to abandon the gold mine he has been digging. He is a hundred feet into the hillside and has hit nothing, so it seems sensible to quit and move his mining operations to another site. And yet, who knows, the next shovelful of dirt might contain the first hints of a mother lode.

In many cases, the great aha moments of mathematics resulted from mathematicians who *did* take that next shovelful, metaphorically speaking, and several shovelfuls after that. Thus, to do mathematics well requires not only brilliance and a tolerance for frustration, but tenacity. This is a character trait that mathematician Andrew Wiles, mentioned in the last chapter, obviously possessed. And yet, for every Andrew Wiles, there are presumably dozens (hundreds?) of mathematicians who spent their careers pursuing proofs that never came.

INCUBATION PLAYS AN IMPORTANT ROLE in mathematical discovery. As a result, some mathematicians, clever people that they are, have made it their business to study the phenomenon, so they can derive maximum benefit from it. Poincaré, for example, took an interest in those occasions on which, after trying unsuccessfully to solve a problem, he took a rest and then returned to the problem. For the next half hour, the dry spell might continue but then, bang, the "decisive idea" would come. He rejects the suggestion that the idea came because the rest period had "given the mind power and freshness." Instead, the unconscious mind continued to work during that period and manifested itself thereafter.[18]

Along similar lines, Littlewood stresses "the importance of giving the subconscious every chance."[19] According to him, mathematicians almost always experience their moment of illumination while *not* doing math. He reports that two of his best times for having mathematical aha moments were when he was walking and when he was shaving.[20] He goes on to offer concrete advice on how mathematicians should structure their workdays to take full advantage of the incubation phenomenon. He advises them to work for at most four or five hours a day, with hourly breaks, perhaps to take a walk. He also advises against ending a session of work, as most people do, by completing a discrete task. It is better, he says, to call it a day when you are "in the middle of something."[21] Then you will have something to get you started the next day. Otherwise, you might waste half an hour trying to regain your concentration.

To most people, the work schedule favored by Littlewood smacks of laziness. Indeed, in most professions, bosses wouldn't tolerate an employee who wanted to work only four or five hours a day, and who insisted on going for walks during that abbreviated workday. But most people don't have to rely on incubation to produce the results they seek. Instead, their intellectual endeavors can be carried out in their conscious mind.

Besides offering advice on how mathematicians should structure their workdays, Littlewood makes recommendations regarding the mathematical workweek. It had been his habit to work seven days a week, but when he experimented with taking Sundays off, he found that Mondays were as a result quite productive: lots of good ideas would come to him. Then he started celebrating the arrival of a good idea on Monday by taking the rest of the day off, only to find that ideas started coming to him on Tuesdays as well.[22] There is, to be sure, a limit to how far this process can be taken. Take enough time off, and your unconscious mind will lose interest in the project you are working on. Your conscious mind, as we have seen, will be helpless without it.

Because incubation plays such an important role in mathematics, a sensible mathematician will spend time determining how best to harness the phenomenon. He will make observations regarding his own aha moments: when do they tend to happen? He will also experiment, the way Littlewood did, and adjust his work habits accordingly. Wouldn't it be a shame, after all, if a mathematician discovered late in his career that if only he had taken more walks or naps, or enjoyed more two-hour-long dinners with pleasant companions, he would have doubled his mathematical output?

WE HAVE ENCOUNTERED the false aha moment: a mathematician has what seems like a genuine insight, only to have it fail the verification process. But sometimes, as I have said, a false aha manages to escape detection and subsequently gets incorporated into a published proof. The proof in question will be defective; it will be what is known, in mathematical circles, as a *spurious proof.*

A proof is a series of assertions, each following from those before it. It can be very, very long—indeed, so long that it is impossible for a mathematician to hold the whole thing in his head at one time. This is not an issue, though, as long as each step in the proof is justifiable. In a spurious proof, one or more steps won't be justifiable. The resulting proof becomes the mathematical equivalent of a three-mile-long bridge with a five-foot-wide gap in the middle. The bridge, although beautiful, won't serve its intended purpose.

I have described mathematical aha moments as being the purest insights a person can have. What makes them special, I have said, is that they can be proven correct, unlike scientific or religious insights. But it should now be clear that in making this claim, I was fudging a bit. Yes, mathematicians can offer a proof that their insight is correct, but the question will remain whether the proof in question is a genuine proof.

Despite the care mathematicians take in avoiding them, spurious proofs do get published. Littlewood describes a case in which he presented a "distinguished class" with a recently published proof. Everyone admired it. Later he discovered a flaw in the proof that he and all his students had missed. And fifteen years after that, in correspondence with the author of the proof, he happened to mention the mistake. It came as news to the author, who all that time had assumed that his proof was correct.[23]

In 1971, a mathematician thought he had proved the Riemann hypothesis. He submitted a copy to the London Mathematical Society for publication, and at the same time sent a copy to Littlewood. Since the Riemann hypothesis was one of the great unproved conjectures of mathematics—it was one of the problems on Hilbert's famous list of unsolved problems—it was likely that the submitted proof was spurious. And indeed, Littlewood found a mistake in it. The referee for the London Mathematical Society also found a mistake, but a different one than Littlewood had found. The referee therefore recommended against publication of the paper. It turned out that the mistake the referee found wasn't in fact a mistake. The one Littlewood found, however, truly was a mistake. Thus, the paper should have been rejected but not for the reason given by the referee.[24]

I have talked about Andrew Wiles's proof of Fermat's last theorem. After seven years of effort, he was convinced that he had proved it and gave a lecture in which he presented his proof. He thereby gained the admiration not only of his fellow mathematicians but the world at large. News of his proof made the front page of the *New York Times*—the headline: "At Last, Shout of 'Eureka!' in Age-Old Math Mystery."[25] Wiles sent the proof off to be published, but in the review process a logical gap was discovered.

Sometimes a logical gap is easily filled. In other cases, a gap turns out to be the heart of the problem in trying to prove a particular theorem. According to Simon Singh, who wrote a book about Wiles's attempt to prove Fermat's last theorem, "Many mathematicians have cried themselves to sleep knowing that they could achieve a major result if only they could establish one missing link in their chain of logic."[26] The gap in Wiles's proof turned out to be a big one, meaning that his proof was spurious.

Wiles, it will be remembered, had worked on Fermat in secrecy, in part to avoid having the world looking over his shoulder. Now he had revealed his secret, only to discover that he had made a mistake. Triumph had turned to tragedy. He was forced to do math in a very public way. It was, for Wiles, a hellish existence. He set to work filling the gap, but progress was slow. During that time, the mathematical world speculated on whether he would be able to fill it, and the press was happy to report this speculation (headline in the *New York Times*: "A Year Later, Snag Persists In Math Proof").[27] After a year and a half of effort, during which time he sought the assistance of mathematician Richard Taylor, Wiles was able to fill the gap.[28]

WHEN MATHEMATICAL IDEAS COME TO US, they come from our unconscious mind. And where, one can reasonably ask, is this located? No one knows the answer to this question. One common suggestion, though, is that the brain has a system dedicated to math. Before I explore this idea further, let me take a moment to talk about brain systems.

Our brain has many systems, and we can detect their presence within us if we pay attention. Suppose someone asks you the name of your first-grade teacher. You ponder the question, but the answer eludes you. You forget about the question and go on with your business. Several hours later, though, the answer pops into your head. The fact that you remembered after a long period of not trying to remember indicates the presence in you of a brain system devoted to memory retrieval. This system, when "turned on" by a request for information, goes into action. You will be unaware of its operation, though, until (and unless) it provides you with the information you requested.

Another brain system is devoted to detecting faces. When you see a photo or painting, this system will immediately draw your attention to a human face, if one is present. And when you walk in front of a large group of people, it will immediately draw your attention to the faces of people you know. It will do this, I should add, whether you ask it to or not. This system presumably evolved to give us the ability to distinguish humans from non-humans, and among humans, to distinguish friend from foe.

The possibility of solving math problems by letting them "incubate" suggests that our brain has a system that does math. It presumably does what the conscious mind does in trying to solve problems—namely, it tries possible solutions. It also screens these solutions, since it will only present our conscious mind with those that look promising. Like the other brain systems I have mentioned, the math system operates without our being aware of its operation, until it sounds an "alarm"—until, that is, it causes us to have a mathematical aha moment. Notice that in one important respect, the brain's math system resembles the memory system more than the face detector. The face detector operates whether we want it to or not. The math system and memory system, in contrast, will usually be dormant unless we turn them on by trying consciously to solve a math problem or remember something.

It makes evolutionary sense that we would have a memory system or a face detector. They would have been quite useful to our evolutionary ancestors on the savannas of Africa one hundred thousand years ago. You needed to remember where you left your hand axe, and you needed to recognize your friends and enemies. In other words, having these brain systems increased your chances of surviving and reproducing—the things with which evolution is concerned. But what about a math system? There was simply no survival advantage to being able to do math on the savannas of Africa one hundred thousand years ago. And even today, a person's survival does not depend on his ability to do higher math—or basic algebra, for that matter. So why do we possess the ability to do (with a bit of training) math?

What we have apparently done is co-opt a brain system; in other words, we are using a brain system for something other than its evolutionary function. And this isn't the only component of our evolutionary inheritance that we have co-opted. Consider, for example, our auditory system. It presumably evolved so that our evolutionary ancestors would be aware of their environment at night and be aware of what was going on outside of their visual field during the day. In particular, it alerted them to approaching predators, a function that clearly had survival value. But modern humans rarely use their auditory system for this purpose. Instead, we might use it to listen to Beethoven. We might also use one physical component of that system—namely, our ears—to hold up eyeglasses, something our evolutionary ancestors would never have done.

Or consider the brain's reward system. It evolved to encourage our evolutionary ancestors to do things that increased their chances of surviving and reproducing. Thus, our ancestors who set ambitious goals for themselves and subsequently attained those goals—something that could dramatically increase their chances of surviving—were rewarded with the rush of success. This rush is caused by the release of the neurotransmitter dopamine in the brain. As the result of a chemical coincidence, though, using cocaine will also trigger a release of dopamine. The cocaine user will experience the delightful rush of success, even though he hasn't succeeded at anything other than obtaining and consuming cocaine. He has thereby co-opted his brain's reward system.

The theory that to do math is to co-opt a brain system presents us with a new question: what brain system are we co-opting? It has to be a system that, besides doing something that would have been useful on the savannas of Africa one hundred thousand years ago, has the capacity to do geometry and linear algebra. What system could possibly have these characteristics?

One candidate is the brain system that does spatial reasoning. It tells us how objects look from different points of view. It is understandable that our evolutionary ancestors would develop such a system. By possessing it, they could recognize landmarks when seen from different points of view and could thereby keep track of where they were.

We use this system every time we predict what, say, a cube will look like when we rotate it in our hand. To be able to make this prediction, though, the spatial-reasoning brain system presumably uses an incredible amount of sophisticated math. As evidence for this claim, consider the software that is used to create computer-generated imagery (CGI). This software begins with a mathematical representation of, say, a tree and then does numerous trigonometrical operations on this representation to reflect changes in the point of view the programmer wants to see it from. It requires a lot of computing power to do this, and an incredibly fast computer to do it in real time.

But this, apparently, is what your brain does all the time. And although your spatial reasoning system is operating whenever you are looking at the world, you are oblivious to its operation; indeed, you take it utterly for granted. Consequently, when you rotate a cube in your hand, you are in no way surprised by what you subsequently see. So maybe when we do math, we are somehow tapping into our brain's ability to do spatial reasoning. But presumably, our ability to do math relies on other brain systems as well. Otherwise, all computer programmers would have to do to get a computer to do higher math is modify their CGI software. One imagines, though, that programming a computer to solve anything but the simplest math problems would be vastly more complicated than this.

FOR OTHER CLUES regarding our brain's math ability, researchers have taken MRI images of people as they do math. The images show where the brain is consuming the most oxygen and therefore where it is most active. Such experiments have significant limitations, though. To begin with, they tell us *where* the brain does math, not *how* it does it. Furthermore, the math in question is math that is being done consciously. But as we have seen, the most interesting math—the kind that generates significant aha moments—is done in the unconscious mind. You can put someone into an MRI machine and tell her to add a column of numbers or think about proving a theorem. You cannot, however, put someone into an MRI machine and instruct her to incubate with respect to a math problem.

It would be wonderful if someone was in an MRI machine when a significant mathematical aha moment struck her: scientists would find out where such moments take place. The chance of this happening, though, is pretty small. It is bad enough to spend half an hour in an MRI machine. No sensible mathematician would be willing to remain in one for the hours, days, or even weeks it might take for an aha moment to come—if it came at all.

Another way to get insight into the mathematical aha moment is to investigate people who are unusually good at math. Are their brains somehow special? Consider, for example, those individuals with savant syndrome, particularly the subgroup of such individuals known as *mental calculators*. Thomas Fuller, an eighteenth-century slave in Virginia, was one such individual. When asked how many seconds a man would have lived who was seventy years, seventeen days, and twelve hours old, it took him only a minute and a half to come up with an answer: 2,210,500,800 seconds. One of the gentlemen who were testing him did the math and came up with a slightly smaller number. On being told that his answer was wrong, Fuller responded that the person who had checked his answer had forgotten about the seventeen leap years a seventy-year-old person would have lived through. On taking account of this, they realized that Fuller's answer was correct.[29]

Strangely enough, these mental calculators appear to be able to do with their unconscious mind what most people can do only with their conscious mind—namely, grind through laborious calculations. It is as if their conscious and unconscious minds have swapped mathematical functions. According to one of these calculators, on being given a problem to solve, "I have often the sensation of somebody beside me whispering the right way to find the desired result."[30] Very strange indeed!

ANOTHER GROUP WE CAN INVESTIGATE to gain insight into the mathematical aha moment are the great mathematicians, some of whom we encountered in this and the previous chapter. One thing that immediately jumps out at us when we undertake this investigation is that they are almost without exception male. What conclusion should we draw from this? Are men's brains simply better at math? And if so, what is it about their brains that makes them more susceptible to mathematical aha moments?

Before we start looking at brain differences between men and women, we would do well to consider another explanation for the near absence of women from lists of great mathematicians. Why are there fewer great women mathematicians than great men mathematicians? In all likelihood, it is a direct consequence of there being fewer women than men who are professional mathematicians.

It is almost unheard of, as we have seen, for an individual to experience a significant mathematical aha moment unless two conditions have been met: first, the person has been extensively trained in mathematics, and second, the person has the time to devote to mathematical research in the hopes of triggering an aha moment. Typically, only professional mathematicians will meet these two conditions. Thus, if someone is not allowed to become a professional mathematician, it is very unlikely that she will have the significant aha moments necessary to be considered a great mathematician. In the past, of course, women *have* been prevented from becoming professional mathematicians—hence the dearth of women on the lists of great mathematicians.

Consider the case of Amalie Emmy Noether (1882–1935), arguably the greatest woman mathematician. Her specialty was abstract algebra. She had the advantage of being the daughter of a mathematician. On completing her doctorate, she worked for seven years, without pay, at the Mathematical Institute of Erlangen in Germany. She was subsequently invited to join the mathematics department at the University of Göttingen, but for four years could serve only as an assistant to David Hilbert. Finally, she was given permission to join the faculty. She never married. This was, in the first decades of the twentieth century, a career path that many women, understandably, would have been reluctant to embark upon.

A similar explanation can be given for the dearth of women in lists of the great scientists. In science, though, two other factors are at work. The first is that in some disciplines, scientists can make discoveries only if they have access to specialized equipment. Women who are not employed by universities or laboratories would be hard-pressed to gain such access. (To do math, of course, you don't need specialized equipment.) Another factor is the relatively subjective standard by which scientific work is judged. In math, whether you did or didn't prove a theorem will, in most cases, be clear. Publish a radical new theory or unexpected experimental result in science, though, and a debate is likely to arise over whether the theory is correct or whether the experiment is somehow flawed. This means that in science you can't simply have a significant aha moment and then relax—not, at any rate, if you want to have an impact on the scientific world. You must instead fight to gain acceptance of your discovery. You must fight to get it published, and then you must counter the storm of skepticism that its publication is likely to unleash.

As we have seen, it takes self-confidence and courage to fight for one's theories or results. Many male scientists lack the self-confidence and courage to do so: they don't publish their controversial findings, or they publish them in obscure journals, where they are unlikely to attract attention and controversy. In the past, women scientists proposing radical theories would have faced even greater resistance to their work. They would have encountered not just the skepticism scientists will express toward almost any new theory but the additional skepticism they would harbor toward a theory proposed by a woman. Thus, for a woman scientist to defend her views took even more self-confidence and courage than for a man to do so. There is little doubt that some significant work by women in the sciences never made it into the history books as a result of their work being dismissed out of hand.

Many male scientists, on contemplating the personal price they may have to pay to defend an unpopular scientific viewpoint, conclude that they have better things to do with their lives. But if female scientists have to pay an even greater price, it is perfectly understandable that they would pass up the opportunity to become a primary combatant in a scientific fight. This is one of the reasons we marvel at the courage of women like Lynn Margulis, the biologist who spent decades defending her endosymbiotic theory, according to which the mitochondria within our cells are the descendants of bacteria that were engulfed by other cells.

So, are female mathematicians less likely to experience aha moments than male mathematicians? It is hard to say. What the above discussion demonstrates is that we should not, in attempting to answer this question, point to the dearth of women on lists of great mathematicians as evidence that this is true. Much the same can be said regarding whether or not female scientists are less likely than male scientists to experience aha moments.

Although we can argue that educational and employment discrimination has prevented women from having as many mathematical and scientific aha moments as men, we cannot develop a similar argument regarding aha moments in religion and morality. This is because having a religious or moral aha moment doesn't require specialized training. We would therefore expect women to have as many of these moments as men. And yet, when we look at the religious and moral aha moments that have transformed the world, we find that they are attributed mostly to men. Why is this? The obvious answer is that society has historically responded differently to the aha moments of men and women. More precisely, the religious and moral insights of men were more likely to be taken seriously than those of women. In other words, discrimination is again a factor.

The above discussion does not get to the bottom of things. We are left with the question of whether men's brains are more susceptible to aha moments than women's brains. However much we want the sexes to be equal, it is possible that because of differences in their brains, men have an advantage when it comes to having, say, mathematical aha moments, and women have an advantage when it comes to having, say, moral aha moments. Whether such differences in fact exist is hard to say. There is just too much that scientists don't understand about the brain processes that yield aha moments.

CHAPTER 12

The After-Math

IN OUR DISCUSSIONS of the aha moment in religion, morality, and science, we ended with an examination of the world's response to an aha moment and the reaction of the person who had the moment to that response. It is difficult to do this for mathematics, though, inasmuch as the world is largely oblivious to mathematical discoveries. People feel, quite correctly, that mathematics has almost no bearing on what they believe and on how they spend their days.

We have also seen how scientists often have to fight to win acceptance, by their fellow scientists, of their discoveries and theories. The same thing can happen in mathematics: if you prove a particularly difficult theorem—one that has defied proof for centuries—the mathematical world will regard your proof with skepticism. Your colleagues will suspect that there is a mistake somewhere. But unless they can find it, they will have little choice but to accept your proof. In mathematics, then, the story about what happens after an aha moment tends to be uninteresting.

There is, however, one striking exception to this generalization. In the late nineteenth century, mathematician

Georg Cantor took on the topic of infinity. The story of what happened next deserves our attention. For one thing, the nonmathematical world took an interest in his research; for another, his research triggered acrimony on the part of his colleagues. Not only that, but his treatment of infinity shows that even a seemingly sound mathematical theory can implode. Finally, Cantor's story has a tragic ending. It is, all things considered, a first-rate tale, but to tell it properly, I will have to introduce a bit of set theory. I shall endeavor to keep the math to a minimum.

IN THE MATHEMATICAL SENSE OF THE WORD, a *set* is simply a collection of things. The things in question can be material objects such as rocks, but they can also be immaterial things such as numbers. The order of the things in a set does not matter. Thus, the sets {1, 2} and {2, 1} are the same set: they are the collection of the numbers 1 and 2, in no particular order.

There are mathematicians who specialize in studying the properties of sets. They might talk about one set being a *subset* of another: {1, 2} is a subset of {1, 2, 4}, since the former set is contained in the latter. They might also talk about the *intersections* of two sets: the set {2, 4} is the intersection of the sets {1, 2, 4} and {2, 3, 4, 5}, since it contains the elements present in both sets. And finally, they might talk about the *size* of sets. Thus, {1, 2, 4} and {7, 11, 41} are the same size, with three members each, whereas {2, 4, 9} and {5, 7} are not the same size.

It was in connection with set size that Cantor made his major mathematical breakthrough. He realized that an effective way to determine whether two sets had the same size is by seeing whether it is possible to put the elements of the two sets into a one-to-one correspondence with each other. You can do this with {1, 2, 4} and {7, 11, 41}. You can, for example, associate the 1 in the first set with the 7 in the second, associate 2 with 11, and associate 4 with 41. (These aren't, to be sure, the only way the associations can be made.) Because this one-to-one correspondence exists, we know that the sets are the same size. (Notice that we made this determination without having to count the elements in the two sets.) If we turn our attention to the sets {2, 4, 9} and {5, 7}, we will find that we cannot put their members into a one-to-one correspondence. We will conclude that they are not the same size.

Mathematicians are used to dealing with infinite sets. Consider, for example, the collection of all positive integers, or *counting numbers*, as they are called: {1, 2, 3, 4, ... }. It will have infinitely many numbers in it. Now consider the set of all even numbers: {2, 4, 6, 8, ... }. It will also have infinitely many numbers in it. Cantor's first important insight is that the two sets are the same size. We can, after all, put the elements of the two sets into a one-to-one correspondence: we associate 1 in the first set with 2 in the second, 2 in the first set with 4 in the second, and so on. What about the number 1023 in the first set? We will associate it with 2046 in the second. It should be clear that every number in the first set will be associated with exactly one number in the second set. Therefore, the two sets, besides being infinite, are the same infinite size.

This result is surprising, though. The set of odd numbers {1, 3, 5, 7, ...} and the set of even numbers {2, 4, 6, 8, ...} are obviously the same size. But the set of counting numbers {1, 2, 3, 4, ...} is the result of *combining* all the odd and even numbers. So shouldn't the set of counting numbers be *twice as large as* the set of even numbers? And yet, if you accept the idea that two sets are the same size if their members can be put into a one-to-one correspondence, it is clearly the case that the set of even numbers is the same size as the set of counting numbers. How exceedingly strange!

Cantor went on to examine other infinite sets, turning his attention first to the set of rational numbers. These are numbers that can be expressed as a ratio of two whole numbers. Thus, 1/3, 5/8, and 57/73 will all count as rational numbers. (Notice that the counting numbers are included in the rational numbers: the counting number 3, for example, can be expressed as the rational number 3/1.) Cantor figured out a way to put the rational numbers into a one-to-one correspondence with the counting numbers and thereby drew the conclusion that the set of all counting numbers is the same (infinite) size as the set of rational numbers.

This result is again surprising. Notice that between any two integers, there are only finitely many integers: between 2 and 7, for example, there are only four integers: 3, 4, 5, and 6. But between any two rational numbers, there are infinitely many rational numbers. Consider 1/2 and 3/4, for example. Between them, we find 5/8; between 1/2 and 5/8, we find 9/16; between 1/2 and 9/16, we find 17/32; and so on. Intuitively, then, the rational numbers are in a sense *doubly* infinite: there are not only infinitely many rational numbers, but between any two rational numbers, there is another infinity of rational numbers. And yet, Cantor showed that there are as many rational numbers as there are counting numbers. Bizarre!

WE HAVE NOW CONSIDERED three infinite sets—the set of counting numbers, the set of even numbers, and the set of rational numbers—and have discovered that they are the same size. On the basis of this sample, we might conclude that all infinite sets will be of this size. But this is where things get even stranger.

After his examination of rational numbers, Cantor turned his attention to the so-called irrational numbers—numbers that *cannot* be expressed as ratios of two whole numbers. Among the irrational numbers, we find the square root of 2, which has the value 1.41421356237 . . . . (According to one story, Pythagoras's student Hippasus first proved the irrationality of the square root of two and was subsequently drowned for having done so.)[1] The famous constant pi, 3.14159265359 . . . , is also demonstrably irrational. (Mathematician Johann Heinrich Lambert proved this in the eighteenth century, but was not subsequently murdered for having done so.) If we combine all the rational numbers and all the irrational numbers, we end up with what are called *real numbers*.

Cantor set about looking for a way to put the set of real numbers into a one-to-one correspondence with the set of counting numbers but could not find one. In the process of looking, though, he had what I have called an anti-aha moment: he stumbled across a proof that the thing he was trying to do couldn't be done—that the real numbers *cannot* be put into such a correspondence with the counting numbers. He concluded that although there are infinitely many counting numbers and infinitely many real numbers, the latter infinity is larger than the former. In other words, there isn't just infinity; there are different sizes of infinity!

CANTOR'S WORK ON INFINITY made his fellow mathematicians uncomfortable. They objected to the way he spoke of infinity, not as an abstraction but as a concrete, albeit nonmaterial entity. It was one thing for theologians to do this, but for a mathematician to do it raised eyebrows. They also objected to the strange things that happen when we talk about infinite sets, such as that the set of all even numbers is the same size as the set consisting of both all even and all odd numbers. But the idea that there could be different sizes of infinity was less plausible still. Even though they could point to no particular mistake Cantor had made, mathematicians in many cases felt that there surely must be one; otherwise, he couldn't reach this absurd conclusion.

Cantor realized that his proofs regarding the various sizes of infinity would be controversial. He also knew that if he put "infinity" in the title of the paper in which he described his proofs, it would attract attention that he was anxious to avoid. He therefore chose a humdrum title: "On a Property of the Collection of All Real Algebraic Numbers." By using this ploy, Cantor could establish his claim of priority in coming up with this result without simultaneously triggering a storm of controversy. As we have seen, this sort of "stealth publishing" also takes place in science. The paper was accepted for publication by *Crelle's Journal* in 1874.[2]

One mathematician who was averse to Cantor's mathematics was Leopold Kronecker, an editor at *Crelle's*.[3] Kronecker began attacks on Cantor's mathematical views. He referred to Cantor's work as "humbug."[4] He also appears to have engaged in a campaign of personal attacks on Cantor, calling him a charlatan and a corrupter of youth—but not to his face.[5] Even such a renowned mathematician as Henri Poincaré found Cantor's results difficult to accept: "Later generations will regard [Cantor's] set theory as a disease from which one has recovered."[6]

In the face of these attacks, Cantor did not back down. He quickly concluded that whether or not his work would be accepted was "a question of power, and that kind of question can never be decided by way of persuasion; the question is which ideas are the most powerful, comprehensive, and fruitful, Kronecker's or mine; only success will in time decide our struggle!"[7] Another thing that gave him courage was his belief that his work on sets had been divinely inspired by God and therefore had to be true.[8]

Cantor was not alone in recognizing the religious overtones of his work. Jews and Christians take God to be a perfect being. A finite being would have limitations, though. Thus, if God is perfect, he must be infinite. More precisely, he is infinitely powerful, infinitely wise, and infinitely good. Thus it was that, in the late nineteenth century, Catholic theologians took interest in and started making use of Cantor's theory of the infinite.[9] Indeed, there seems to have been more support for his theory of infinity among Catholic theologians than among mathematicians.[10]

Cantor was sympathetic to this interest in his work: "From me, Christian philosophy will be offered for the first time the true theory of the infinite."[11] Cantor felt he had a duty to make sure the Church used his doctrines correctly.[12] And according to one biographer, he also felt he had a duty to "keep on, in the face of all adversity, to bring the insights he had been given as God's messenger to mathematicians everywhere."[13]

Cantor's discoveries regarding infinite sets were slow to gain acceptance. In 1885, for example, he sent two papers to a journal edited by Gösta Mittag-Leffler, who was sympathetic toward him and his work. This editor, however, was reluctant to publish the papers, for the simple reason that Cantor was so far ahead of his time: "It may well be that you and your theory will never be given the justice you deserve in our lifetime. Then the theory will be rediscovered in a hundred years or so by someone else, and then it will subsequently be found that you already had it all. Then, at least, you will be given justice."[14]

When we start examining aha moments, we are struck by two things: their power to transform the world and the remarkable extent to which the world resists being transformed by them. Such resistance is fairly common in the other domains we have explored. The story of Cantor shows that it can also take place in mathematics. But it is premature for me to talk about the "story of Cantor," since the story is not yet over.

IN MUCH THE SAME WAY THAT EUCLID axiomatized geometry, Cantor axiomatized set theory. One of his axioms, known as the *axiom of abstraction*, asserted that for any property P, we can form the set consisting of all and only those things that have P. We can, for example, form the set of all even numbers, the set of all unicorns (it would be an empty set), or the set of all blue-eyed people. Although this axiom seems intuitively correct and utterly harmless, it turned out to be so deeply flawed that it caused Cantor's axiomatization of set theory to implode.

In 1897, mathematician Cesare Burali-Forti showed that Cantor's axiomatization is inconsistent.[15] In 1901, philosopher and mathematician Bertrand Russell found a much simpler way to reveal the flaw. He considered the rather unusual property of being a set that does not contain itself and invoked Cantor's axiomatization to create the set of all and only those things that had this property—the set, in other words, of all sets that don't contain themselves. And finally, he asked a simple question: does this set contain itself? If it *doesn't* contain itself, then it belongs in itself: it is, after all, the set of all sets that don't contain themselves. And if, on the other hand, it *does* contain itself, then it doesn't belong in itself, since it is supposed to contain only those sets that don't contain themselves. This became known as *Russell's paradox*. The discovery of this paradox—which doubtless yielded a first-class aha moment for Russell—was the death blow to Cantor's axiomatization of set theory.

Cantor seems not to have been terribly concerned about these paradoxes.[16] (The reason for his indifference is technical in nature and need not concern us here.) But in 1904, mathematician Jules König came up with what looked like another serious flaw in Cantor's set theory, which he revealed at the Third International Congress, in front of much of the mathematical world. A humiliated Cantor felt God had wronged him by allowing this to happen.[17] He refused to accept König's argument but could find no mistakes in it.

We have encountered inconsistent beliefs, both in our discussion of morality and our discussion of science. We have seen that people tend to "deal with" their inconsistencies by ignoring them, only to pay a price in the form of an uncomfortable bout of cognitive dissonance. Mathematicians, however, are unusual for their willingness to take drastic action when they detect an inconsistency in their mathematical beliefs. In particular, if an axiomatic system proves to be inconsistent, they will quickly abandon it. And thus it was that Cantor's axiomatization of set theory was supplanted by other axiomatizations that avoided making use of the intuitively plausible but logically toxic axiom of abstraction. Will inconsistencies someday be discovered in these new, improved axiomatizations? Perhaps.

While one part of the mathematical world was attacking Cantor's theories, another part was acknowledging his contributions. In 1904, England's Royal Society awarded him the very prestigious Sylvester Medal.[18] It is unfortunate that this recognition was so late in coming, since by then, Cantor was spending much of his time in sanatoriums.[19] It appears that at the same time as he was wrestling with infinity, he had been doing battle with a bipolar disorder.[20] He suffered a nervous breakdown in 1884,[21] and his mental health remained fragile for the rest of his life. Presumably, his mathematical endeavors placed him under considerable intellectual and emotional stress. Did they thereby trigger the breakdown? One can only speculate.

I WILL END THIS STORY of a mathematical aha moment and its aftermath by describing one last twist. We have seen that although the set of counting numbers and the set of real numbers are both infinite, the latter is a bigger infinity than the former. This leaves us with an interesting question: is there an infinity between these two infinities? Is there a set of numbers that is bigger than the set of counting numbers but smaller than the set of real numbers? This was a question Cantor pondered for decades. Many times he thought he could prove that such a set existed, only to find a flaw in the proof. He also thought, on occasion, that he had proved that there was no such set.[22] It was a frustratingly indeterminate state of affairs.

The question about the sizes of infinite sets morphed into what became known as the *continuum hypothesis*, according to which there was no set bigger than the counting numbers but smaller than the real numbers. Either proving or disproving this hypothesis became a major concern of mathematicians; indeed, it was significant enough to make the top of Hilbert's list of twenty-three unsolved problems. (Hilbert, by the way, described Cantor's work on infinity as "the most astonishing product of mathematical thought, one of the most beautiful realizations of human activity in the domain of the purely intelligible."[23])

The question was finally answered in 1963, when Paul J. Cohen proved that the continuum hypothesis could not be proved. He also proved that it couldn't be disproved! He proved, in other words, that it is an example of what mathematicians call an *independent statement*. Standard axiomatizations of set theory—ones that have been reformulated to avoid triggering the paradox that Russell found—are compatible with the continuum hypothesis being either true or false. A proof that the continuum hypothesis was true would have afforded a mathematician a first-rate aha moment, as would a proof that it was false. It was Cohen's luck, though, to experience what might be called a *double anti-aha moment*: he proved that neither proof was possible.

And how did this moment feel? Somewhat different from the other aha moments I have described. Cohen says, "I feel very strongly that great mathematics...is simple and comes as a flash." It appears, however, that his own discovery regarding the continuum hypothesis involved not a single insight but an insightful period. His breakthrough idea was to use a mathematical technique known as *forcing*, but he didn't experience instant bliss, for the simple reason that, as he puts it, "I didn't know what I had." It was only after further work that he concluded, "My God, this thing [forcing] is crazy, but it actually seems to work." But even at this point, he wasn't convinced that his proof was correct. Consequently, when famed mathematician Kurt Gödel approved of his proof, Cohen experienced "an incredible relief."[24]

And yet, there was an emotional component to Cohen's discovery process: "I can only say, at the risk of being a little bit overly emotional, that it was frightening, almost, when I did my own work, when suddenly I could construct all these universes [through the use of forcing]. I just couldn't believe it, that you could do this much." He adds, "I suddenly felt that I had understood things no one had ever seen."[25] It was, one imagines, a wonderful moment to have experienced.

PART FIVE

The Aha Moment in the Arts

CHAPTER 13

Lots of Little Ahas

IN THE 1970S, DANIEL S. GODFREY was working on a Ph.D. in music composition at the University of Iowa when the Tanglewood Music Center gave him an important commission. By fulfilling this commission, he would not only meet one of the more difficult requirements for his doctorate but would embark on what was, for young American composers, one of the most desirable career paths possible: it put him on the "stairway to Nirvana."[1]

After working on the composition for nearly a year, though, he had gotten nowhere. Two months before the Tanglewood deadline, he informed the center of the situation. They graciously extended the deadline by a year, but it was no use: Godfrey remained creatively blocked. He finally gave up and made arrangements with Tanglewood to pay back his advance. He had, in a very public way, blown the opportunity of a young composer's dreams. "It was," as he recalled, "the most humiliating thing." Godfrey then turned his attention simply to finishing his Ph.D., but by now he was so demoralized that he spent another year in a state of creative paralysis.

At this point, he got a shot at redemption: Steven Schick, a conductor who was not directly connected to Tanglewood, offered him a commission to write a percussion piece. He took a stab at writing it, but whatever he put down on paper seemed silly. "It was painful," he says. "I had headaches and nausea, and part of me was writing the music, while another part of me was saying, 'You can't do this, this stinks, this is no good.'" Then he had an important aha moment: "I realized that some composers who were getting significant attention were writing music without a lot of creativity or intelligence. I knew that at the very least I wasn't stupid—that even if I pursued what seemed like a really dumb idea, I could do something intelligent with it."[2] No longer held back by the voice of his inner critic, he forged ahead and finished the piece, thereby completing a requirement for his dissertation. The resulting piece was well received. He went on to have a successful career, both as a composer and teacher.

Godfrey's story is instructive. Take a highly intelligent person with considerable musical talent and deprive him of musical inspiration. The music will not come. Or if it does come, it won't be "inspired"; it will merely be—groan!— "workmanlike." Indeed, in Godfrey's case, his intelligence seems to have been an impediment to his compositional ability. It was nipping in the bud whatever ideas his unconscious mind came up with.

THE QUESTION THAT CONFRONTS anyone attempting to produce a work of art is where to begin. A painter who completed a painting the day before walks into her studio. Before her is a blank canvas. How should she fill it? A novelist, faced with the declining sales of his previous book, decides to write another. He turns on his computer and rests his fingers on the keyboard. What story will he tell?

Composers also encounter this problem. Frederick Delius reported that "I, myself, am entirely at a loss to explain how I compose—I know only that at first I conceive a work suddenly, thro' a feeling."[3] Tchaikovsky's *Sixth Symphony* was inspired by a musical theme that suddenly appeared in his head.[4] In other cases, a musical composition is based on an involuntary mental image. Igor Stravinsky, for example, described "a fleeting vision which came to me as a complete surprise, my mind at the moment being full of other things. I saw in imagination a solemn pagan rite; sage elders, seated in a circle, watched a young girl dance herself to death. They were sacrificing her to propitiate the god of spring."[5] The "Rite of Spring" he visualized translated into one of the great musical works of the century. Novels can also begin in images. Michael Ondaatje said that his novel *The English Patient* was inspired, in part, by a mental image of a thief stealing a photograph of himself.[6]

Sometimes the inspiration that sets an artistic journey in motion is powerful enough to carry it to its destination. While traveling on a ship, poet Robert Nichols (1893–1944) experienced an excruciatingly painful duodenal ulcer. One morning, when the pain had subsided, he forced himself to leave his cabin and go up on deck. It was then that he noticed that "a tiny voice within was saying: 'You're in fine fettle, so refreshed, that undoubtedly a poem will be waiting for you.

By and large I'd say that it will probably be about the rising sun.'" Nichols's initial reaction was to argue, mentally, with this inner voice: "Now look here, . . . can't you leave a fellow alone awhile? I'm hearty, but not as hearty as all that." But the voice was insistent: "Enjoy the illusion of liberty if you will and can. Remember however that the sun will soon be highest above the horizon and that, once it is, the light will be of quite a different quality. Get out there as soon as you can."

Watching the light of the newly risen sun reflect on the ocean swells, Nichols experienced an extraordinary sense of physical exhilaration, followed by a moment of poetic inspiration: "'Of course!' I said to myself—'Arabic.' It was at that moment . . . that I understood I had only to yield to the emotion evoked by what I beheld to discover a poem." And indeed, a few moments later, "there formed in my mouth the line 'The sun an ancient, serene poet.'" As he stood on deck, the rest of the poem was delivered to him by the inner voice, one line at a time,[7] and within twenty minutes, his twenty-eight-line "Sunrise Poem" was complete.

Cases like this are unusual, though. After realizing what her work is going to be about, an artist is typically faced with a series of difficult decisions. Consider the predicament of an artist who has been commissioned to paint a portrait. She knows who her subject is, but she is left with the task of filling a blank canvas with paint. Before she can do anything, she needs to come up with an artistic vision for the portrait. She needs, in particular, to decide on the background for the portrait, the way the subject will be posed, what the subject will be wearing and holding, and of course, the style in which the portrait will be painted. The artist will likely rely on inspiration, in the form of artistic gut feelings, to help her make these artistic choices.

The painter will then have an idea of where she is headed, but she won't yet know what the portrait will end up looking like. When she is putting paint on the canvas, she isn't simply making a copy of a picture that is already in her head; she is instead trying to discover a picture while creating one. This discovery will be made through an extended process of experimentation. She will probably do some sketches to see which composition works best. She will then try things on canvas to see what works. She will repaint things that don't work and retain things that do.

For novelist Michael Ondaatje, having the mental image of a thief stealing a picture of himself was the easy part. To turn this initial inspiration into a novel, he had to decide when and where his novel would be set; what characters would populate it, how they would relate to each other, what their back stories would be, what they would look like, and what personalities they would have; which character, if any, would be the narrator of the story; what events would take place; and what style the novel would be written in. He would also have to decide the structure of the novel: would he, for example, simply offer a chronological account of what happened or would flashbacks be more effective?

Even when these decisions had been made, many questions would remain. Where would the chapter breaks be? What paragraphs would be in those chapters, and what words would be in those paragraphs? Unskilled writers are content simply to put words on paper; skilled writers, though, take every sentence they write to be a little puzzle that needs to be solved. What are the best words to use, and in what order?

To make things more complicated, the choices a novelist makes in one place will affect the choices he can and should make at other places. The whole novel ends up resembling an incredibly convoluted puzzle that he will spend his working days trying to solve.

IN OUR DISCUSSION OF MATHEMATICS, we saw that inspiration usually strikes in the form of what might be called a thunderbolt aha moment, in which a mathematician has a single important insight that lets him solve the problem he is working on. This sort of thing can happen in art, but according to composer Jonathan Harvey, "the experience of musical inspiration...is generally more complex and varied than the 'thunderbolt' image would lead us to believe. It is rare for a single moment to supply the inspiration needed for an entire work, unless the work is very short."[8]

Instead of one grand aha moment, then, an artist must typically rely on a long chain of little aha moments to guide him. On experiencing one of them, the artist is not likely to cry out, "Eureka! I have found it!" Instead, he might pause and mutter, "Hmmm...that seems to work." In other words, rather than experiencing ecstasy, an artist will experience at best a momentary feeling of satisfaction, combined with a feeling of relief at having cleared another small step on a long creative stairway.

If an author does experience a major aha moment while writing a novel, it is likely to be what I call an anti-aha moment—a sudden realization that she has been doing something wrong. Along these lines, Booker Prize–winning novelist Hilary Mantel had reached an impasse in the novel she was working on: how could she possibly fit in everything that she needed to? During a shower, she had an important aha moment: "It's two books!"[9]

Mantel was lucky, inasmuch as her insight allowed her to keep all the work she had done: it became *Wolf Hall* and *Bring Up the Bodies*. In other cases, though, an author is forced to abandon thousands of written words. This was the plight of novelist Kate Christensen. It took her two years of writing to figure out what her first novel was *really* about, at which point her 150-page manuscript had to undergo radical surgery.

It may seem odd that an artist can, in response to an initial inspiration, embark on a project only to discover that the inspiration was a false lead. Why would an artist embark on a project when she wasn't really sure what the project was? Because that is the only way for artists to proceed!

ASK A NOVELIST WHAT HE SPENDS his time doing, and he will likely answer that he spends some of it writing but much more time revising what he has already written. Thus, a writer might try several words at a particular point in a sentence before finding the one that works best. He will realize that, as Mark Twain put it, the difference between the almost right word and the right word is as big as the difference between a lightning bug and lightning. He will also fiddle with entire sentences in an attempt to improve them. Nobel laureate Orhan Pamuk tells of rewriting the first line of a novel fifty to one hundred times. Readers might think this level of fastidiousness sort of makes sense: the first sentence will create, after all, the reader's first impression of the novel. But then we are told that novelist Amitav Gosh rewrites *every sentence* at least twenty times. Successful writers are, almost without exception, compulsive *re*writers.

Besides fiddling with individual words and sentences, novelists will spend time experimenting with the structure of their novel. They might move material—maybe even whole chapters—around to see what arrangement works best. They might test a character's contribution to a moment in the story by removing him from a scene to see what happens—Michael Ondaatje has done this. And Booker Prize–winning author Kazuo Ishiguro, on figuring out who the characters in a novel are, uses "auditions" to determine which character gets to play the role of first-person narrator. To do this, he writes different versions of a few chapters, with different characters taking the role of narrator, to see what works best.[10]

Sometimes, an author will conclude that where a chapter really belongs is in the waste basket. The willingness to discard material that doesn't work is a sign of literary maturity. Indeed, a mature author will be willing to discard sentences, paragraphs, or chapters that she worked long and hard to write, and that *do* in some sense work—just not as well as they might. She will be willing, as the saying goes, to kill her darlings.[11] She will eliminate material that is merely good so she can wind up with material that is better than good. She will agree with Ernest Hemingway's assertion that "the test of a book is how much good stuff you can throw away."[12]

What are we to make of all this rewriting? Why can't novelists simply write down what they have to say and be done with it? Novelists would love to be able to do this: it would result in an incredible increase in their productivity. The problem is that this way of writing simply doesn't work. Imagine a writer who decided to follow the mind-to-paper-to-publisher route. He would think long and hard before writing down any words, so that thereafter he would not have to change them. He would doubtless be a very long time sitting, with precious little to show for it. He would, in other words, be vastly less productive than if he used, as almost every writer does, a process of trial and error: try things, keep what works, and discard what doesn't.

Many people have the idea that poets write their poems in a single sitting, by taking dictation, as it were, from their muse. As we shall see in the next chapter, this sort of thing can happen. Most of the time, though, poets rewrite as compulsively as novelists do. Consider again Robert Nichols. As we have seen, his "Sunrise Poem" took him only twenty minutes to write. This makes it sound like instant poetry, but we need to realize that a good part of that twenty minutes was spent fiddling with the choice of words and their location within the poem. Realize, too, that the poem was not very long and that Nichols doesn't tell us what tweaking might have taken place after the poem was "finished."

Along similar lines, Lord Byron—a poet's poet if ever there was one—felt compelled to rewrite. Manuscripts of his poems reveal that the first words he put to paper, in the process of writing a poem, had little chance of making it into the final draft of that poem.[13] Samuel Taylor Coleridge also understood the importance, after words had flowed from his pen, of taking a second look at them. Poetry, he said, has "a logic of its own as severe as that of science; and more difficult, because more subtle, more complex, and dependent on more and more fugitive causes. In the truly great poets . . . there is a reason assignable, not only for every word, but for the position of every word."[14]

Musical composers also find it necessary to revise extensively. Composer Steve Reich reports that 95 percent of his compositions require a lot of revising and trashing of material.[15] Composer James Mobberley estimates that only 2 percent of his time is spent coming up with an idea and that the other 98 percent is spent tweaking, reworking, and extending that idea. "It's funny," he says, "how some ideas can take a minute to come up with, then six months to execute."[16]

Choreographers likewise revise the moves in a dance they are creating. What makes a choreographer's revision process tricky is that the best way to see if dance moves work is to have dancers try them out. And while he has the assistance of these dancers, he needs to be ready to make changes on the spot. According to Andy Blankenbuehler, choreographer for the 2012 revival of *Annie*, "bringing something simple in art to an audience is very complicated. You have to make your mistakes. You have to understand why it doesn't work to get you to what does work."[17]

Likewise, a playwright might revise a play many, many times before turning it over to a theatrical company, but some of the play's shortcomings will become apparent only when he watches it being rehearsed. He will then have an opportunity to correct these shortcomings but will have to make the corrections under a tight deadline and under the watchful eyes of many people. It is one thing to create; it is quite another to have to create *now*.

Painters are also revisers. In much the same way as novelists might experiment with the characters in their novel, a painter might experiment with the figures in a painting. Consider Rembrandt's 1662 *Syndics of the Drapers' Guild*, which depicts five drapers and a servant. X-ray studies reveal that Rembrandt tried four different positions for the servant on the canvas before finding the one that worked. The rejects were simply painted over.[18] This is an example of what art historians call a *pentimento*, an Italian word that is derived from the verb *pentirsi*, meaning to repent. In preliminary sketches for a painting, the process of artistic trial and error will be obvious: we might see the same figure drawn in different ways. In a painting, though, it will usually take high-tech equipment to reveal the "repentances" an artist experienced in the production of the work.

Besides making corrections in part of a work, painters are perfectly capable of painting over an entire canvas and starting it again—and again. In the early 1960s, writer James Lord sat for a portrait by painter and sculptor Alberto Giacometti. Lord took notes on Giacometti's artistic process, with the plan of perhaps writing an article about it. The result was instead the book *A Giacometti Portrait*. Lord had assumed that the portrait would take only one or two sittings to complete, but he was quite mistaken. Giacometti kept ending sessions, not with a finished portrait but by instructing Lord to come back again. In the subsequent meeting, Giacometti would paint out much or all of what he had done during the previous sitting because it wasn't what he wanted. By their seventeenth meeting, the paint was so thick on the canvas, from all the painting over, that it was becoming difficult to apply more paint.

Finally Lord, who had repeatedly delayed his flight back to New York, could delay no longer. On what was supposed to be their final meeting, Giacometti again announced that he was going to start over. But instead of painting over the portrait, he kept working on it. It was at this point that Lord, who wanted *something* to result from all this posing, devised a plan. He by now was thoroughly familiar with Giacometti's artistic process: he could tell, by his choice of brushes and colors, what stage of the creative process Giacometti was in. More important, he knew that when Giacometti was adding highlights, it was a sign that the creative process was drawing to an end. He also knew that in the past, this had been the point at which the destructive process would begin.

During this session, though, when Giacometti reached this point, Lord announced that he needed a rest from posing. He stood up and went over to look at the painting. "It was superb. . . . Never before had the picture looked just as it did then, and it had never looked better. I said, 'It looks fine. Why not leave it as it is now?'" Giacometti agreed but complained, "It's too bad. We'd only started. We could have gone on for a long time."[19]

If this behavior seems obsessive, realize that compared to Leonardo da Vinci, Giacometti was speedy. Leonardo spent over ten years on his *Leda* and on his *St. John*, and over twelve years on his *St. Anne*. He spent "only" four years on his masterpiece, the thirty-by-twenty-one-inch *Mona Lisa*. But in thinking about these time spans, it is important to keep in mind that, according to Vasari, Leonardo never regarded his paintings as "finished."[20]

When is a work of art finished? In most cases, not when it has reached a state of perfection but when the artist is unable to think of any way to make it better.

ARTISTS AND MATHEMATICIANS are often taken to be polar opposites, intellectually speaking: artists are the ultimate right-brain people, and mathematicians are the ultimate left-brain people—although research suggests that there is less to the right-brain/left-brain distinction than once was thought.[21] It turns out, though, that artists and mathematicians have a lot in common.

In our discussion of the mathematical aha moment, we found that one of the things that motivates mathematicians is the austere beauty of a mathematical proof. We might think that mathematical beauty was different from artistic beauty, but recent research suggests otherwise. Neurologists did an experiment in which they asked fifteen mathematicians to rate the beauty of various equations. They discovered that when mathematicians found an equation to be beautiful, the same part of their brain was activated as when they found a work of art to be beautiful.[22]

If we watch their working routines, we will notice another striking similarity between mathematicians and artists. Both spend their days trying things in an attempt to find something that works. Most of the things they try don't work, but they nevertheless benefit from their failed attempts: they learn important lessons that can help them find what does work. The biggest difference between mathematicians and artists is in how they determine whether or not something "works." Mathematicians can prove that something does or doesn't work; artists must rely on their aesthetic sense to make this determination, and this sense is quite subjective.

Most mathematicians would be comfortable hearing their workday routine characterized as involving a process of trial and error. Artists, one suspects, would be less comfortable with this characterization. In going through their extensive revision process, they might claim, they aren't simply using trial and error to solve artistic problems; they are instead waiting for inspiration to strike—waiting, some would say, for their muse to pay them a visit. An artist might go on to describe how emotionally difficult her work is and then add that it is a price she is willing to pay, for the sake of her art.

I would like to suggest that both the mathematician and the artist use a process of trial and error and that both require moments of inspiration for their work to progress. Furthermore, the process of trial and error is what makes these moments of inspiration possible. By trying things in a search for something that works, a person is using his conscious mind to solve a problem. By employing his conscious mind in this manner, the person can get his unconscious mind interested in the problem. He can then benefit from the process of incubation, which I described in my discussion of mathematical aha moments. With luck, his unconscious mind will start supplying him with ideas on how to solve the problem or maybe even supply him with the perfect solution to the problem. It is a technique that works, regardless of whether the problem in question is mathematical or artistic.

In the introduction to this book, I told the story of Gustav Mahler's breakthrough aha moment in the composition of his *Seventh Symphony*. He had just gotten into a boat, and on the first stroke of the oars, his mind filled with the musical theme that he needed. After that, progress on the symphony was rapid. This sounds like magic—like he had won the musical lottery—but had he not previously spent time and energy trying, unsuccessfully, to write the symphony, it is unlikely that inspiration would have struck. Mahler's conscious effort triggered unconscious incubation, which in turn yielded his aha moment.

We have seen that mathematicians can solve difficult problems in their sleep. So can composers. Daniel S. Godfrey describes spending twelve hours trying to solve a composition problem before collapsing, completely distraught, at one o'clock in the morning. After five hours of sleep, he woke up, only to realize that his problem had been solved: "Of course. How obvious! This is the way the piece should go."[23] Mahler was also capable of composing in his sleep. Progress on his *Third Symphony* came to a standstill until a voice in a dream instructed him to "let the horns come in three measures later!" It was, he said, "the most wonderfully simple solution of my difficulty!"[24] And what if a composer needs inspiration in the middle of the day? A nap, says Aaron Jay Kernis, might come in handy.[25]

THE BIGGEST ARTISTIC PAYOFF is when a project comes alive for an artist. When this happens, an artist can experience unconscious incubation—on steroids. When writers begin a novel, they typically have to tell their characters what to do and say. The hope is that by bossing characters around in this manner, the novelist can make them "come alive," at which point they will take control and start telling the novelist what they are going to do and say. This makes it much easier for the novelist to proceed since he is, in a sense, just taking dictation. If it sounds strange that fictional characters would start dictating plot and dialogue to a novelist, realize that even non-novelists experience this phenomenon nearly every night. We have dreams in which people appear, speak, and act. We have no control over who shows up in our dreams, or what they say or do. When they are deep in a novel, artists seem to trigger a waking version of this same phenomenon.

When a project comes alive, artistic productivity can skyrocket. Novelist Irving Wallace describes his sprint to the finish at the end of his novel *The Prize*: "As I came nearer and nearer to the climax and to the end, I wrote more and more steadily, entirely absorbed, totally pulled, and I started passing up meals, limiting my time with my family, canceling social engagements." He says that he wrote the last chapter of the book with such intensity that he completed its 127 pages in only six days. By way of contrast, in his early work on this novel, he worked six or seven hours a day, and on one day out of five, would finish the day without a single page of writing to show for it.[26] What a difference the participation of the unconscious mind makes!

ARTISTS RELY ON VISITS from their muse (which in fact resides in their unconscious mind) to make their living. The problem is that muses are not very reliable. They don't always respond to invitations, preferring instead to stop by on a whim. On some days they show up, brimming with great ideas. Then, without warning, they disappear for days or even weeks, leaving artists with ravaged self-confidence and precious little to show for their efforts.

Many an artist has pondered this predicament. Wouldn't it be wonderful if there was something an artist could do to improve his relationship with his muse and thereby encourage visits from her? In the next chapter, we will explore some of the ways—including the use of drugs and alcohol—in which artists have attempted to do this.

CHAPTER 14

On Managing One's Muse

BEING AN ARTIST is like trying to run a restaurant with unreliable employees. Some days the waiters show up; other days they don't. Some days the chef works her whole shift; other days she arrives only to announce that she will have to leave in an hour to attend her daughter's birthday party. The restaurant owner will spend his days trying desperately to get the customers fed.

Because they can't count on inspiration showing up as needed, artists often experience work-related anxiety. Novelist Joan Didion, for example, describes the "low dread" she experiences each morning as she contemplates the day of writing that awaits her.[1] Novelist Kate Christensen often deals with the start of her workday by delaying it: she might play thirty games of solitaire before attempting her first sentence of the day.[2]

Christensen isn't alone among writers in resorting to procrastination. Journalist Megan McArdle experienced enough of it herself that she decided to do some research. She asked a colleague how he managed to turn out well-written eight-thousand-word features on deadline. His response: "Well, first, I put it off for two or three weeks. Then I sit down to write. That's when I get up and go clean the garage. After that, I go upstairs, and then I come back downstairs and complain to my wife for a couple of hours. Finally, but only after a couple more days have passed and I'm really freaking out about missing my deadline, I ultimately sit down and write." As McArdle observes, "most writers manage to get by because, as the deadline creeps closer, their fear of turning in nothing eventually surpasses their fear of turning in something terrible."[3]

It is one thing to procrastinate when you have all the time in the world to do something. If an artist is on deadline, though, procrastination will likely make an artistic undertaking much more difficult. This is because artists who rush the creative process won't have time enough to take advantage of incubation, meaning that their conscious mind will have to do the job all by itself. The end product will, in many cases, be uninspired.

TO BECOME A GREAT ARTIST, one must undertake challenging works, and what makes a work challenging is the artistic problems that must be overcome to complete it. This means that an artist who aspires to greatness will almost certainly encounter problems that bring his work to a standstill. He might spend a day trying, unsuccessfully, to solve a problem. If he is a mature artist, he will know from experience that artistic tenacity can pay off. He will therefore continue to hammer away at the problem, for another day, followed by yet another.

Suppose, though, that despite resolute hammering, the problem resists solution not for a matter of days, but for weeks, months, or even years—as was the case with Daniel Godfrey and his Tanglewood commission. After experiencing such a dry spell, an artist might become despondent. Composer Carl Maria von Weber certainly did: "Shall I ever again find a single thought within me? Now there is nothing—nothing. I feel as if I had never composed a note in my life, and that the operas could never have been really mine."[4]

In making this last comment, by the way, Weber might have been manifesting what psychologists call *imposter syndrome*. People with this syndrome feel that their successes aren't genuine—that they have simply gotten lucky or that they have somehow faked their way to success. It might seem odd that a highly accomplished artist like Weber would think such a thing. Then again, he knew how hard it was for him to do what he did. He also knew how often he had been bailed out of a tight spot by an unpredictable and inexplicable aha moment. If Weber didn't realize that his fellow artists were in this same situation, he might conclude that, unlike them, he wasn't a true artist.

It is bad enough that artists have to cope with the absence of an inspirational voice that provides them with solutions to their artistic problems. In many cases, though, they also have to cope with the presence of a critical voice that ridicules whatever ideas they come up with. We saw that Daniel Godfrey had this problem. So does composer Aaron Jay Kernis, who reports, "The first couple of weeks with any piece are the hardest, because I usually hate everything I come up with."[5]

Likewise, composer Libby Larsen complains not only about hating every note in a work she is writing but about hating the fact that she hates it.[6] It requires tremendous artistic courage to carry on under these circumstances, in the hope that the critical voice will finally be assuaged.

Because an act of will can't make the inspirational voice speak or muzzle the critical voice, artists' work can have a nightmarish aspect, and the frustration of their struggles with the absent muse or the outspoken inner critic can spill over into the rest of their lives. To deal with the pressures brought on by their attempts to create, artists might resort to drink or drugs during their off hours, and they might become abusive to the people around them.

IS THERE ANYTHING AN ARTIST CAN DO to increase his chances of being artistically inspired? It turns out that there is, but it comes at a price that many would-be artists will be unwilling to pay: they will have to live their artistic lives in accordance with the "Knickerbocker Rule."

Writer Richard Rhodes was introduced to this rule while working on Hallmark Cards' daily employee newspaper. His boss, one Conrad Knickerbocker, had published a bit of fiction on the side. Rhodes asked him what he had to do to become a "real" writer, one who wrote books rather than newspaper columns. Knickerbocker replied, "You apply ass to chair."[7] In other words, to become a writer, you must spend a lot of time writing, and to be a writer, you must do more of the same. You must spend lots of time putting words on paper, and then moving those words around and replacing them, until you can't think of a better way for them to be situated. Do this and, if you have some talent, you will be a writer.

The common belief, says novelist Irving Wallace, is that "a writer writes only when he feels like it, only when he is touched by mystic inspiration." When we look at successful novelists, though, we find that they work long hours: Gustave Flaubert worked seven hours a day, Joseph Conrad eight, and Somerset Maugham four. And not only do novelists spend many hours writing, but when they are working on a book, they tend to work every day of the week.[8] We think of Ernest Hemingway as someone who liked to eat, drink, fish, and hunt. But besides doing these things, he wrote for six hours each day. What about the days he took off to fish? He would, in essence, put in a double shift the day before.

Hemingway's daily work quota, by the way, was about five hundred words.[9] A skilled typist could have typed those words in ten minutes, and yet it took Hemingway six hours to write them—an average rate of about a word a minute! So what was he doing during the other five hours and fifty minutes of his workday? He was engaged in the kind of trial and error I described in the previous chapter. He was writing words, sentences, and paragraphs only to delete them. He was sitting there waiting for inspiration to strike—or in his case, maybe standing there, since he sometimes wrote standing up. He also spent time altering or throwing out material that had previously passed muster.

Most people have an externally imposed schedule of working hours to tell them when their workday starts and ends. This is not the case with artists. There is no boss breathing down their necks and checking their timecards. This means that it takes self-discipline to do art, but self-discipline is a trait that even mature artists have trouble with. As a result, they might resort to drastic measures to keep themselves at work. When, for example, Victor Hugo was up against a deadline, we are told that he would give his clothes to his valet with instructions not to bring them back until the story he was working on was finished.[10]

Like novelists, composers must obey the Knickerbocker Rule if they are to succeed. Bright Sheng compares writing music to running an antiques shop: "You have to keep the shop open every day. Some days nobody comes, but you still have to be there. Once in a while somebody comes in and purchases a precious object for a large amount of money. If you are not there that day, you will not make the sale. It's very important to be mentally ready to receive when the inspiration comes."[11]

Suppose an artist has a bad day at the "antiques shop": she spends several hours working on a project with no creative output to show for it. Does it make sense to protract her frustration for a few more hours? It is understandable that she would want to "leave work early."

An artist with self-discipline will have strategies for dealing with such days. She might, for example, have several projects in the works at any one time. If she hits a creative wall with respect to one of them, she will turn her attention to another. This is what Giacometti did: during the time he was working on his portrait of James Lord, he was also working on a sculpture.[12] Scientists employ a similar technique for coping with frustration: they work on many research projects at the same time, so that when they are stymied on one, they can turn their attention to another.

In some cases, an artist might leave work a bit early one day for a legitimate reason—namely, to ensure that the next day has a good start, artistically speaking. She will quit for the day just after inspiration has struck, leaving her with an idea of what she must do next to advance the project she is working on. By quitting at that point, she will have something to do when she shows up for work the next day. Not only that, but the "something" in question might benefit from having been slept on. By doing this, she can avoid the kind of pre-work anxiety I described above.

AT THIS POINT, SOME OBSERVATIONS are in order about artists' use of drink and drugs. It is easy to come up with examples of such artists, particularly among writers. Hemingway was an alcoholic, as was Norman Mailer. Jack Kerouac used Benzedrine in order to write. Hunter S. Thompson not only used a wide variety of drugs while writing but wrote about using drugs while writing. And of course the Romantic poets of the nineteenth century were famous for their use of opium. On hearing of such cases, it is easy to assume that they are a representative sample of writers. We need to keep in mind, though, that we hear about these cases because they are dramatic. We don't hear about all the artists who soberly turned out great bodies of inspired work—about the regular hours they kept and the wild parties they didn't attend. It is therefore a mistake to assume that most or even many artists have drinking or drug problems.

Whenever we hear about great writers who were alcoholics, we need to ask two questions. First, when in the day did they do their drinking, while they were working or afterward? Lots of writers who drank did so after they had finished working; this is what Hemingway did. We would find the same thing, of course, if instead of looking at writers we looked at lawyers, brain surgeons, or factory workers. Second, at what stage of their career did they do their drinking? Many artists with reputations for being alcoholics didn't start their careers that way. In some cases, they were led to drink excessively by the pressures brought on by the literary success they enjoyed as young, sober artists.

By way of illustration, consider Norman Mailer. To write his first novel, *The Naked and the Dead*, he worked four days a week. On those days, he would wake up at eight or eight-thirty and be at his typewriter at ten. At twelve-thirty, he would break for lunch and then work for two more hours. He admitted to indulging in a mid-afternoon beer, but it isn't clear whether this was before or after he had quit writing for the day. Thanks to his work ethic, he managed to turn out, on average, seven typewritten pages a day.[13] Drinking seems to have become a problem only after the success of *The Naked and the Dead*.

Now consider the process by which Jack Kerouac wrote *On the Road*. It was written on a 112-foot roll of teletype paper, fed into a typewriter. This unorthodox manuscript—which in 2001 was sold at auction for \$2.4 million—was completed in only three weeks, a feat that was possible because Kerouac spent them buzzed on Benzedrine.

Kerouac's creation tale is, I think you will agree, vastly more interesting than Mailer's. His tale is also mostly fictional, though. For one thing, there was a lot more to the creative process, both before and after his three-week stint at the typewriter, than Kerouac let on.[14] Also, it isn't clear how much Benzedrine was used in the making of *On the Road*—lots of coffee, for sure, but maybe not so much Benzedrine. And why would Kerouac allow such a story to be told? Because it makes it sound like he has remarkable creative ability. It is the literary equivalent of a painter claiming to have painted a detailed landscape in under twenty minutes or while blindfolded. What remarkable talent!

We readers don't want our novelists to keep regular working hours. We don't want to think of them sitting at a desk, tapping away at a keyboard as if they were secretaries. We instead want them to have complex lives, punctuated by astonishing creative outbursts. It is also fine with us if they suffer to produce their art. And so, some novelists, besides obliging us by coming up with stories about the characters in their novels, are perfectly willing to further oblige us by coming up with stories about their creative process.

BECAUSE THEY DON'T UNDERSTAND the comings and goings of inspiration, artists can be superstitious about their working conditions. French novelist Colette would write only with pens with Flamant No. 2 nibs.[15] Rudyard Kipling was also picky about his writing implement: he could not write with a pencil but needed a pen with the blackest ink obtainable. If possible, he preferred that the ink had been freshly made by an ink boy.[16] Novelist William Styron liked to write longhand on yellow pads with a Venus Velvet No. 2 pencil.[17] Vladimir Nabokov wrote his posthumously published novel, *The Original of Laura*, on index cards.[18]

Some writers can write almost anywhere. Other writers care very much about their writing environment. Friedrich Schiller liked to compose poetry surrounded by the scent of rotten apples.[19] French novelist Georges Simenon wrote in an office at his home. The room had a "Do Not Disturb" sign on the door, and inside, things had to be just so. On the day he began a new novel, the room had to be stocked with a pot of coffee and a freshly cleaned pipe; four dozen freshly sharpened new pencils and a new pad of yellowish paper; a freshly cleaned typewriter; a pile of railway guides; and an envelope with the names, ages, and addresses of his characters. And while he was writing, the curtains of the room had to be drawn.[20]

Simenon realized that in being obsessive about his work environment, he was indulging in superstition. The fact that he succeeded in penning two hundred novels, though, suggests that he benefited from this indulgence: believing that he would be more creative in a certain environment somehow enabled him to be more creative. More generally, if an artist is convinced that he is incapable of doing inspired work, it almost guarantees that he won't do any. If, however, he believes that inspiration is possible, he significantly increases his chance of experiencing it.

Simenon, with his coffee and his pipe, was not alone among novelists who relied on stimulants in order to work. Honoré de Balzac appears to have needed only coffee, but lots of it and very strong. Indeed, he liked it as strong as it can possibly be made—without any water added! He would simply eat the grounds—or so he would have us believe.[21]

Besides being affected by their work environment, writers' creativity can be affected by what they do in their off hours. Along these lines, Ray Bradbury advises his fellow novelists not just to read poetry but to read it every day. "Poetry is good," he says, "because it flexes muscles you don't use often enough. Poetry expands the senses and keeps them in prime condition. It keeps you aware of your nose, your eye, your ear, your tongue, your hand." And what poetry in particular should novelists read? "Any poetry that makes your hair stand up along your arms."[22]

ASPIRING ARTISTS WILL NATURALLY LOOK to established artists for guidance on how to be creative. Some would-be artists will be lucky enough to be exposed, early in their career, to the Knickerbocker Rule and will subsequently try to follow it in their artistic endeavors. Many more, though, will look for a shortcut to artistic excellence, one that doesn't require them to work hard and endure frustration. One such shortcut, they might think, is to imitate the workday idiosyncrasies of their favorite artist. A would-be novelist, for example, might stop using a word processor in favor of fountain pens with a certain color ink. Other artists will imitate not their favorite artist's workday idiosyncrasies but his recreational activities.

They might start drinking heavily on the assumption that this is where their artistic model derives his inspiration. This assumption is dangerous, though, since as we have seen, it is quite possible that their model doesn't drink to become inspired; he drinks because inspiration has failed him.

Young, aspiring artists are exposed to the work of the greats who have preceded them and are told that these artists needed both talent and inspiration to accomplish what they did. In many cases, though, art students aren't told about the frustration even great artists likely had to experience before they found inspiration. They aren't told, in other words, about the days spent with nothing to show for them, or even worse, the days spent undoing previous days' labor. This is unfortunate, since no amount of posing as one's favorite novelist or painter can allow one to bypass this inevitable, unglamorous part of pursuing a career as an artist.

IN *ZEN AND THE ART OF WRITING*, Ray Bradbury explains that he doesn't actually believe in the existence of muses; for him, *muse* is just a fancy word for "subconscious mind."[23] Nevertheless, he includes a chapter titled "How to Keep and Feed a Muse." Other artists also know muses don't exist but choose to think in terms of them anyway—and with good reason, as we shall see.

In ancient Greece, there were said to be nine muses. Among them were Calliope, the muse of epic poetry, and Terpsichore, the muse of dance. Other muses were connected with what we moderns would not classify as art: consider Clio, the muse of history, and Urania, the muse of astronomy.

(There was, perhaps significantly, no muse of math.) People were perfectly willing to attribute artistic creativity not to an artist, but to the muse who had visited him. Thus, in his *Ion*, Plato tells us that "poets are simply inspired to utter that to which the Muse impels them." The ancient Romans, when thinking about artistic creativity, invoked the notion not of a muse, which was a kind of goddess, but of a genius, which was a kind of spirit. According to the Romans, if an artist was creative, it wasn't because *he* was a genius, it was because he had been visited by one.

Talk of muses raises a new question. Suppose we accept that humans lack the power to come up with creative breakthroughs and must instead turn to a goddess for them. We can then ask how a goddess comes up with *her* creative breakthroughs. Does she have to try? Does she have dry spells? Maybe that's why she fails to visit us—she has run out of material! Or is she simply a fountain of creative insights that pour forth without any effort on her part? If so, where do they come from? Do they just come out of thin air—by magic, as it were? These are interesting questions, and ones that ancient Greeks and Romans seem not to have asked.

This brings us back to the question of why artists would pretend to believe in muses. For one thing, it gives them a nonscientific and entertaining way to explain where their inspired ideas come from. It is also an explanation that has impressive literary credentials. But besides this justification, there is an important psychological benefit to be derived from believing in muses. An artist depends in her work on creative aha moments that might or might not arrive. It is easy for an artist, on unproductive days, to blame herself. Such blame, though, can be artistically debilitating. By "believing in" muses, an artist can place the blame elsewhere—on the muse who failed to show up for work.

Elizabeth Gilbert, although a successful novelist, has experienced the usual number of dry spells during her writing career. During one such spell, she fell into what she describes as a "pit of despair." She responded by speaking her mind to her imaginary muse:

> Listen, you thing, you and I both know that if this book isn't brilliant, that is not entirely my fault, right? Because you can see that I am putting everything I have into this. I don't have any more than this. So if you want it to be better, then you've got to show up and do your part of the deal, okay? But if you don't do that, you know what? The hell with it: I'm going to keep writing anyway because *that's my job.* And I would please like the record to reflect today that I showed up for my part of the job.[24]

This is clearly a mind game, but if playing it enables an artist to maintain her creative flow, so what?

IF IT'S NOT AN ACTUAL MUSE that comes to visit us and bestow on us our creative insights, then how *do* we arrive at artistic aha moments? We can find answers—or rather, partial answers—to this question in the psychology and neuroscience of art.

Consider music. From an evolutionary point of view, the ability to make it seems worse than useless. Notice, in particular, that if our ancestors on the savannas of Africa had gone around playing flutes or banging drums, they would have drawn attention to themselves that might have invited an attack by animals or by other, unfriendly humans.

At the same time, music is the source of great delight. The appeal of music seems to be universal. You can play Western music for Mafa farmers in the Extreme North region of Cameroon. They are sufficiently isolated that they have never been exposed to our music, and yet the first time they hear it, they will recognize it to have the same emotional content— happy, sad, and scared/fearful—as we do.[25] Not only that, but music is capable of delighting us at any age: even newborn babies appreciate it.[26]

Indeed, according to neuroscientist Istvan Molnar-Szakacs, brain imaging studies reveal that listening to music activates more of the brain than any other known stimulus. When you are listening to music, he says, "it's like the brain is on fire."[27] Neurologists have also determined that listening to music triggers the same part of the brain's reward circuitry as is involved in activities like eating and having sex, and that the reward is delivered in the form of the neurotransmitter dopamine.[28] One of the things the brain does, on being exposed to music, is predict what is going to happen next. It rewards us both when our prediction is correct and when, much to our surprise, it isn't.[29]

Besides working at an emotional level, music can work at an intellectual level, but for this to happen, an understanding of music theory is usually necessary. We saw in Chapter 5 how the moral code was an attempt to explain our moral sense. Music theory can be understood as an attempt to do something similar with music. Some music sounds good because of the way it triggers our emotions or teases our brain, and other music sounds bad. Music theory helps us predict what will and won't sound good. Many musical aha moments are the result of musicians realizing how, within the confines of music theory, they can accomplish a musically satisfying effect.

It would appear that we gained our ability to appreciate music by co-opting one of the brain's many systems without realizing that we were doing so: we took a system that evolved to enable us to do one thing and used it to do something else. We saw an example of this phenomenon in our discussion of math, when we explored the possibility that we gained our ability to do math by unwittingly tapping into the brain system that tells us how objects will look from different points of view. It is likewise possible, cognitive scientist Steven Pinker has suggested, that our ability to appreciate music is the result of our having co-opted part of our language processing ability. He states this thesis in blunt terms: "Music is auditory cheesecake. It just happens to tickle several important parts of the brain in a highly pleasurable way, as cheesecake tickles the palate."[30]

Neuroscientist Daniel Levitin has argued otherwise. He suggests, more precisely, that musical ability is adaptive: possessing it increases one's chances of reproducing. In support of this claim, he points to the sexual prowess of modern musicians. Perhaps the most memorable evidence he offers is the sexual experience of Robert Plant, lead singer for Led Zeppelin and generally acknowledged to be one of the gods of rock music. Plant reports that during his concert tours, when his band was at the peak of its popularity, "I was on my way to love. Always. Whatever road I took, the car was heading for one of the greatest sexual encounters I've ever had."[31]

To be sure, Levitin also offers other explanations for our musical ability. Furthermore, both Levitin and Pinker have modified their views on music since the debate between them broke out in 2006.[32]

BESIDES BENEFITING FROM A VISIT by their muse, artists can benefit from a mood disorder.[33] In particular, poets can benefit from manic-depressive illness.[34] For poets to be touched with madness is not a modern phenomenon. Indeed, according to Plato, "if a man comes to the door of poetry untouched by the madness of the Muses, believing that technique alone will make him a good poet, he and his sane compositions never reach perfection, but are utterly eclipsed by the performance of the inspired madman."[35]

Among the mad poets we find Percy Bysshe Shelley. "Mad Shelley" as he was called by his Eton schoolmates, seems to have suffered from manic-depressive illness, and as a result, apparently heard voices and saw visions.[36] Lord Byron, too, was called mad by his contemporaries. According to a friend, "the mind of Lord Byron was like a volcano, full of fire and wealth, sometimes calm, often dazzling and playful, but ever threatening. It ran swift as the lightning from one subject to another, and occasionally burst forth in passionate throes of intellect, nearly allied to madness."[37] In a manic state, Byron was able to write the poem *The Corsair* at an astonishing rate of more than two hundred lines a day.[38] This led critic John Ruskin to observe that "Byron wrote, as easily as a hawk flies."[39]

It isn't just poets who can benefit from bipolarity. Robert Schumann, in his manic phases, was spectacularly productive. Before taking an interest in music, he wrote seven novels in eighteen months; in 1840, he composed more than 130 songs; and in 1841, he wrote an entire symphony in four days. Apparently, he couldn't understand why doing this was in any way remarkable.[40] During these phases, Schumann reported that his mind was "always working" and that he was "so fresh in soul and spirit that life gushes and bubbles around me in a thousand springs. This is the work of divine fantasy and her magic wand."[41] Indeed, his mind was, if anything, too busy, causing him to complain, "Sometimes I am so full of music, and so overflowing with melody, that I find it simply impossible to write down anything."[42] Schumann arguably benefited from his mental illness. He also paid a price for it: he died in an insane asylum in 1856. Many artists and writers before and after Schumann have paid a price for the mood disorder that enabled them to create the works for which they are remembered. They are, in particular, rather more likely than other people to commit suicide.[43]

It is clear that being bipolar can benefit an artist. In the manic phase, he will be full of energy. He will probably need less sleep and while awake will want to work. He will be brimming with self-confidence that will enable him to overcome whatever artistic obstacles he encounters. Not only that, but a manic state will enable him to experience

combinatory thinking, in which seemingly incongruous per-
cepts, ideas, or images merge or are elaborated.[44] According
to Kay Redfield Jamison, who has written with great insight
about manic-depressive artists, manic states can result in "a
formidable combination of imagination, adventurousness,
and a restless, quick, and vastly associative mind."[45]

But then comes the depressive phase, during which the artist is likely to become critical of what he has done and edit it,
perhaps too severely. Fortunately, there is a good chance that
whatever damage is done in this phase can be corrected when
the artist is neither manic nor depressed. He can then put his
work into its final order.[46]

Medication makes it possible for artists who suffer from
manic-depressive illness to eliminate or at least moderate
mood swings, but it has some drawbacks. Artists complain, for example, that drugs to prevent manic behavior
put a "brake" on their creative abilities.[47] There have also
been cases in which artists on medication lose their ability
to paint, only to regain it when the medication dosage is
adjusted.[48]

ONE WAY TO DISCOVER the neurological source of artistic creativity would be to systematically tamper with various parts
of an artist's brain to see how her creativity is affected. For
obvious reasons, artists would be unlikely to volunteer as
subjects for such experiments. We must instead resort to
what are called *natural experiments* to obtain this information.
The subjects of these experiments are people whose brains

have been "tampered with," not by an experimenter but by disease or injury.

French organist and composer Jean Langlais inadvertently became the subject of one such experiment. He experienced a cerebral hemorrhage that interfered with his ability to speak, read, and write words, but not his ability to compose music. This rather curious mix of abilities and inabilities attests to the complexity of the way functions are distributed within the brain.[49] In another case, a painter, after suffering a left hemisphere infarct, lost the ability to do symbolic pictures but retained the ability to do realistic drawings.[50] This suggests that the left hemisphere of his brain, which is where language processing takes place, is also a source of symbolic thinking.

Besides altering already-existing artistic ability, brain disease and injury can apparently trigger an interest in art. In the first four decades of her life, Sandy Allen was an organized, analytical person, adept at math and science. At age forty, doctors discovered a golf-ball-sized tumor in the left temporal lobe of her brain. Soon, she developed an incredible passion for art and went around decorating walls, pencil cups, salt shakers, and even light switches. (Some would quibble that she had developed an interest not in art but in crafts.) She was as amazed as anyone by this turn of events: "I couldn't even draw a stick figure before."[51] In cases like this, the prevailing theory is that the artistic ability that seems to have "developed" was always present but was suppressed by the parts of the brain that are responsible for a person's inhibitions. If the operation of these parts is compromised, people at last are free to express their artistic side.

In other cases, though, brain disease and injury appear to give rise to genuinely new artistic ability. Derek Amato was a mediocre guitar player, until, at age forty, a head injury transformed him into a keyboard sensation, despite the fact that he had never had a single lesson. He sat down at a friend's house and found himself performing wonderful music, as if by magic. He could not only play and compose music on the keyboard, but could easily replay anything he had previously played.[52] He was able to do this because the injury caused him to experience synesthesia, a condition in which sensory input gets mixed. Amato had developed the ability to "see" music. He explained, "As I shut my eyes, I found these black and white structures moving from left to right, which in fact would represent in my mind, a fluid and continuous stream of musical notation."[53] This somehow enabled his fingers to find the right keys to play.

SCIENTISTS' UNDERSTANDING of how brains make thoughts can best be described as basic, but their understanding of how brains can give rise to paintings, dances, poems, and symphonies is more basic still—indeed, it is primitive. That we humans would possess such an ability is astonishing. It is conceivable that regardless of all the things computers can do, the creation of art—that is inspired rather than formulaic—is something that will always remain beyond their ability.

Most of us appreciate what a magical thing artistic ability is, and as a result we like to read a novel, and we enjoy the occasional trip to the art museum. At the same time, though, we are perfectly capable of treating contemporary artists in much the same way as we treat moral reformers: we reject their insights, perhaps so vehemently that we take steps to silence them. It is to this phenomenon that we will, in the following chapter, turn our attention.

CHAPTER 15

But Is It Art?

MANY VISITORS TO NEW YORK'S Metropolitan Museum of Art go there to see the Impressionist galleries. On their way to them, they might walk past *1807, Friedland*, a painting by French artist Jean-Louis-Ernest Meissonier that depicts Napoleon's victory at the Battle of Friedland. The huge (fifty-three by ninety-five inch) canvas is filled with horses and their riders, some stationary and some galloping, painted in a realistic manner and in astonishing detail.

Visitors might be brought to a halt by this canvas, but probably only for a moment. They will then move on to the Impressionist paintings that are just around the corner. Visitors may be astonished by the *Friedland*, but they know they will be delighted by the canvases of Manet, Monet, and Cezanne. Yet if these very same viewers could be transported back in time, their artistic tastes would quite likely have been different. They would very much have appreciated the *Friedland*, but if they came across, say, Edouard Manet's *Dejeuner sur l'Herbe*, they would have wondered whether it was even art.

When he painted the *Friedland*, Meissonier was the world's wealthiest and most successful painter. He had the admiration of critics, the public, and even his fellow artists. Eugène Delacroix remarked, "Amongst all of us, surely it is he who is most certain to survive."[1] Manet, by way of contrast, was a struggling young artist who had funny ideas about what should happen on a canvas and was therefore mocked by both critics and the public. But within two decades of his death, Meissonier had, to a considerable extent, disappeared from art history, and Manet was on his way to becoming an Impressionist superstar.

EARLY IN HIS CAREER, Manet embraced Realism, as did essentially all the painters of the time. Their canvases resemble what we today would describe as high-definition photographs, without any subsequent Photoshop modification. An artist, after choosing the subject matter—maybe something biblical, mythological, or historical—and a composition, would simply have painted what the eye would have seen. In an aesthetically satisfying realist painting, the painting would look like real life, and it would look this way not just when seen from across the room but when inspected from a distance of a few inches.

In 1861, twenty-nine-year-old Manet had some of his paintings accepted by the Salon. Since the early 1700s, the Salon had been the official art exhibition of the French Académie des Beaux-Arts. To have a painting shown in one of its exhibitions was a major honor. It not only signaled acceptance by one's fellow artists but likely meant commercial success as well. The Salon's jury had at one time been composed of painters, elected by their peers. Starting in 1857, though, jurists had to be members of the Académie, a change that dramatically raised the average age of the jury. These older jurors preferred historical and mythological works that taught a moral lesson. They disliked landscapes. Even though Manet's paintings lacked the tight brushwork expected of a Realist painting, two of his submissions were accepted, and one of them received an honorable mention.

Spurred on by this success, Manet submitted his *Le Bain* (later to be known as *Le Déjeuner sur l' Herbe*) to the Salon of 1859. In the two years since the previous salon, Manet's style of painting had drifted even further from the Realist mainstream. His brushwork was even looser, and his subject matter was radical: *Le Bain* showed a naked woman lying beside two fully dressed—one might even say overdressed—men, with another somewhat-clothed woman wading in water in the background. It was rejected.

Manet challenged this rejection, as did several other artists whose submissions had met a similar fate. Emperor Napoleon III decided that the best way to settle the dispute was to allow the rejected artists to display their works in what became known as the Salon des Refusés—the "exhibition of the rejects." Manet's *Le Bain*, on being shown there, was met with confusion and condemnation. It was mocked by both critics and the public, who wondered what this painting could possibly be about. To many, the brushwork seemed slapdash. One critic suggested that *Le Bain* could have been done with a floor mop. The sneaking suspicion was that Manet's painting was a joke being played on the art world. The painting did draw some praise, mostly from Manet's friends.

Many artists would have withered under this kind of criticism. After having his work attacked at the Salon of 1834, French Neoclassical painter Jean-Auguste-Dominique Ingres closed his studio, left Paris for seven years, and stopped showing work in the Salon until 1855, at which time the old attacks were renewed. One of his paintings, a critic for *Le Figaro* wrote, was "like the taste of a sick man's handkerchief."[2] In other cases, artistic criticism had fatal consequences. After the Salon of 1835, painter Antoine-Jean Gros, partly in response to merciless reviews, drowned himself in a river. Decades later, painter Jules Holtzapffel, after having gotten a work into every Salon in the preceding ten years, had his submission rejected. He thereupon blew his brains out with a gun. In his suicide note, he offered this explanation: "The members of the jury have rejected me, therefore I have no talent . . . I must die."[3]

However stung he might have been by the attacks on his work, Manet not only kept painting but moved deeper into the style he was developing. He showed two paintings in the Salon of 1864, only to have both attacked, by critics and the public alike. Manet responded by cutting one of them, *Incident in a Bull Ring*, into pieces. In the Salon of 1865, he showed two paintings, *Jesus Mocked by the Soldiers* and *Olympia*. When the show opened, a number of people came up to congratulate him for his wonderful seascapes. The problem was that neither of his paintings showed the sea. On further investigation, Manet discovered that an artist named Monet was responsible for the paintings that were being praised.

Manet's own paintings at this Salon, by way of contrast, were the subjects of withering insults. Said one critic: "Never has a painting excited so much laughter, mockery, and cat-calls as this *Olympia*."[4] It again triggered a suspicion that the painting was bad on purpose—that Manet was just trying to get attention. Extra guards were posted to protect *Olympia*, and when that seemed insufficient, the painting was moved to a higher, and therefore safer, location on the gallery wall. In a letter, Manet complained, "Insults are beating down on me like hail. I've never been through anything like this."[5]

Undaunted, Manet submitted two works to the Salon of 1866, and both were rejected. In 1867, he decided not to sub-mit paintings to the Salon but instead staged, at considerable personal expense, a one-man exhibition at the Pont de l'Alma. This exhibition received some critical praise but far more ridicule. According to one friend, "husbands escorted their wives to the Pont de l'Alma. Wives brought their children. The entire world had to avail itself of this rare opportunity to shake with laughter."[6]

Manet had paintings accepted in subsequent Salons, only to have them attacked by critics who published reviews with titles such as "Manet's Horrors." His work was described as provoking only "laughter or pity."[7] In 1870, one unflattering review caused Manet to fight a duel with swords. It wasn't the hostility of the review that irked him—he was used to criti-cism. What bothered him was that the review had been writ-ten by someone he regarded as a friend. The resulting duel left the two combatants more bruised than bleeding.

By 1872, Manet—who was then forty—had sold only a cou-ple of paintings, and both times to friends. (One had paid with a case of cognac.) In January of that year, though, it looked like Manet's fortunes were starting to turn. He was visited by Paul Durand-Ruel, a gallery owner, who bought several of his paintings. Durand-Ruel did not, however, buy *Le Déjeuner sur l'Herbe* and *Olympia*, which are now regarded as two of Manet's greatest paintings. In that same year, Manet submitted his *Battle of the U. S. S. "Kearsarge" and the C. S. S. "Alabama"* to the Salon. It was not only accepted but garnered praise. And in the summer of that year, Manet got a major commission to do a painting of horse racing at the Hippodrome de Longchamp.

In 1873, his good luck continued. Although many avant-garde artists had abandoned the Salon, Manet submitted two paintings, both of which were accepted. One of them, *Le Bon Bock*, showed a gentleman enjoying a beer and pipe. It was much less provocative than earlier work and became one of the most popular pieces in the Salon. Manet read in a newspaper that someone had offered 120,000 francs to buy the painting. On further investigation, though, he discovered that it had been a typo: the offer was for 12,000 francs. In the end, the painting sold for 6,000 francs—a letdown, but still a sale. After that, Manet continued, with mixed success, to submit paintings to the Salon. In the 1881 Salon, he was finally awarded a medal. The 1882 Salon was to be his last; he died the next year.

Had he lived longer, Manet might have been able to witness, finally, public and critical acceptance of his art. In the early 1880s, Paul Durand-Ruel, who had bought many of his paintings, started putting on Impressionist exhibitions in London and New York. Thanks to the New York shows,

American money came pouring into Impressionist art. And after Manet's death, his *Olympia* finally sold, for a very respectable 10,000 francs, to Manet's brother-in-law.

Even then, though, artistic acceptance was mixed with indifference. Claude Monet raised nearly 20,000 francs to buy *Olympia* so that it could be donated to the French nation. The French government accepted the painting but wasn't quite sure what to do with it. *Olympia* was first sent to the Musée de Luxembourg. It was finally displayed in the Louvre in 1907. *Le Déjeuner sur l' Herbe* got similar treatment. It had been sold in 1878 for 3,000 francs and resold two decades later for 55,000. It was subsequently donated to the French nation and hung in the Louvre—not in the gallery space, but in an office occupied by the Ministry of Finance. In 1934, it was finally put on public display.

FOR AN ARTWORK to change the world, it is not enough that it be created; it must also be shared widely or, we might say, "published." Publication will take different forms in different arts. Paintings and sculptures must be displayed in public places, films must be screened, dances and symphonies must be performed before audiences, and architectural designs must be built.

This means that in most cases, the publication of art will require the cooperation of other people. Publication of a symphony, for example, will require the cooperation of nearly a hundred musicians. Likewise, for an architect's creations to be "published" requires the cooperation of a client, engineers, and builders. To be sure, architects can publish in a more limited manner, by publicly displaying the drawings for their unbuilt designs, and composers can publish the score of a symphony that has never been performed. This sort of restricted publication, however, will limit the impact their work will have on the world.

Publishing an artistic work is much easier today than was once the case. In the late 1990s, musicians realized that they didn't need recording studios and record companies to publish their songs; they could instead record them on a personal computer and distribute them as compact discs. Authors likewise gained the ability to publish novels without needing the assistance of an agent, editor, or publishing company. They could instead make their work available through a print-on-demand Internet publisher or distribute it as an e-book. Filmmakers no longer needed distribution through theaters; they could instead post their works online. The increased ability to publish art meant a dramatic increase, at the turn of the century, in the quantity and diversity of the art that was available to the public. Much of that art was bad, but some of it was quite wonderful.

Once a work of art has been published, the world can respond to it. In particular, the artistic community—consisting of other artists, critics, and academics—can pass judgment on it. In a perfect world, this judgment would be based purely on aesthetic grounds. But since members of the artistic community are only human, we can expect them to have mixed motives for the judgments they deliver. Manet's paintings, as we have seen, were rejected by the old guard of French painting. His works challenged their artistic values. Also, those on the jury of the Académie probably envied their younger rival. As we have seen, scientists can experience similar feelings when a younger scientist proposes a radical new theory.

The public also can respond to the publication of art but in most cases does not do so, in large part because people are simply unaware of its existence. Most art must be sought out. You must go to a theater to watch a ballet, you must buy or borrow a novel to read it, and you must go to a museum to see a painting—or at least see the original of it. Much of the public is disinclined to do these things and therefore remains oblivious to current artistic trends. And if ordinary people do go to an art museum, they will be unlikely to go to one that specializes in avant-garde art. Instead they will visit one with "classical" art, and in that museum, they might bypass the art of the second half of the twentieth century in favor of art that they feel more comfortable with.

PERIODICALLY, THE PUBLIC FEELS compelled to attack works of art. This can happen when art is thrust upon them against their will. They might be walking through their fair city when they encounter what they take to be a particularly pointless modern sculpture. If they subsequently learn that they were taxed to pay for it, they might be upset enough to protest. In other cases, the work that offends them won't be on public display but will instead be tucked away in a gallery somewhere. They will be made aware of its existence not by seeing it but by being told about it. And what will likely offend them about the work is its attack on their values—not their aesthetic values, but their moral or religious values.

Consider Andres Serrano's *Piss Christ*, a photograph showing a crucifix immersed in what looks like urine. Serrano claimed that this work was a protest not against Christianity but against the commercialization of Christian icons.[8] Many Christians, however, doubted his sincerity in making this claim. They were also upset that Serrano's work was funded in part by tax dollars.

Artists aren't necessarily averse to being attacked by the public. Many artists feel that their work is sufficiently highbrow that members of the general public should not be able to understand or appreciate it. These artists therefore take public attacks as evidence that they are working at the cutting edge of art, which is precisely where they want to be.

When the government funds specific works of art or the work of specific artists, there will usually be a government-appointed panel that decides what or who gets funded. One might think that artists would find it disturbing that such a panel would have this kind of power over their creative lives, but this is not the case. They are usually happy to have the funding—or at least happy to have a chance at getting funded.

One reason art is subject to public attacks is because artistic aha moments are so subjective. We can prove that a mathematical aha moment is correct, we can assemble a body of evidence that a scientific aha moment is correct, and we can use logic to show that a moral aha moment is inconsistent with our other moral beliefs. We cannot, of course, prove that religious revelations are genuine, even if we ourselves experience them. This is in large part why we think it is important that it should be up to us to decide which religious prophet we follow—if we follow any at all—and why we would find it disturbing to be taxed to support the religion started by one particular prophet.

When we are taxed to support the work of a particular artist, we are likely to have similar misgivings. In particular, we can question the "authenticity" of a funded artist. Is he a serious artist, or is his art some kind of inside joke? Is the artist trying to mock us? Is he laughing at us for taking his art seriously, and laughing even harder at us for paying his salary? Artists will sometimes defend their legitimacy by pointing to the aesthetic theory—sometimes spelled out in a manifesto—under which they labor. But this just moves the question of legitimacy back one step: how can we know which of the rival theories is correct? And if they are all "correct," what can meaningfully be called art?

It is this sort of thinking that gives rise to many of the attacks, by members of the public, on contemporary art. And while intellectuals are likely to dismiss such attacks as being philistine, I think that for them to do this is to take the easy way out. They are right in thinking that art enriches our lives, a claim that almost everyone will accept. But from this it does not follow that unless we climb aboard whatever avant-garde train is currently leaving the station, we are dooming ourselves to lives of artistic deprivation.

Besides supporting the work of particular artists, the government can play a more direct role in the art world by commissioning works of art with a political purpose in mind. Dictators are perfectly willing to pay artists to produce portraits and statues of themselves. Governments might also commission art intended to sway popular opinion in favor of their policies. They might pay filmmakers to create propaganda films—think of Leni Riefenstahl's *Triumph of the Will*. Or they might pay painters to do paintings that glorify a political viewpoint—think of socialist realist art under Stalin. Again, you might think that artists would be reluctant to lend their talents to such efforts, but history shows the opposite. In some cases, artists cooperate because they fear what will happen if they don't; in other cases, they might be in agreement with the political purpose of the art; and in yet other cases, they are simply happy to have the work.

SO FAR, WE HAVE DISTINGUISHED between aha moments in the arts and aha moments in morality, but the two moments can be connected. Artists are as capable as anyone of experiencing moral epiphanies, and in doing so are capable of having a second aha moment in which they realize that they have a moral duty to fight the wrong they discovered in their epiphany. In many cases, being artists, they will fulfill this duty by creating an appropriate work of art.

Usually, it is an artistic aha moment that launches a novel. As we saw in Chapter 4, though, *Uncle Tom's Cabin* was launched by Harriet Beecher Stowe's aha moment regarding slavery. Along similar lines, Picasso's painting *Guernica* was a protest against the bombing of Guernica, Spain. Crosby, Stills, Nash, and Young's song *Ohio* was a protest against the Kent State shootings. Other protest songs seem to be protesting not a specific government policy or action but the status quo; consider, for example, Bob Dylan's *Blowin' in the Wind* and *The Times They're A-Changin'*. Stanley Kubrick's movie *Dr. Strangelove* was a protest against US militarism.

To be sure, some art forms make better vehicles for protest than others. It is conceivable that someone could write a protest symphony or protest opera, but it isn't clear how effective it would be. Protest songs, on the other hand, can be quite effective, partly because they make their case not so much with logic as with poetry accompanied by a musical hook. Novels allow a more thoughtful form of protest, since they allow artists to explore an issue in great depth and allow characters to personify various plights or viewpoints. *Uncle Tom's Cabin* did this so well that it played a significant role in fomenting abolitionism in pre-Civil-War America. When Stowe later met Abraham Lincoln, he greeted her as "the little woman who wrote the book that started this great war."

When a government is particularly powerful and vindictive, artists who protest government policies do so at great personal risk. They might try to avoid political persecution by publishing their works in underground form. This is what happened in the old Soviet Union: through the practice of *samizdat*, censored articles were reproduced by individuals and passed from person to person. Artists might also attempt to disguise their protests as apolitical art—think of Arthur Miller's play *The Crucible*, written when artists were being blacklisted for their political views.

BESIDES PLAYING A ROLE in creating art, governments can play a role in preventing its creation or destroying art that already exists. They can engage, in other words, in censorship.

Sometimes this censorship is brought about by citizens who demand that their government "do something" about a particular kind of art. In other cases, the government plays a paternalistic role and decides what sort of art the public should or shouldn't be exposed to.

The ensuing censorship might result in books being burned, as was commonplace in Germany in the 1930s. The Nazi government also confiscated works of modern art that were deemed degenerate. In Cuba in the 1960s, it was, as Christopher Hitchens discovered, unwise for a writer to criticize Castro. In the Soviet Union in the late 1940s, it was inadvisable to draw a caricature of Joseph Stalin. And in Saudi Arabia today, it is risky to write a play sympathetic to homosexuals. Artists who ignore a government's censorship decrees might be fined, jailed, or even executed.

How does the artistic community respond to censorship? In order to explore this question, let us consider a particular case from the not-too-distant past. In 1989, Ayatollah Ruhollah Khomeini issued a fatwa calling for the death of Salman Rushdie, author of *The Satanic Verses*, a novel that Khomeini took to be blasphemous. With the support of the British government, Rushdie went into hiding and remained there for nine years.

This was admittedly an unusual form of censorship. Khomeini was not an official of the Iranian government at the time, although he wielded considerable political power. Rushdie was not a citizen of Iran, and Khomeini was not trying to ban the sale of the book outside of Iran—something he would have had a hard time doing. But by decreeing that Rushdie be killed, Khomeini was able to make publishers and booksellers think twice about whether they should be involved in the distribution of the book. It also made novelists around the world reconsider whether they wanted to say anything about Islam in their books. It resulted, in other words, in self-censorship on the part of authors. Thus, the effect of the fatwa on the literary world was arguably much greater than if a government official had simply announced that the book was banned.

The fatwa turned out to be no idle threat, and although Rushdie did not die, many others did. Some died in riots that took place shortly after the fatwa was announced. The Japanese translator of *The Satanic Verses* was murdered, and another translator and a book publisher were attacked but did not die. There is also reason to think the massacre in Sivas, Turkey, in which thirty-seven people died when a mob burned down a hotel, was triggered by the fatwa. What drew protestors to the hotel was the presence there of the Turkish translator of *The Satanic Verses*.

Some artists responded to the fatwa by coming out in support of Rushdie. Christopher Hitchens was one of them. He and some other writers publicly declared themselves to be co-responsible for the book, a bold thing to do. Hitchens subsequently read from *The Satanic Verses* at a bookstore at which Rushdie, before the fatwa had been issued, had been scheduled to speak. A crudely assembled pipe bomb was later found at that store.

Most writers, though, were not so bold. Many said nothing at all about the fatwa. Others—including, most prominently, novelist John le Carré—agreed with Khomeini that

Rushdie had crossed an important line and repercussions—but not murder—were to be expected. Le Carré subsequently backtracked from this position, but in doing so he resembled, wrote Hitchens, "a man who, having relieved himself in his own hat, makes haste to clamp the brimming chapeau on his head."[9]

What we have in the case of the fatwa against Rushdie is a collision between aha moments. The second was the artistic aha had by Rushdie at the conception of *The Satanic Verses*. The first was had long ago by Mohammed. In this case, artistic inspiration eked out a victory over a religious revelation, but only barely, and perhaps only for the time being.

WE BENEFIT FROM THE PRESENCE among us of people who are willing to spend their days thinking about morality or art, and to some extent, we admit as much. At the same time, though, we experience a curious kind of ambivalence with respect to these individuals. We tend to admire moralists and artists who lived in the past, in particular those whose insights we were exposed to as we grew up. But we tend to feel threatened by the moralists who live among us. They challenge our moral values, and for reasons I explained in Chapter 6, we don't like having them challenged. We feel much the same way about our aesthetic values.

In my discussion of the moral aha moment, I argued that by overcoming our aversion to moral challenges, we become more moral. Likewise, by overcoming our aversion to artistic innovation—or for that matter, to certain forms of art—we can enrich our lives. Realize that in the same way that you like the art you were exposed to in the past, you can come to like the art you choose to expose yourself to in the future. Unless you are an unusual person, there are worlds of art left for you to explore.

And where should you begin your exploration? You might, for starters, take Ray Bradbury's advice and read a poem that "makes your hair stand up along your arms." After that, head off in whatever artistic direction strikes your fancy. It's hard to go wrong if you keep an open mind.

Conclusion
Food for Thought

WHEN DID HUMANKIND have its first aha moment? It is hard to say because aha moments themselves leave no direct physical evidence. They can at best leave indirect evidence, in the form of material objects that came into existence as the result of them.

Stone tools are the earliest known artifacts created by our hominid ancestors. We can therefore conclude that 2.6 million years ago they realized that it was possible to shape and sharpen stones. But it is unlikely that they would have had this epiphany unless they had realized, at some earlier time, that sharp stones could cut meat. We can imagine how this might have happened: after an ancestor accidentally cut himself on a sharp stone, it dawned on him that this same stone could be used to cut meat from the carcass before him. Aha! This is, by any measure, a modest insight, but in the history of humanity, it turned out to be profoundly important.

Once our ancestors figured out that stones could be shaped and sharpened, a long series of aha moments led to improved production techniques. By at least 1.76 million years ago,[1] our ancestors had invented the hand axe. In their more refined form, hand axes, which are about the size of a computer mouse, are teardrop shaped, with the round part comfortable to hold and the pointed part wickedly sharp. This design proved to be quite popular: hand axes have been found throughout Africa and western Eurasia.

Astonishingly, though, after our ancestors invented the hand axe, its design remained essentially unchanged for a million years; and when change finally did come, about 600,000 years ago, it was minor: the hand axe became a bit more symmetrical. After that, it remained pretty much unchanged for another 500,000 years.[2] Imagine, then, an ancestor of 650,000 years ago misplacing his hand axe. He goes to where he last saw it and, after looking around for a while, finds one in the bushes that isn't the one he lost but is just as good. He happily takes possession of it and heads on his way. It is conceivable that the hand axe he found was manufactured not by a contemporary but by someone who lived a million years earlier—by, perhaps, his great-times-forty-thousand grandfather!

ABOUT 50,000 YEARS AGO, humans seem to have made a great leap forward, intellectually and culturally speaking.[3] As a result, they became more innovative in their manufacture of tools. About 45,000 years ago, our ancestors figured out how to make long, slim stone blades. Bone points for spears came 34,000 years ago, and spear throwers (atlatls) 18,000 years ago.[4] The pace picked up even more when, about 10,000 years ago, our ancestors figured out how to domesticate plants and animals. Such domestication made food more abundant and reliable, and gave people an incentive to stay put and live among other people. Settlements increased in size, and by 6,000 years ago, there were what might be called cities. People started coming into regular contact with lots of other people. This allowed sharing of ideas, which in turn gave rise to new ideas.

We have today reached a stage at which the pace of innovation can best be described as hectic. There wasn't a lot of difference, in terms of daily existence, between the life *my* great-great-grandfather lived and the life *his* great-great-grandfather lived. They both would have regarded horses as the primary means of transportation and the letter as the primary means of interpersonal communication. But I am living a life that my great-great-grandfather would have had trouble imagining. I wake up in a bed in a centrally heated—and in summer, centrally air-conditioned—house. I use an indoor flush toilet and then take a shower with hot water. I cook oatmeal in a microwave oven. I drive to work in a car, and as I drive, my smartphone gives me traffic updates. This same smartphone can tell me my current altitude, latitude, and longitude; can make high-definition videos; can play Beethoven's *Sixth Symphony*; and can tell me the current temperature on the Greek island of Mykonos. At work, I use a computer that can remember what I have written, right-justify it, check it for spelling errors, change its font, read it back to me, and even take dictation from me (but not very well).

IN THE LAST THREE MILLION YEARS, as man's innovative ability was improving, his brain was increasing in size. It is tempting to think that these events are linked—more precisely, that the bigger brain made it possible for him to have better, more productive aha moments. But the connection is rather more interesting than this. In particular, a case can be made that having more aha moments also made it possible for him to grow a bigger brain. Allow me to explain.

The brain is, as we saw in our discussion of religion, a resource-hungry organ. Big brains are nutritionally expensive things to have, and we wouldn't have them unless doing so yielded a significant payoff in terms of evolutionary fitness. What was this payoff? Before we attempt to answer this question, it will be useful for us to consider some other cases in the animal world in which bigger is better.

Consider the peacock. Why do peacocks have such big tails? Because peahens like them. Thus, a peacock with a bigger tail will have more sex, meaning more offspring who will inherit his big-tail genes. Now consider blue whales, the heavyweight champions of the animal world. Why are they so big? In this case, the answer probably isn't because this is how female whales like them. Notice, after all, that female whales also got bigger—they can in fact be bigger than males—which suggests that if you are a whale, there is an intrinsic value to being big. Peahens, in contrast, did not grow bigger tails.

One reason blue whales got bigger is because they are filter feeders and as such can get their lunch simply by opening their mouth while swimming forward. For such an animal, the bigger its mouth is, the more food it will take in. So yes, it requires lots of food to get big, but in the case of the blue whale, getting big makes it possible to get lots of food. Thus, for a blue whale, growing a bigger body is nutritionally self-supporting. It is an evolutionary change that, although expensive, pays its own way.

Now consider the human brain. Why did it get bigger? One reason is that growing bigger brains was a nutritionally self-supporting strategy. Yes, growing and then operating a bigger brain requires more food, but if a bigger brain increases the innovative ability of its owner, it will make it easier for him to meet his nutritional needs. In nutritional terms, then, a bigger brain can pay its own way.

Consider again our early ancestors' use of sharp stones to butcher animals. It is, as I have said, a modest innovation but one that is nutritionally quite significant, inasmuch as it dramatically improved our ancestors' access to meat. By including meat in their diet, they increased their intake of both protein and calories.

A 100-gram steak might have 280 calories. To get this same number of calories from bananas, you would have to consume three of them, and whereas three bananas would provide you with only four grams of protein, the steak would provide you with twenty-seven. And if all you were interested in was calories, you could get 280 calories by eating only 30 grams of fat. Because of their raw-food vegetarianism, chimps have to eat a lot of food in the course of a day; indeed, they might spend six hours a day chewing,[5] compared to maybe an hour for us humans. By including meat in their diet, our ancestors gained the "surplus" protein and calories they would need to grow and operate a bigger brain.

Some readers might at this point accuse me of inconsistency. I announced in Chapter 4 that I am a moral vegetarian, and now I am extolling the virtues of a diet high in meat. I will respond by pointing out that because we don't live on the savannas of Africa, we can get a diet with sufficient calories and protein without eating meat. In other words, we have choices that our evolutionary ancestors lacked.

Here, then, is a theory about how our hominid ancestors came to grow bigger brains. Starting about three million years ago, they used their minimal intelligence to figure out that by using stones as cutting implements, they could improve their access to meat. This improved access meant that they could afford to evolve, over many generations, a bigger brain. This bigger brain, however, made it easier for them to come up with yet other nutrition-enhancing innovations. Thus, their innovative ability literally gave them food for thought. By figuring out how to use stones as tools, they inadvertently put themselves on a feedback loop: innovation led to more and better food, which led to bigger brains, which led to more innovation.

Many subsequent innovations involved killing at a distance. The first such innovation involved throwing ordinary rocks. It was effective against small animals. Later, our ancestors would have thrown spears. The first spears were presumably wooden, but later someone came up with the idea of lashing a stone blade to the tip of a wooden spear—aha! After that came the use of an atlatl, a device for throwing spears that dramatically increased their velocity. This enabled our ancestors to bring down large game animals. Then came the bow and arrow, which allowed them to kill from an even greater distance. (And of course, we are still coming up with innovative ways to kill at a distance. In recent decades, we have added the nuclear-tipped ICBM to our arsenal.)

The hand axes our ancestors invented let them butcher any carcasses they came across and thereby access the meat they contained. By inventing techniques for killing at a distance, though, our ancestors made hunting animals much safer and more efficient, and thereby increased their access to carcasses to butcher. It represented a great leap forward, nutritionally speaking.

One other important innovation was cooking. The first cooking would have been done on fires found in nature. As they got smarter, our ancestors would have figured out how to keep these fires going and then how to start them. Cooking not only makes meat tastier but makes it easier for humans to access the nutrients it contains.

In summary, by improving their access to meat and the nutrients it contains, our hominid ancestors inadvertently placed themselves on a feedback loop. With each circuit around this loop, their nutrition improved, as did their brain size, as did their ability to innovate. Our current ability to have aha moments is in part the result of having spent a few million years on this loop. But there is more to the story than this.

CONSIDER THE RHINOCEROS. Suppose that as the result of a mutation, a rhino developed an oversized brain. As a result, this rhino might be remarkably intelligent and might therefore develop a profound understanding of the world. In material terms, though, this understanding would be useless. Yes, he can figure out how to make a smart phone, but because he is inhabiting what can charitably be described as a clumsy body, he will never be able to build one. He won't even be able to make a hoof axe, the rhino equivalent of a hand axe. Indeed, even if he found a sharp rock, he wouldn't be able to do anything with it.

Our hominid ancestors, by way of contrast, had dexterous fingers with opposable thumbs. This let them turn ideas into objects that could be used to increase their access to meat. And equally important, they were, as of perhaps four million years ago, bipedal. This meant that they could carry with them the tools they manufactured. This was more convenient than having to make a new tool whenever one was needed.

If the wrong sort of body can prevent a brain from taking material advantage of its aha moments, so can the wrong sort of personality. To see why I say this, consider again hand axes. Modern individuals known as *knappers* have figured out how to manufacture them. It turns out that it isn't an easy thing to do: there are lots of ways the process can go wrong, resulting either in the knapper getting hurt or in a hand axe getting ruined. To be a successful knapper, then, requires a tolerance for frustration. It is therefore unlikely that a hominid ancestor who was easily frustrated would have been able to translate his aha moment regarding hand axes into physical hand axes that could improve his access to meat.

A tolerance for frustration was also necessary if our ancestors were to start fires so they could cook their food. I found this out through personal experience when I took a class, a few years ago, on how to start a fire without a match. We used what are called *bow drills*. To make one, you tie together a stick and a string to make a bow. Then you wind the string of the bow around another stick, called the *drill*. You put the drill into a hole in another piece of wood, pile tinder around it, and then vigorously pull the bow back and forth. It is what is commonly called "making a fire by rubbing two sticks together," a description, I should add, that is utterly misleading.

The instructor succeeded in starting a fire, but none of his students did. It was frustrating and somewhat humiliating. The instructor attempted to cheer us up with the observation that if we ever found ourselves in a situation in which our life depended on starting a fire, we would have days and days to perfect our technique and would, as a result, succeed. I'm not so sure.

One other thing that would have improved our ancestors' access to meat is a good throwing arm. We humans take our throwing ability for granted, but in fact, we are exceptionally good throwers—indeed, the best in the animal world. Our throwing ability is, of course, an evolutionary accident. A good throwing arm will be long, and we are blessed with arms that are long in proportion to our bodies. They evolved not so we could throw rocks or spears, but so we could swing through trees. Not only that, but the tendons and ligaments in our shoulders are arranged—again by coincidence—so that during the windup for a throw, they store energy that is released during the throw. As a result, we can throw things fast. Adult chimpanzees, although strong and athletic, can throw a baseball at only twenty miles per hour.[6] A twelve-year-old little-league pitcher might throw it three times as fast, and a big-league pitcher can throw it five times as fast and with exquisite accuracy.

Had it not been for their throwing ability, our hominid ancestors would not have been able to kill at a distance. Chimps, I should add, are sufficiently innovative to come up with the concept of harming something at a distance. This is demonstrated by the fact that they sometimes throw things in anger. But this insight is of little use to them, for the simple reason that their bodies lack the requisite throwing ability.

We are led to the somewhat surprising conclusion that man would not have his present ability to experience aha moments if, despite having a somewhat innovative brain, he lacked hands with dexterous fingers and opposable thumbs, if he hadn't been bipedal, if he hadn't been even tempered, and—perhaps most surprising of all—if he had lacked a good throwing arm! Without these characteristics, his ability to procure meat would have plateaued at a lower level, thereby limiting further growth of his brain. A smaller brain, though, would translate into fewer aha moments.

It is also important to keep in mind that even though our ancestors possessed traits conducive to brain growth, it was by no means a sure thing that their brains would grow. This is because the evolutionary process is *sensitive*, by which I mean that small differences in environment can result in big differences in evolutionary outcome. Humans and chimps evolved from a common ancestor that lived about seven million years ago. Had environmental influences been a bit different during that period, it is entirely possible that it would have been chimps rather than us who gained the ability to experience aha moments.

I HAVE ARGUED THAT WE OWE, our ability to have aha moments to our having inadvertently placed ourselves on a feedback loop, in which innovative ability meant better access to food, which meant bigger brains, which in turn meant improved innovative ability. I also argued that what made this loop work was the fact that we possessed a body and personality that let us transform our insights into changes in our material circumstances. Even now, though, we haven't gotten to the bottom of things.

In our discussion of religious and moral aha moments, I explained that as our brains got bigger in the last three million years, much of the growth involved an increase in the size of our cerebrum. What was significant about this growth is that our cerebrum did not *supplant* our primitive brain; it grew around it and thereby *supplemented* it. We humans are therefore owners of a curious kind of dual brain with one part highly rational and the other reflexive and emotional. As we have seen, it is the primitive part of the brain that to a considerable extent is responsible for religious revelations. It is also responsible for our moral sense, and therefore for many of our moral epiphanies.

Besides having a dual brain, we humans have two minds, one conscious and one unconscious. In our discussion of science, mathematics, and art, we saw that the aha moments that occur in these domains "come to us." By *us*, of course, we mean our conscious mind. But notice that for us to have an aha moment, we cannot be aware of the contents of that moment until it arrives; otherwise, there would be no feeling of surprise associated with the moment. It is therefore convenient that the source of our aha moments—namely, our unconscious mind—is very good at keeping us in the dark about them until it judges us worthy of receiving them: "Surprise!"

Notice, too, that our conscious mind is not clever enough, all on its own, to come up with important new ideas. Furthermore, although our unconscious mind is up to this task, it will undertake it only if the conscious mind requests that it do so by struggling valiantly to come up with an idea. And finally, notice that without the conscious mind to play the role of spokesperson, the unconscious mind would be unable to share with the world the brilliant ideas it comes up with. The relationship between the conscious and unconscious mind is thus both quite strange and exceedingly wonderful.

SO WHAT, IN THE END, do we know about aha moments as they are experienced in the various domains? With regard to religious revelations, I have described the predicament we humans are in. For whatever reason, God (assuming that he exists) has not seen fit to give us all revelations. Instead, only a select few experience them, and the rest of us are faced with choosing among reported revelations to determine which—if any!—are authentic. I have been careful not to come out in favor of or in opposition to any particular revelation. I instead counsel skepticism toward them all.

Regarding moral aha moments, I have argued that although we cannot avoid being morally indoctrinated while growing up, we can, on reaching adulthood, re-evaluate our moral beliefs to see if they are correct. As part of this process, we can learn more about the world around us. In some cases, this self-education will lead us to an epiphany like the one Gandhi experienced. We can also go out of our way to expose ourselves to people whose moral beliefs are at odds with our own. Doing this can trigger in us a somewhat unpleasant episode of cognitive dissonance, but such episodes can lead to moral growth. And if, as a result of our moral re-evaluation, we conclude that the people around us are mistaken in their moral beliefs, we might, if we are sufficiently courageous, undertake a campaign to enlighten them.

In my exploration of aha moments, I gained some important insights about the creative process. Many people seem to think that if you are a truly creative person, creative thoughts will just come to you. All you need to do is collect them when they arrive at your doorstep and incorporate them into the mathematical proof you are working on, the scientific theory you are formulating, or the symphony you are composing. This sort of thing can happen, but it is very rare. More often, to be creative you must, besides having talent, work very hard. Spend enough time on a project, and your unconscious mind will start incubating. It is this incubation process that gives you your best chance at coming up with something profound.

This means that creative people will be in the habit of spending significant amounts of time trying things, in the full realization that most of the things they try won't work. To keep their frustration level down, they will regard their errors not as personal failures but as milestones that must be passed on the way to success. They will learn what they can from their errors and try again. They might also make a point of having multiple creative projects going, so that when one bogs down, they can turn their efforts to another.

Of course, to show up for work each day in the knowledge that at the end of that day you will likely have little to show for your effort takes self-discipline. This, however, is only one of the character traits of a person who is likely to have a world-changing aha moment. Two others are courage and persistence. The more important an insight is, the more reluctant the world usually will be to accept it. It requires both courage and persistence to overcome this reluctance.

AS I EXPLAINED in the introduction, this is the second book in which I've explored the relationship between the conscious and unconscious mind. The first was my *On Desire: Why We Want What We Want*. As the result of doing the research for that book, I became acutely aware of the way desires pop into my head. They are like door-to-door salespeople. I would send them packing only to have them back at my door five minutes later, as eager to talk me into buying whatever they were selling as they had previously been. They just wouldn't take no for an answer!

As the result of that research, I also became aware of the dangerous role desire can play in people's lives. The problem is that people tend to think that the desires they discover within themselves must be an indication of what they genuinely want, but this often isn't the case. Rather, our "spontaneous" desires are the result of wiring we acquired hundreds of thousands of years ago. We want sex. We want social status. We want sweet, fattening food. And not only that, but we are insatiable. A person who embraces whatever desires pop into his head is therefore likely to live a life of perpetual dissatisfaction. To avoid this fate, he needs to treat the desires he discovers within him in much the same way as he would treat a salesperson who turns up, uninvited, at his door—namely, with profound skepticism!

Doing research about aha moments made me acutely aware that desires aren't the only things that pop into my head; ideas do as well. But whereas I found my spontaneous desires to be a source of distress, I found my "spontaneous" ideas—which of course weren't truly spontaneous, since if my conscious mind hadn't sought them, they wouldn't have happened—were a source of delight. Being capable of having aha moments, I realized, is like being a child with a front-row seat at a magic show. You know that the magician's hat is empty, and yet he pulls a rabbit out of it! You know the magic box is empty, and yet there she is, the magician's beautiful assistant, emerging from it!

As magicians go, our unconscious mind is unorthodox. What he causes to pop into existence will depend on who is in "the audience." If a mathematician is before him, it might be the key step in a proof that suddenly appears; if it is a physicist, it might be a new theory about the behavior of subatomic particles; and if it is a composer, it might be the opening notes of a symphony. What is also striking is that the magician will not expect to be paid for putting on his show. He asks only that his audience be dedicated in their pursuit of whatever insight it was he provided them with—and maybe that they tell the rest of the world about the trick he performed.

So yes, our creative endeavors can be demanding, frustrating, and humbling. But they give us a chance to experience a very special kind of magic, in which we simultaneously play the role of magician and audience. It is a tradeoff, most creative people would agree, that is very much worth our while.

NOTES

Introduction

1. Clarkson 1808, n.p.
2. Clarkson 1808, n.p.
3. Quoted in Brian 1996, 61.
4. Quoted in Harvey 1999, 10.
5. Poincaré 2004, 24.
6. Stillwell 1985, 1.
7. Quoted in Vitruvius 1914, 253–54.
8. Joseph Smith n.d., 1.16–17.

Chapter 1

1. Lewis 1955, 229.
2. Quoted in James 1929, 210.
3. Ullman 1989, 157.
4. Exodus 3:2–6. (*New English Bible*).
5. Augustine 1991, 8:28–29.
6. Quoted in James, 246–47.
7. Acts 9: 3–6.
8. Landsborough 1987, 662.
9. Matthew 1:20–21.
10. Ibn Ishāq 1955, 106.
11. Andrae 1936, 50.
12. Luhrmann 2012, xv–xvi.
13. Luhrmann 2012, 39.
14. Krakauer 2003, 159.
15. Quoted in Krakauer 2003, 161.
16. Krakauer 2003, 182–86.

17. Exodus 25:10.
18. *Doctrines and Covenants*, 124: 62–64.
19. *Doctrines and Covenants*, 124: 56–83.
20. *Doctrines and Covenants*, 107: 91–92.
21. Lattin 1997.

Chapter 2

1. Bonenfant 2000, 103–104.
2. Pasricha 1993, 165.
3. Pasricha 1993, 163.
4. Pasricha 1993, 167.
5. Pasricha 1993, 162.
6. Wettach 2000, 75.
7. Whinnery 1990, 774.
8. Bonenfant 2000, 105.
9. Bonenfant 2000, 105.
10. Bonenfant 2000, 107.
11. Wasson 1957, 114, 117.
12. Wasson 1957, 109.
13. Wasson 1957, 104.
14. Doblin 1991, 1.
15. Doblin 1991, 13.
16. Griffiths 2006, 278.
17. Sacks 2012, 144.
18. Sacks 2012, 141.
19. Quoted in Sacks 2012, 146.
20. Ogata 1998, 322.
21. Quoted in Ogata 1998, 322.
22. Sacks 2012, 159.
23. Sacks 2012, 162–63.
24. Quoted in Sacks 2012, 161.
25. Altschuler 2002, 561.
26. Dostoevsky (1868) 2004, 265.
27. Ibn Ishāq 1955, 223.
28. Quoted in Andrae 1936, 50.
29. Quoted in Andrae 1936, 49–50.
30. Devinsky and Lai 2008, 638.
31. Hughes 2005, 531.
32. Dostoevsky (1868) 2004, 263–64.

33. Quoted in Landsborough 1987, 660.
34. Hansen and Brodtkorb 2003, 672.
35. Quoted in Landsborough 1987, 659.
36. Landsborough 1987, 662.
37. Penfield 1978, 31.
38. Penfield 1978, 12.
39. Penfield 1978, 12–13.
40. Penfield 1978, 21–22.
41. Penfield 1978, 24–25.
42. Sacks 2012, 153.
43. Rahachadran and Blakeslee 1998, 175.
44. Rahachadran and Blakeslee 1998, 175.

Chapter 3

1. Genesis 2:15–17.
2. Genesis 3:8.
3. Isaiah 53:2.
4. Genesis 17:1.
5. Genesis 36:6.
6. 2 Corinthians 11:14.
7. Joseph Smith n.d., 1.19.
8. Joseph Smith n.d., 1.21.
9. Ibn Ishāq 1955, 117.
10. Ibn Ishāq 1955, 117–18.
11. Ibn Ishāq 1955, 118.
12. Ibn Ishāq 1955, 191.
13. Ibn Ishāq 1955, 145.
14. Ibn Ishāq 1955, 120.
15. Ibn Ishāq 1955, 143.
16. Ibn Ishāq 1955, 131.
17. Matthew 13:57–58.
18. Armstrong 2006, 106–107.
19. Brodie 1971, 92.
20. *Doctrine and Covenants*, 28:2.86.
21. Quran 33:40.
22. *Doctrine and Covenants*, 132:61.
23. *Doctrine and Covenants*, Official Declaration 1.
24. Brodie 1971, 467.
25. Brodie 1971, 76–77. See also Joseph Smith, 1.54–55.

26. Brodie 1971, 398.
27. Krakauer 2003, 199n.

Chapter 4

1. Gandhi 1957, 112.
2. Clarkson 1808.
3. Quoted in Ellen Gibson Wilson 1990, 17.
4. Clarkson 1808.
5. Ellen GibsonWilson 1990, 20.
6. Ellen GibsonWilson 1990, 1.
7. Quoted in Hitchens 2001, 27.
8. Stowe 1889, 93.
9. Quoted in Stowe 1889, 145.
10. Quoted in Stowe 1889, 146.
11. Quoted in Hitchens 2010, 10.
12. Nation Institute.
13. Hitchens 2010, 11.

Chapter 5

1. Haidt.
2. For this argument, see my *On Desire*.
3. de Waal.
4. Foot 2002, 23.
5. Thomson 1985, 1409.
6. Singer 2005, 347–48.
7. Singer 2005, 348.

Chapter 6

1. Russell 1950, 101.
2. Plato, *Apology*, 31d.
3. Plato, *Apology*, 40a.
4. Plato, *Symposium*, 220c3–d5.
5. Plato, *Apology*, 21b.
6. Plato, *Apology*, 21d.
7. Plato, *Apology*, 23b.
8. Plato, *Apology*, 30e.
9. Plato, *Apology*, 23b–c.
10. Plato, *Apology*, 32b–32c.
11. Plato, *Apology*, 32d.

12. Hitchens 2010, 117.
13. Hitchens 2001, 3.
14. Hitchens 2001, 95–96.
15. Hitchens 2001, 81.
16. Hitchens 2001, 96.
17. Hitchens 2001, 12.
18. Hitchens 2001, 35.
19. Hitchens 2001, 45.
20. Hardy 1967, 46.
21. Hitchens 2001, 29.
22. Hitchens 2001, 122.
23. Hitchens 2001, 20.
24. Mill (1859) 1978, 42.
25. Mill (1859) 1978, 34.
26. Plato, *Apology*, 31a.

Chapter 7

1. Brian 1996, 61.
2. Einstein 1982, 46–47.
3. Quoted in Isaacson 2008, 145.
4. Einstein 1982, 47.
5. Quoted in Highfield 1993, 174.
6. Rhodes 1986, 13, 28.
7. Smolin 1997, 81.
8. Guth 1997, 167.
9. Guth 1997, 176, 179.
10. Guth 1997, 19–20.
11. Feynman 1973.
12. Smolin n.d.
13. Merton 1973a, 401.
14. Quoted in Hadamard 1954, 34.
15. Quoted in Merton 1973a, 402.
16. Feynman 1999, 12.
17. Feynman 1973.
18. Watson 1953, 737.
19. Weinberg 1992, 90.
20. Quoted in Chandrasekhar 1987, 65.
21. Chandrasekhar 1987, 66.
22. Quoted in Dawkins 2008, 378.

23. Quoted in Meyers 2012, 33.
24. Quoted in Meyers 2012, 33.
25. Alfred Russel Wallace 1908, 191.
26. Ferris 2002, 144.
27. Ferris 2002, 148–49.
28. Ferris 2002, 148.
29. Ferris 2002, 150.
30. Glasser 1993, 223–24.
31. Shapiro 1986, 50.
32. Shapiro 1986, 44–45.
33. Coyne 2009, 219.

Chapter 8

1. Firestein 2012, 160.
2. Quoted in Lowenstein 1994, 94.
3. Park 2004, 609.
4. Wilde 1905, 58.
5. Quoted in Johnson 1999, 168.
6. Westfall 1993, 35.
7. Csikszentmihalyi 1996, 110–13.
8. Edward O. Wilson 2008.
9. Firestein 2012, 21.
10. Zimmer 1998, 145.
11. Lane 2005, 87, 90.
12. Hull 1988, 160.
13. Quoted in Schopenhauer 1995, 58.
14. Hallam 2004, 2.
15. Quoted in Sachs 2007, 84.
16. Grant 2014.
17. Bartusiak 1990, 89.
18. Bartusiak 1990, 90.
19. Rubin 1995.
20. Rubin 1995.
21. Walker 2003, 71.
22. Walker 2003, 98–99.
23. Kirschvink 1992, 52.
24. Walker 2003, 99.
25. Edward O. Wilson 1994, 319–20.
26. Hoffman 2007.

27. Ferris 2002, 179–80.
28. Medawar 1972, 16.
29. Quoted in Hadamard 1954, 34.
30. Crick 1995.
31. Lankester 1896, 4391–92.
32. Quoted in Wood 1985, 73.
33. Marshall 2005.

Chapter 9

1. For the mathematics behind this claim, see http://hudsonvalleygeolo
   gist.blogspot.com/2011/12/scale-of-atoms.html.
2. Davis 2006.
3. Pollock 2006, 3.
4. Quoted in Ferris 2002, 195.
5. Quoted in Barber 1961, 597.
6. Firestein 2012, 22.
7. Margulis 1995, 136.
8. John Maynard Smith, "Hamilton."
9. John Maynard Smith, "Haldane's Reaction."
10. Quoted in Edward O. Wilson 1994, 337.
11. Edward O. Wilson 1994, 337–38.
12. Edward O. Wilson 1994, 331.
13. Hallam 2004, 8.
14. Arthur Miller 2005, 9.
15. Arthur Miller 2005, 108.
16. Arthur Miller 2005, 10.
17. Arthur Miller 2005, 12.
18. Quoted in Arthur Miller 2005, 128.
19. Arthur Miller 2005, 109–10.
20. Arthur Miller 2005, 111, 115, 132.
21. Quoted in Arthur Miller 2005, 177.
22. Quoted in Arthur Miller 2005, 259.
23. Arthur Miller 2005, 173.
24. Arthur Miller 2005, 210.
25. Arthur Miller 2005, 262.
26. Merton 1973c, 318.
27. Quoted in Morell 1997, 701–2.
28. Quoted in Morell 1997, 702.
29. Quoted in Morell 1997, 702.

30. Martin 2010.
31. Margulis 1995, 135.
32. Smolin 1995, 142.

Chapter 10

1. Singh 1997, 223.
2. Quoted in Singh 1997, 225.
3. Singh 1997, 227.
4. Singh 1997, 122–23.
5. Landers 2003.
6. Quoted in Schecter 1998, 51.
7. Hardy 1967, 149.
8. Hardy 1967, 88.
9. Rota 1997, 130.
10. Rota 1997, 70.
11. Quoted in Singh n.d.
12. Russell 1917, 60.
13. Quoted in Singh 1997, 62.
14. Singh 1997, 209–10.
15. Quoted in Singh 1997, 146.
16. Wiles 1997.
17. Rota 1997, 93.
18. Rota 1997, 202.
19. Quoted in Merton 1973b, 335.
20. Rehmeyer 2007.
21. Hardy 1967, 81.
22. Schecter 1998, 127–28.
23. Schecter 1998, 128.
24. Rota 1997, 116.
25. Loomis 1940.
26. Quoted in Robin J. Wilson 2002, 208.
27. Schecter 1998, 137.
28. de Lange 2012.
29. Rota 1997, 209–10.
30. This example is borrowed from Singh 1997, 159.
31. Jackson 2002, 1247.

Chapter 11

1. Littlewood 1986, 93.
2. Littlewood 1986, 93.

3. Littlewood 1986, 93.
4. Littlewood 1986, 145.
5. Littlewood 1986, 191. In making this claim, Littlewood appears to be borrowing from Graham Wallas's *Art of Thought*.
6. Littlewood 1986, 191–92.
7. Poincaré 2004, 21–22.
8. Quoted in Hersh 1997, 36.
9. Littlewood 1986, 144.
10. Littlewood 1986, 196.
11. Cohen 2006.
12. Hersh 1997, 36.
13. Littlewood 1986, 160–61.
14. Jackson 2002, 1246.
15. Quoted in Jackson 2002, 1249.
16. Poincaré 2004, 26.
17. Littlewood 1986, 192.
18. Poincaré 2004, 25.
19. Littlewood 1986, 196.
20. Littlewood 1986, 192.
21. Littlewood 1986, 198.
22. Littlewood 1986, 197.
23. Littlewood 1986, 145.
24. Bollobás 1986, 16.
25. Kolata 1993.
26. Singh 1997, 66.
27. Kolata 1994.
28. Kolata 1995.
29. Scripture 1891, 3.
30. Quoted in Hadamard 1954, 59.

Chapter 12

1. Crew n.d.
2. Hellman 2006, 127.
3. Hellman 2006, 127.
4. Quoted in Dauben 1979, 134.
5. Hellman 2006, 129.
6. Quoted in Hellman 2006, 168.
7. Quoted in Hellman 2006, 130.
8. Dauben 1979, 298.
9. Dauben 1979, 142–44.

10. Hellman 2006, 135.
11. Quoted in Hellman 2006, 122.
12. Dauben 1979, 147.
13. Dauben 1979, 291.
14. Quoted in Dauben 1979, 138.
15. Dauben 1979, 259.
16. Dauben 1979, 246.
17. Dauben 1979, 248.
18. Dauben 1979, 248.
19. Hellman 2006, 138–39.
20. Hellman 2006, 133.
21. Dauben 1979, 135.
22. Dauben 1979, 137.
23. Quoted in Hellman 2006, 117.
24. Cohen 2006.
25. Cohen 2006.

Chapter 13

1. Quoted in McCutchan 1999, 99.
2. Quoted in McCutchan 1999, 99–100.
3. Quoted in Harvey 1999, 3.
4. Harvey 1999, 26.
5. Quoted in Harvey 1999, 30.
6. Alter 2009.
7. Nichols 1948, 150–53.
8. Harvey 1999, 25.
9. Quoted in Alter 2009.
10. Alter 2009.
11. For a brief history of "killing one's darlings," see Wickman 2013.
12. Quoted in Overbey 2010.
13. Jamison 1994, 187.
14. Quoted in Jamison 1994, 98.
15. Quoted in McCutchan 1999,18.
16. Quoted in McCutchan 1999,183.
17. Blankenbuehler 2013.
18. Mole 2014.
19. Lord 1965, 63–64.
20. Clark 1973, 145–46.
21. Nielsen 2013.
22. Zeki et al. 2014.

23. Quoted in McCutchan 1999, 102–3.
24. Quoted in Harvey 1999, 23.
25. McCutchan 1999, 242.
26. Irving Wallace 1977, 519–21.

Chapter 14

1. Davidson 1977.
2. Alter 2009.
3. McArdle 2014.
4. Quoted in Harvey 1999, 11.
5. Quoted in McCutchan 1999, 239.
6. Quoted in McCutchan 1999, 145.
7. Rhodes 1995, 3.
8. Irving Wallace 1977, 518.
9. Irving Wallace 1977, 518.
10. Irving Wallace 1977, 518.
11. Quoted in McCutchan 1999, 205.
12. Lord 1965, 5.
13. Mailer 1964.
14. Shea 2007.
15. Colette 1957, 65.
16. Kipling 1955, 158–59.
17. Styron 2002.
18. Christies.
19. Spender 1955, 113.
20. Simenon 1971, 136, 319.
21. Balzac n.d.
22. Bradbury 1996, 36–37.
23. Bradbury 1996, 33.
24. Gilbert 2009.
25. Fritz, 573.
26. Zentner 2009.
27. Quoted in Gaidos 2010.
28. Salimpoor 2013, 216.
29. Salimpoor 2013, 217.
30. Quoted in Levitin 2006, 242.
31. Quoted in Levitin 2006, 246.
32. For an update on this debate, see Levitin 2009.
33. Jamison 1994, 56.
34. Jamison 1994, 60–62.

35. Plato, *Phaedrus* (254A).
36. Jamison 1994, 91.
37. Quoted in Jamison 1994, 105.
38. Jamison 1994, 178.
39. Quoted in Jamison 1994, 188.
40. Jamison 1994, 202–5.
41. Quoted in Jamison 1994, 203.
42. Quoted in Jamison 1994, 203.
43. Jamison 1994, 249.
44. Jamison 1994, 107.
45. Jamison 1994, 109.
46. Jamison 1994, 6.
47. Jamison 1994, 246.
48. Jamison 1994, 247.
49. Sergent 1994, 170.
50. Bruce Miller 2000, 461.
51. Carol Smith 2006.
52. Neal 2012.
53. Neal 2012.

Chapter 15

1. Quoted in King 2006, 2.
2. Quoted in King 2006, 90.
3. Quoted in King 2006, 171.
4. Quoted in King 2006, 152.
5. Quoted in King 2006, 151.
6. Quoted in King 2006, 201.
7. Quoted in King 2006, 270.
8. Seeley 2002.
9. Quoted in Flood 2012.

Conclusion

1. Lepre et al. 2011.
2. Ridley 2010, 49.
3. Klein 2002, 231.
4. Ridley 2010, 70.
5. Wrangham 2009, 139.
6. George Washington University 2013.

WORKS CITED

Alter, Alexandra. 2009. "How to Write a Great Novel." *Wall Street Journal*, November 13. http://online.wsj.com/article/SB10001424052748703740 004574513463106012106.html.

Altschuler, Eric Lewin. 2002. "Did Ezekiel Have Temporal Lobe Epilepsy?" *Archives of General Psychiatry* 59: 561–62.

Andrae, Tor. 1936. *Mohammed: The Man and His Faith*. Translated by Theophil Menzel. London: George Allen & Unwin.

Armstrong, Karen. 2006. *Muhammad: A Prophet for Our Time*. New York: HarperCollins.

Augustine. 1991. *The Confessions*. Translated by Henry Chadwick. Oxford: Oxford University Press.

Balzac, Honore de. N.d. "The Pleasures and Pains of Coffee." Translated by Robert Onopa. http://blissbat.net/balzac.html.

Barber, Bernard. 1961. "Resistance by Scientists to Scientific Discovery." *Science* 134 (3479): 596–602.

Bartusiak, Marcia. 1990. "The Woman Who Spins the Stars." *Discover*, October: 88–94.

Blankenbuehler, Andy. 2013. Interviewed on PBS's documentary *ANNIE: It's the Hard-Knock Life, From Script to Stage*. First aired on June 28. http://video.pbs.org/video/2365032177.

Bollobás, Béla. 1986. Forward to *Littlewood's Miscellany*. Edited by Béla Bollobás. Cambridge: Cambridge University Press.

Bonenfant, Richard J. 2000. "A Near-death Experience Followed by the Visitation of an Angel-like Being." *Journal of Near-Death Studies* 19 (2): 103–12.

Bradbury, Ray. 1996. *Zen in the Art of Writing*. Santa Barbara, CA: Joshua Odell Editions.

Brian, Denis. 1996. *Einstein: A Life*. New York: John Wiley.

Brodie, Fawn. 1971. *No Man Knows My History: The Life of Joseph Smith, the Mormon Prophet*. New York: Knopf.

Chandrasekhar, Subrahmanyan. 1987. *Truth and Beauty: Aesthetics and Motivations in Science*. Chicago: University of Chicago Press.

Christies. Catalog entry for the sale of the autograph manuscript of *The Original of Laura*. http://www.christies.com/lotfinder/books-manuscripts/nabokov-vladimir-autograph-manuscript-of-the-5370926-details.aspx.

Clark, Kenneth. 1973. "Mona Lisa." *The Burlington Magazine* 115 (840): 144–51.

Clarkson, Thomas. 1808. *The History of the Rise, Progress and Accomplishment of the Abolition of the African Slave Trade by the British Parliament*. Vol. I. http://www.gutenberg.org/files/10633/10633-h/10633-h.htm.

Cohen, Paul. 2006. Video of a talk given at the Gödel Centennial in Vienna. http://www.youtube.com/watch?v=VBFLWk7k1Zo.

Colette. 1957. *My Apprenticeships*. Translated by Helen Beauclerk. New York: Farrar Straus Giroux.

Coyne, Jerry A. 2009. *Why Evolution Is True*. New York: Oxford University Press.

Crew, Richard. N.d. "Pythagoras, Hippasos, and the Square Root of Two." http://www.math.ufl.edu/~rcrew/texts/pythagoras.html.

Crick, Francis. 1995. "The Impact of Linus Pauling on Molecular Biology." http://oregonstate.edu/dept/Special_Collections/subpages/ahp/1995symposium/crick.html.

Csikszentmihalyi, Mihaly. 1996. *Creativity: Flow and the Psychology of Discovery and Invention*. New York: Harper Perennial.

Dauben, Joseph Warren. 1979. *Georg Cantor: His Mathematics and Philosophy of the Infinite*. Cambridge, MA: Harvard University Press.

Davidson, Sara. 1977. "A Visit with Joan Didion." *New York Times Book Review*, April 3. http://www.saradavidson.com/NytDidion.html.

Davis, Raymond. 2006. Transcript of "The Ghost Particle" episode of PBS's *NOVA* television series. First aired on February 21. http://www.pbs.org/wgbh/nova/transcripts/3306_neutrino.html.

Dawkins, Richard. 2008. Introduction to "John Archibald Wheeler with Kenneth Ford from Geons, Black Holes, and Quantum Foam." *The Oxford Book of Science Writing*. New York: Oxford University Press.

de Lange, Catherine. 2012. "Superdoodles: The Science of Scribbling." *New Scientist*, December 28. http://www.newscientist.com/article/mg21628962.000-superdoodles-the-science-of-scribbling.html.

Devinsky, Orrin, and George Lai. 2008. "Spirituality and Religion in Epilepsy." *Epilepsy & Behavior* 12: 636–43.

de Waal, Franz. N.d. YouTube video showing part of a TED talk given by him. http://www.youtube.com/watch?v=meiU6TxysCg.

Doblin, Rick. 1991. "Pahnke's 'Good Friday Experiment': A Long-term Follow-up and Methodological Critique." *The Journal of Transpersonal Psychology* 23: 1–28.

Doctrines and Covenants. http://www.lds.org/scriptures/dc-testament/dc/124.45-55?lang=eng.

Dostoevsky, Fyodor. (1868) 2004. *The Idiot.* Translated by David McDuff. London: Penguin.

Einstein, Albert. 1982. "How I Created Relativity." *Physics Today* 35: 45–47.

Ferris, Timothy. 2002. *The Red Limit: The Search for the Edge of the Universe.* New York: HarperCollins.

Feynman, Richard. 1973. "Take the World from Another Point of View." Abridged transcript of an interview with Yorkshire Television. http://calteches.library.caltech.edu/35/2/PointofView.htm.

———. 1999. "The Pleasure of Finding Things Out." In *The Pleasure of Finding Things Out: The Best Short Works of Richard P. Feynman.* Cambridge, MA: Perseus.

Firestein, Stuart. 2012. *Ignorance: How It Drives Science.* Oxford: Oxford University Press.

Flood, Alison. 2012. "Salman Rushdie and John le Carré End Fatwa Face-off." *The Guardian*, November 12. http://www.theguardian.com/books/2012/nov/12/salman-rushdie-john-le-carre.

Foot, Philippa. 2002. "The Problem of Abortion and the Doctrine of the Double Effect." In *Virtues and Vices and Other Essays in Moral Philosophy.* Oxford: Oxford University Press.

Fritz, Thomas, et al. 2009. "Universal Recognition of Three Basic Emotions in Music." *Current Biology* 19: 573–76.

Gaidos, Susan. 2010. "More than a Feeling." *Science News* 178 (4): 24–29.

Gandhi, Mohandas K. 1957. *Autobiography: The Story of My Experiments with Truth.* Translated by Mahadev Desai. Boston: Beacon Press.

George Washington University. 2013. "How Throwing Made Us Human." *ScienceDaily*, June 26. www.sciencedaily.com/releases/2013/06/130626142710.htm.

Gilbert, Elizabeth. 2009. TED talk given in February. http://www.ted.com/talks/elizabeth_gilbert_on_genius.html.

Glasser, Otto. 1993. *WilhelmConrad Röntgen and the Early History of the Roentgen Rays.* San Francisco: Norman Publishing.

Grant, Andrew. 2014. "Nobel's Sharp Cuts: How Gerald Guralnik Just Missed the Physics Prize." *ScienceNews*, January 19. https://www.sci encenews.org/article/nobels-sharp-cuts.

Griffiths, R. R., et al. 2006. "Psilocybin Can Occasion Mystical-type Experiences Having Substantial and Sustained Personal Meaning and Spiritual Significance." *Psychopharmacology* 187(3): 268–83.

Guth, Alan H. 1997. *The Inflationary Universe*. Cambridge, MA: Helix Books.

Hadamard, Jacques. 1954. *An Essay on the Psychology of Invention in the Mathematical Field*. New York: Dover.

Haidt, Jonathan, Fredrik Björklund, and Scott Murphy. N.d. "Moral Dumbfounding: When Intuition Finds No Reason." Unpublished paper.

Hallam, Tony. 2004. *Catastrophes and Lesser Calamities: The Causes of Mass Extinctions*. Oxford: Oxford University Press.

Hansen, Bjørn Åsheim, and Eylert Brodtkorb. 2003. "Partial Epilepsy with 'Ecstatic' Seizures." *Epilepsy & Behavior* 4: 667–73.

Hardy, G. H. 1967. *A Mathematician's Apology*. Cambridge: Cambridge University Press.

Harvey, Jonathan. 1999. *Music and Inspiration*. Edited by Michael Downes. New York: Faber and Faber.

Hellman, Hal. 2006. *Great Feuds in Science: Ten of the Liveliest Disputes Ever*. Hoboken, NJ: John Wiley.

Hersh, Reuben. 1997. *What Is Mathematics, Really?* New York: Oxford University Press.

Highfield, Roger, and Paul Carter. 1993. *The Private Lives of Albert Einstein*. New York: St. Martin's Press.

Hitchens, Christopher. 2001. *Letters to a Young Contrarian*. New York: Basic Books.

——. 2010. *Hitch-22: A Memoir*. New York: Twelve (The Hachette Book Group).

Hoffman, Paul. 2007. Interviewed by William Irvine on October 8.

Hughes, John R. 2005. "The Idiosyncratic Aspects of the Epilepsy of Fyodor Dostoevsky." *Epilepsy and Behavior* 7: 531–38.

Hull, David L. 1988. *Science as a Process: An Evolutionary Account of the Social and Conceptual Development of Science*. Chicago: University of Chicago Press.

Ibn Isḥāq, Muhammad. 1955. *The Life of Muhammad*. Translated by A. Guillaume. Lahore: Oxford University Press.

Irvine, William. 2006. *On Desire: Why We Want What We Want*. New York: Oxford University Press.

Isaacson, Walter. 2008. *Einstein: His Life and Universe*. Pocket Books: London.

Jackson, Allyn. 2002. "The World of Blind Mathematicians." *Notices of the AMS* 49 (10): 1246–51.

James, William. 1929. *The Varieties of Religious Experience*. New York: The Modern Library.

Jamison, Kay Redfield. 1994. *Touched with Fire: Manic-Depressive Illness and the Artistic Temperament*. New York: Free Press Paperbacks.

Johnson, George. 1999. *Strange Beauty: Murray Gell-Mann and the Revolution in Twentieth-Century Physics*. New York: Vintage.

King, Ross. 2006. *The Judgment of Paris: The Revolutionary Decade that Gave the World Impressionism*. New York: Walker.

Kipling, Rudyard. 1955. "Working Tools." In *Creative Process: A Symposium*. Edited by Brewster Ghiselin. New York: New American Library.

Kirschvink, Joseph. 1992. "Late Proterozoic Low-latitude Global Glaciation: The Snowball Earth." *The Proterozoic Biosphere: A Multidisciplinary Study*. Edited by J. William Schopf and Cornelis Klein. Cambridge: Cambridge University Press.

Klein, Richard G., with Blake Edgar. 2002. *The Dawn of Human Culture*. New York: John Wiley & Sons.

Kolata, Gina. 1993. "At Last, Shout of 'Eureka!' In Age-old Math Mystery." *New York Times*, June 24.

———. 1994. "A Year Later, Snag Persists in Math Proof." *New York Times*, June 28.

———. 1995. "How a Gap in the Fermat Proof Was Bridged." *New York Times*, January 31.

Krakauer, Jon. 2003. *Under the Banner of Heaven: A Story of Violent Faith*. New York: Doubleday.

Landers, Peter. 2003. "Dying Mathematician Spends Last Days on Area of Polygon." *The Wall Street Journal*, June 29. http://online.wsj.com/articl e/0,,SB105943075045962600,00.html.

Landsborough, D. 1987. "St Paul and Temporal Lobe Epilepsy." *Journal of Neurology, Neurosurgery, and Psychiatry* 50: 659–64.

Lane, Nick. 2005. *Power, Sex, Suicide: Mitochondria and the Meaning of Life*. New York: Oxford University Press.

Lankester, E. R. 1896. "Charles Robert Darwin." In *Library of the World's Best Literature Ancient and Modern*. Vol. 2. Edited by C. D. Warner. New York: R. S. Peale & J. A. Hill. http://darwin-online.org.uk/ content/frameset?itemID=F2113&viewtype=text&pageseq=1.

Lattin, Don. 1997. "Musings of the Main Mormon." *SFGate*, April 13. http:// www.sfgate.com/news/article/SUNDAY-INTERVIEW-Musings-of-the-Main-Mormon-2846138.php.

Lepre, Christopher J., et al. 2011. "An Earlier Origin for the Acheulian." *Nature* 477: 82–85.

Levitin, Daniel. 2006. *This Is Your Brain on Music: The Science of a Human Obsession.* New York: Dutton.

———. 2009. Interview for "The Music Instinct blog." http://www.pbs.org/wnet/musicinstinct/blog/interview-with-daniel-levitin/part-two/27/.

Lewis, C. S. 1955. *Surprised by Joy: The Shape of My Early Life.* New York: Harcourt, Brace.

Littlewood, John E. 1986. *Littlewood's Miscellany.* Edited by Béla Bollobás. Cambridge: Cambridge University Press.

Loomis, Elisha Scott. 1940. *The Pythagorean Proposition.* National Council of Teachers of Mathematics, Inc.: Washington, DC. http://files.eric.ed.gov/fulltext/ED037335.pdf.

Lord, James. 1965. *A Giacometti Portrait.* New York: Farrar, Straus and Giroux.

Lowenstein, George. 1994. "The Psychology of Curiosity: A Review and Reinterpretation." *Psychological Bulletin* 116 (1): 75–98.

Luhrmann, T. M. 2012. *When God Talks Back: Understanding the American Evangelical Relationship with God.* New York: Alfred A. Knopf.

Mailer, Norman. 1964. Interviewed by Steven Marcus. *The Paris Review* 31: 28–58. http://www.theparisreview.org/interviews/4503/the-art-of-fiction-no-32-norman-mailer.

Margulis, Lynn. 1995. "Gaia Is a Tough Bitch." In *The Third Culture: Beyond the Scientific Revolution.* Edited by John Brockman. New York: Touchstone.

Marshall, Barry J. 2005. "Barry J. Marshall—Biographical." http://www.nobelprize.org/nobel_prizes/medicine/laureates/2005/marshall-bio.html.

Martin, Douglas. 2010. "Leigh Van Valen, Evolution Revolutionary, Dies at 76." *New York Times,* October 30. http://www.nytimes.com/2010/10/31/us/31valen.html?_r=3&src=twt&twt=nytimesscience&pagewanted=all&.

McArdle, Megan. 2014. "Why Writers Are the Worst Procrastinators." *The Atlantic,* February 12. http://www.theatlantic.com/business/archive/2014/02/why-writers-are-the-worst-procrastinators/283773/.

McCutchan, Ann. 1999. *The Muse that Sings: Composers Speak about the Creative Process.* New York: Oxford University Press.

Medawar, Peter B. 1972. *The Hope of Progress: A Scientist Looks at Problems in Philosophy, Literature and Science.* London: Methuen.

Merton, Robert K. 1973a. "The Ambivalence of Scientists." In *The Sociology of Science: Theoretical and Empirical Investigations*. Edited by Norman W. Storer. Chicago: University of Chicago Press.

———. 1973b. "Behavior Patterns of Scientists." In *The Sociology of Science: Theoretical and Empirical Investigations*. Edited by Norman W. Storer. Chicago: University of Chicago Press.

———. 1973c. "Priorities in Scientific Discovery." In *The Sociology of Science: Theoretical and Empirical Investigations*. Edited by Norman W. Storer. Chicago: University of Chicago Press.

Meyers, Morton A. 2012. *Prize Fight: The Race and the Rivalry to be the First in Science*. New York: Palgrave Macmillan.

Mill, John Stuart. (1859) 1978. *On Liberty*. Indianapolis: Hackett.

Miller, Arthur I. 2005. *Empire of the Stars: Obsession, Friendship, and Betrayal in the Quest for Black Holes*. Boston: Houghton Mifflin.

Miller, Bruce L., Kyle Boon, et al. 2000. "Functional Correlates of Musical and Visual Ability in Frontotemporal Dementia." *British Journal of Psychiatry* 176: 458–63.

Mole, Beth. 2014. "X-Rays Uncover Hidden Faces in Rembrandt Painting." *ScienceNews*, February 16. https://www.sciencenews.org/article/x-rays-uncover-hidden-faces-rembrandt-painting.

Morell, Virginia. 1997. "Microbiology's Scarred Revolutionary." *Science* 276 (5313): 699–702.

Nation Institute. N.d. http://www.nationinstitute.org/prizes/1066/the_ridenhour_prizes/.

Neal, Meghan. 2012. "'Acquired Savant' Derek Amato Becomes Musical Prodigy." *New York Daily News*, June 7. http://www.nydailynews.com/news/national/acquired-savant-derek-amato-musical-prodigy-hitting-head-hard-diving-shallow-pool-article-1.1091812.

New English Bible with the Apocrypha. 1970. Oxford: Oxford University Press.

Nichols, Robert. 1948. "Birth of a Poem." Appendix to *An Anatomy of Inspiration and an Essay on the Creative Mood*. Cambridge: W. Heffer & Sons.

Nielsen, Jared A., et al. 2013. "An Evaluation of the Left-brain vs. Right-brain Hypothesis with Resting State Functional Connectivity Magnetic Resonance Imaging." *PLoS ONE* 8 (8): e71275. http://www.plosone.org/article/info%3Adoi%2F10.1371%2Fjournal.pone.0071275.

Ogata, Akira, and Taihei Miyakawa. 1998. "Religious Experiences in Epileptic Patients with a Focus on Ictus-related Episodes." *Psychiatry and Clinical Neurosciences* 52: 321–25.

Overbey, Erin. 2010. "Eighty-five from the Archive: Lillian Ross." *New Yorker* blog, April 13. http://www.newyorker.com/online/

blogs/backissues/2010/04/eighty-five-from-the-archive-lillian-ross.html.

Park, Nansook, Christopher Peterson, and Martin E. P. Seligman. 2004. "Strengths of Character and Wellbeing." *Journal of Social and Clinical Psychology* 23 (5): 603–19.

Pasricha, Satwant. 1993. "A Systematic Survey of Near-death Experiences in South India." *Journal of Scientific Exploration* 7 (2): 161–71.

Penfield, Wilder. 1978. *Mystery of the Mind: A Critical Study of Consciousness and the Human Brain.* Princeton, NJ: Princeton University Press.

Plato. *Symposium.* Translated by Benjamin Jowett. http://www.gutenberg.org/files/1600/1600-h/1600-h.htm.

——. 1973. *Phaedrus and Letters VII and VIII.* Translated by W. Hamilton. London: Penguin.

——. 1993. "Apology." In *Plato: The Last Days of Socrates.* Translated by Hugh Tredennick and Harold Tarrant. New York: Penguin.

Poincaré, Henri. 2004. "Mathematical Invention." In *Musings of the Masters: An Anthology of Mathematical Reflections.* Edited by Raymond G. Ayoub. [Washington, DC]: Mathematical Association of America.

Pollock, Ethan. 2006. *Stalin and the Soviet Science Wars.* Princeton, NJ: Princeton University Press.

Rahachadran, V. S., and S. Blakeslee. 1998. *Phantoms of the Brain.* New York: HarperCollins.

Rehmeyer, Julie. 2007. "A Prayer for Archimedes." *ScienceNews,* October 3. https://www.sciencenews.org/article/prayer-archimedes.

Rhodes, Richard. 1986. *The Making of the Atomic Bomb.* New York: Simon and Schuster.

——. 1995. *How to Write: Advice and Reflections.* New York: HarperCollins.

Ridley, Matt. 2010. *The Rational Optimist: How Prosperity Evolves.* New York: HarperCollins.

Rota, Gian-Carlo. 1997. *Indiscrete Thoughts.* Edited by Fabrizio Palombi. Boston: Birkhäuser.

Rubin, Vera Cooper. 1995. Transcript of interview by David DeVorkin at the Department of Terrestrial Magnetism, Carnegie Institution of Washington, on September 21. Session II. http://www.aip.org/history/ohilist/5920_2.html.

Russell, Bertrand. 1917. "The Study of Mathematics." *Mysticism and Logic and Other Essays.* London: George Allen and Unwin.

——. 1950. "An Outline of Intellectual Rubbish." *Unpopular Essays.* London: George Allen & Unwin.

Sachs, Jessica Snyder. 2007. *Good Germs, Bad Germs: Health and Survival in a Bacterial World.* New York: Hill and Wang.

Sacks, Oliver. 2012. *Hallucinations*. New York: Alfred A. Knopf.

Salimpoor, Valorie N., et al. 2013. "Interactions between the Nucleus Accumbens and Auditory Cortices Predict Music Reward Value." *Science* 340 (6129): 216–19.

Schecter, Bruce. 1998. *My Brain is Open: The Mathematical Journeys of Paul Erdős*. New York: Simon and Schuster.

Schopenhauer, Arthur. 1995. *The Wisdom of Life and Counsels and Maxims*. Amherst, NY: Prometheus Books.

Scripture, E. W. 1891. "Arithmetical Prodigies." *The American Journal of Psychology* 4 (1): 1–59.

Seeley, Bill. 2002. "But Is It Art?" *Metapsychology Online Reviews* 6 (19). http://metapsychology.mentalhelp.net/poc/view_doc.php?type=book&id=1124.

Sergent, Justine. 1993. "Music, the Brain and Ravel." *Trends in Neurosciences* 16 (5): 168–72.

Shapiro, Gilbert. 1986. *A Skeleton in the Darkroom: Stories of Serendipity in Science*. San Francisco: Harper & Row.

Shea, Andrea. 2007. "Jack Kerouac's Famous Scroll, 'On the Road' Again." NPR's *All Things Considered news show*. First aired on July 5. http://www.npr.org/templates/story/story.php?storyId=11709924.

Simenon, Georges. 1971. *When I Was Old*. New York: Harcourt Brace Jovanovich.

Singer, Peter. 2005. "Ethics and Intuitions." *The Journal of Ethics* 9 (3/4): 331–52.

Singh, Simon. N.d. "Mathematicians, Romantic Heroes of the Past, Present and Future." Blog posting. http://simonsingh.net/media/articles/maths-and-science/mathematicians-romantic-heroes-of-the-past-present-and-future/.

———. 1997. *Fermat's Enigma: The Quest to Solve the World's Greatest Mathematical Problem*. New York: Walker and Company.

Smith, Carol. 2006. "Brain Tumor Opens Her Mind to Art." *Seattle Post-Intelligencer*, March 12. http://www.seattlepi.com/local/article/Brain-tumor-opens-her-mind-to-art-1198236.php.

Smith, John Maynard. N.d. "Haldane's Reaction to the Lysenko Affair." An interview on the webofstories.com website. http://www.webofstories.com/play/john.maynard.smith/33.

———. N.d. "Hamilton: Political and Ideological Commitment." An interview on the webofstories.com website. http://www.webofstories.com/play/john.maynard.smith/39.

Smith, Joseph. N.d. "History." In *Pearl of Great Price*. https://www.lds.org/scriptures/pgp/js-h/1?lang=eng.

Smolin, Lee. N.d. Transcript of "Creative Problems in Physics." An interview by Steve Paulson. *To the Best of Our Knowledge* radio show/podcast.http://www.ttbook.org/book/transcript/transcript-lee-smolin-creative-problems-physics.

———. 1995. Introduction to "Gaia Is a Tough Bitch." In *The Third Culture: Beyond the Scientific Revolution.* Edited by John Brockman. New York: Touchstone.

———. 1997. *The Life of the Cosmos.* Oxford: Oxford University Press.

Spender, Stephen. 1955. "The Making of a Poem." In *Creative Process: A Symposium.* New York: New American Library.

Stillwell, John. 1985. Translator's introduction to *Papers on Fuchsian Functions.* New York: Springer-Verlag.

Stowe, Charles Edward. 1889. *Life of Harriet Beecher Stowe.* Boston and New York: Houghton, Mifflin and Company. Republished by Detroit: Gale Research Company, 1967.

Styron, William. 2002. Interview on C-SPAN's *BookTV* on March 14. http://www.c-span.org/video/?169935-2/random-house-75th-anniversary.

Thomson, Judith Jarvis. 1985. "The Trolley Problem." *Yale Law Journal* 94 (6): 1395–415.

Ullman, Chana. 1989. *The Transformed Self: The Psychology of Religious Conversion.* New York: Plenum Press.

Vitruvius, 1914. *The Ten Books on Architecture.* Translated by Morris Hicky Morgan. Cambridge, MA: Harvard University.

Walker, Gabrielle. 2003. *Snowball Earth: The Story of a Maverick Scientist and His Theory of the Global Catastrophe That Spawned Life As We Know It.* New York: Three Rivers Press.

Wallace, Alfred Russel. 1908. *My Life: A Record of Events and Opinions.* London: Chapman & Hall.

Wallace, Irving. 1977. "Self-Control Techniques of Famous Novelists." *Journal of Applied Behavior Analysis* 10 (3): 516–19.

Wasson, R. Gordon. 1957. "Seeking the Magic Mushroom." *Life*, May 13: 101–20.

Watson, James D., and Francis Crick.1953. "A Structure for Deoxyribose Nucleic Acid." *Nature* 171 (4356): 737–38.

Weinberg, Steven. 1992. *Dreams of a Final Theory: The Scientist's Search for the Ultimate Laws of Nature.* New York: Pantheon Books.

Westfall, Richard S. 1993. *The Life of Isaac Newton.* Cambridge: Cambridge University Press.

Wettach, George E. 2000. "The Near Death Experience as a Product of Isolated Subcortical Brain Function." *Journal of Near-death Studies* 19 (2): 71–90.

Whinnery, J. E. 1990. "Acceleration-induced Loss of Consciousness: A Review of 500 Episodes." *Archives of Neurology* 47 (7): 764–76.

Wickman, Forrest. 2013. "Who Really Said You Should 'Kill Your Darlings'?," October 18. http://www.slate.com/blogs/browbeat/2013/10/18/_kill_your_darlings_writing_advice_what_writer_really_said_to_murder_your.html.

Wilde, Oscar. 1905. *The Soul of Man under Socialism*. Portland, ME: Thomas B. Mosher.

Wiles, Andrew. 1997. Interviewed on "The Proof" episode of PBS's *NOVA* series. First aired on October 12.

Wilson, Edward O. 1994. *Naturalist*. Washington, DC: Island.

——. 2008. Interviewed on "Lord of the Ants" episode of PBS's *NOVA* series. First aired on May 20.

Wilson, Ellen Gibson. 1990. *Thomas Clarkson: A Biography*. New York: St. Martin's Press.

Wilson, Robin J. 2002. "Hardy and Littlewood." In *Cambridge Scientific Minds*. Edited by Peter Harman and Simon Mitton. Cambridge: Cambridge University.

Wood, Robert Muir. 1985. *The Dark Side of the Earth*. London: George Allen & Unwin.

Wrangham, Richard. 2009. *Catching Fire: How Cooking Made Us Human*. New York: Basic Books.

Zeki, Semir, John Paul Romaya, Dionigi M. T. Benincasa, and Michael F. Atiyah. 2014. "The Experience of Mathematical Beauty and Its Neural Correlates." *Frontiers in Human Neuroscience*, February 13. http://www.frontiersin.org/human_neuroscience/10.3389/fnhum.2014.00068/abstract.

Zentner, Marcel, and Tuomas Eerolab. 2010. "Rhythmic Engagement with Music in Infancy." *PNAS* 107 (13): 5768–73.

Zimmer, Carl. 1998. *The Water's Edge: Fish with Fingers, Whales with Legs, and How Life Came Ashore but Then Went Back to Sea*. New York: Touchstone.

INDEX